Palgrave Studies on Norbert Elias

Series Editor
Tatiana Savoia Landini
Universidade Federal de Sao Paulo
Sao Paulo, Brazil

More information about this series at
http://www.palgrave.com/gp/series/16153

John Connolly • Paddy Dolan

Gaelic Games in Society

Civilising Processes, Players, Administrators and Spectators

John Connolly
DCUBS
Dublin City University
Dublin, Ireland

Paddy Dolan
Technological University Dublin
Dublin, Ireland

ISSN 2662-3102   ISSN 2662-3110   (electronic)
Palgrave Studies on Norbert Elias
ISBN 978-3-030-31698-3   ISBN 978-3-030-31699-0   (eBook)
https://doi.org/10.1007/978-3-030-31699-0

This Palgrave Macmillan imprint is published by the registered company Springer Nature Switzerland AG.
The registered company address is: Gewerbestrasse 11, 6330 Cham, Switzerland

Ray McManus/Sportsfile via Getty Images

John dedicates this book to the three hurlers Mossy, Tadhg and Fiachra
Paddy dedicates this book to Jakki and Kate

PREFACE

In many ways, it is difficult to identify the genesis of this book. We first began to study Gaelic games in 2005, when we were both based at what was then Dublin Institute of Technology—now Technological University Dublin (John's introduction to Elias was via Paddy, who had been introduced to Elias's work by Professor Stephen Mennell in 1994 while studying for a master's in sociology at University College Dublin). Extended lunchtime discussions on Eliasian understandings of violence (and violence in sport) were soon considered in relation to the sport of hurling. The subsequent research project culminated first in a conference paper delivered at the European Association for the Sociology of Sport conference in Munster, Germany, in 2007. A revised paper would later be published in the journal *Sport in Society*. In the years that followed, we extended the remit of the research on both Gaelic games and the Gaelic Athletic Association (GAA). The fruits of this research work were subsequently published as journal articles and book chapters, replete with their specific requirements and focus. Yet that is not quite the full story of how this book has come about; as Elias stressed, there are no absolute origins! The fact that we found Elias's approach compelling certainly ensured we began from a figurational perspective but it still leaves the question of why study hurling (our initial focus) and the GAA? We could have sought to collaborate around questions concerning many social phenomena, sports related or otherwise. Beyond our academic lives, sport (of varying kinds) did, and continues to, stir our emotions with moments of great pleasure (and pain too!). And, as for many people in contemporary society, it is a source for collective identification and meaning for us. In that sense, for most of our lives, sport has provided mimetic, motility and sociability functions for both of us. We have also been familiar with Gaelic games for most of our lives to varying degrees, and this familiarity and 'involvement' has been helpful in writing this book.

We emphasise these diverse yet interconnected social threads because it is these processes which contributed to a desire to sociologically investigate Gaelic games back in 2005. The programme of research that followed and which has culminated in this book was not driven by modern university metrics. During much of the time working on our research programme we were both based in Business departments—a locale where the sociology of sport has yet to register high in perceived functional importance, relative to what is seen as the more 'essential' world of 'business'! Our motivation was simply to make a small contribution to the social fund of knowledge on a sport and a society—Gaelic games and Ireland. In doing so we also believe we have contributed to the further development of figurational theory, particularly in respect of the relationship between violence and state legitimacy.

The book addresses several of the questions and themes covered in our previous publications on Gaelic games and the GAA, bringing them together 'under one roof' so to speak. However, the book goes well beyond our previous work, linking and extending the range of questions and topics. Consequently, new research angles have been integrated, while previous syntheses have been expanded. It concludes many years of collaboration on Gaelic games and the GAA. It is important to stress too that this book is not about making value judgements or normative pronouncements on the direction of the GAA; we have eschewed that territory. Our aim was to explain how and why specific developments occurred. Whether these are deemed 'positive' or 'negative' is not the concern of this book; our task was to explain how and why they have come about.

It also needs to be recognised that this book, as the title suggests, is also concerned with changes in Irish society—both social structures and the social habitus of people in Ireland. This aspect has been a focus for one of us, Paddy Dolan, for almost 20 years now and this book draws from much of that work also. Paddy completed his PhD in Goldsmiths College, University of London, in 2005 using Elias's concepts and theories. While the topic concerned the development of consumer culture in Ireland, the examination of changing social interdependences and the national habitus proved as relevant to the study of Gaelic games.

In the Preface to his book *The Combat Soldier*, Anthony King makes the insightful observation that 'any programme of research necessarily involves a conversation with a multiplicity of scholars both living and dead' (pp. x–xi). That has been our experience too. On the latter point of conversations with the dead, there was an element of this also, for while we never met Elias and he is long deceased, we have had in ways many conversations with him through his writings in the course of researching this book.

Researching and writing any book brings with it its own set of challenges and frustrations, but it has also been a very enjoyable experience. As we said, we began this research over a decade ago. Along the way we have encountered many historians, sociologists, archivists and others who have been sources of inspiration and assistance. Back then no official archive of the GAA existed in Croke Park, the administrative and playing headquarters of the association. Despite this, various individuals at Croke Park were extremely helpful and accommodating. While we cannot name all of them individually, we thank and acknowledge their assistance and for facilitating the not infrequent visits in those early years of the research. In addition, we were given access to the minutes of the Leinster council of the GAA which were then held in the office of the Leinster Council in Portlaoise. We also sourced material from the Cardinal Tomás Ó Fiaich Library and Archive in Armagh. Again we acknowledge the assistance of staff at all these locations and others, including the National Library of Ireland; Pearse Street library, Dublin; Limerick City library; and Dublin City University Library. We are also grateful to the following sociologists, historians and various members of the GAA, and others, who over the years provided helpful sources, suggestions and ideas: Dr Dónal McAnallen, Professor Stephen Mennell, Mark Reynolds, John Cotter, Michael Delaney and Joan Cooney. We thank Palgrave and in particular Madison Allums and Mary Al-Sayed for their assistance and patience in particular! Finally, for their love, support and encouragement, Paddy thanks his wife Jakki, and John thanks his wife Kate. Paddy also thanks his daughter Kate for her own unique approach to motivation.

Dublin, Ireland   John Connolly
                                                                                          Paddy Dolan

Contents

1 Introduction: Gaelic Games in Society   1

2 Gaelic Games and Player Violence   19

3 Spectators, Emotions and the Individualisation of Violence   39

4 The Sociogensis and Development of the GAA:
Centralising and Decentralising Tensions   69

5 The Amateur–Professional Tension Balance   93

6 The Amplifying of Professionalism and Amateurism, and
the Emergence of 'Player Power'   117

7 Integrating Irish Youth, National Identification and
Diminishing Displays of Superiority   139

8 Cultural Hybridisation as an Essentialising Strategy:
The Development of a New Sport—International Rules
Football   161

9   Conclusion: Some Thoughts on Contemporary
    Developments   181

Bibliography   191

Index   203

ABBREVIATIONS

AAA	Amateur Athletic Association
AFL	Australian Football League
CPA	Club Players Association
DMP	Dublin Metropolitan Police
EEC	European Economic Community
ESRI	Economic and Social Research Institute
FAI	Football Association of Ireland
GAA	Gaelic Athletic Association
GPA	Gaelic Players Association
IAAA	Irish Amateur Athletic Association
IFA	Irish Football Association
IRA	Irish Republican Army
IRB	Irish Republican Brotherhood
IRFU	Irish Rugby Football Union
LGFA	Ladies Gaelic Football Association
RIC	Royal Irish Constabulary
RTÉ	Radió Teilifís Éireann
UK	United Kingdom
US	United States
USA	United States of America

CHAPTER 1

Introduction: Gaelic Games in Society

The Study of Gaelic Games and Irish Society

This book is about Gaelic games, the Gaelic Athletic Association (GAA), the body that governs Gaelic games, and Irish society. The term 'Gaelic games' refers to a number of ball games—hurling, Gaelic football, rounders and Gaelic handball—which fall under the governance and administration of the GAA. The two more widespread and popular, and perhaps more familiar, of these ball games are Gaelic football and hurling, which are the games examined in this book.

Many readers, though perhaps to varying degrees, will be familiar with Gaelic games—hurling and football in particular. However, given the sociological focus and relevance of this text there will also be some readers perhaps less familiar with them. For that reason, the following is a short summary of the sports; however, we would suggest a quick view on YouTube would perhaps give one a better grasp! Hurling is a field game of fifteen-a-side played with a wooden stick, with a broad base known as the bas (pronounced 'boss'), called a hurley and a small ball known as a sliotar, which is similar in size to a tennis ball. The game is played both on the ground and 'in the air' (unlike field hockey). The ball can be propelled long distances through the swinging action of the player with the hurley. The ostensible object of the game is to accrue scores through propelling the ball between goalposts, either under the bar to score a goal (worth three points) or over the bar to score a single point. Each team has a goalkeeper, and the goalposts resemble the H structure of rugby,

© The Author(s) 2020
J. Connolly, P. Dolan, *Gaelic Games in Society*, Palgrave Studies on Norbert Elias, https://doi.org/10.1007/978-3-030-31699-0_1

though with netting in the lower part as with soccer, which is minded by the goalkeeper. It has a long history in Ireland, though its precise form has changed over time. Similarly, Gaelic football has a related structure. A field game involving two teams of fifteen-a-side, the goalposts are the same as in hurling and each side has a goalkeeper. The ball can be kicked, fisted and caught 'in the air'. The scoring structure of both hurling and football is the same, while the playing surface is wider and longer than of either soccer or rugby.

As the title implies, the book is also about Irish people—how they think, feel and act has changed over the course of the last 150 years—and how this relates to Gaelic games and the GAA. It is generally acknowledged that the formation of the GAA in 1884 was related to broader changes involving the rise of cultural nationalism in Ireland[1] during the late nineteenth century (Mandle, 1987). Yet more contemporary developments in both Gaelic games and in the organisational structure of the GAA tend not to be linked with wider social changes to the same extent. Thus, underpinning this book is the belief that to understand and explain developments in Gaelic games and the GAA we must simultaneously examine the changes in Irish society. As Elias (2008b, p. 26) argues, 'studies of sport which are not studies of society are studies out of context'.

A large body of academic work (Cronin, Duncan, & Rouse; 2009 Cronin, Murphy, & Rouse, 2009; De Búrca, 1989, 1999; Mandle, 1987; McAnallen, Hassan, & Hegarty, 2009)[2] and more journalistic-style texts (e.g., Corry, 1989, 2005; Fullam, 1999) on Gaelic games and the GAA now exists. Indeed, the number and diversity of such manuscripts have grown exponentially in recent years. Most of these emanate from historians, journalists, players, former players and managers, many of the latter in the form of autobiographies. In contrast, only a relatively small pool of sociologically informed work exists (Mullan, 1995), including our own which we build upon here (Connolly & Dolan, 2010, 2011, 2012, 2013a, 2013b; Dolan & Connolly, 2009, 2014b). This book provides sociologically informed explanations of particular developments in Gaelic games and the GAA. More specifically, we explain:

- the shift in the direction of more rounded and even self-restraint and more advanced thresholds of repugnance towards violence in relation to the playing of Gaelic football and hurling.
- changes in the structure of spectator violence and how these changes are connected to changes in the structure of Irish society.

- the greater suppression of displays of superiority feelings and animosity towards the competing sports of soccer and rugby.
- decentralisation and centralisation forces in the organisational development of the GAA.
- the relationship between the increasing seriousness of involvement and achievement orientation and the change in the tension balance between amateurism/volunteerism and professionalism at playing and administrative levels.
- shifting balances of power between players and administrators and the emergence of the concept of 'player power'.
- how and why the discourses of amateurism and professionalism were amplified or de-amplified over the years by different groups constituting the GAA.
- changes in how GAA administrators sought to attract and integrate young people into the GAA and how this was connected with increasing social interdependences and shifting intergenerational power balances.

Overall, this book is an attempt to sociologically theorise developments in Gaelic games, the GAA and Irish society. It is in this way too that this book is much more than a mere sociological study of Gaelic games and Irish society, for it involves an examination of Elias's (2010, 2012a, 2012b) ideas and theories.

While this book is written from a sociological perspective, we hope it will be read beyond academia, and become a vehicle for public discussion about Gaelic games, the GAA and Irish society itself. It was clear to us in writing this book that the developments we sought to explain were matters of public interest. The subject matters—player 'violence', the amateur–professional tension, the rise of what is referred to as 'player power', spectator behaviour, the structure of decision-making within the GAA, the relationship between GAA functionaries and those of other sporting organisations—are perennial issues of discussion in Irish society. They resurface regularly within the media and public discourse, as well as being formally debated issues within the various organisational units of the GAA itself. Within mainstream contemporary media many of these issues are treated a-socially, a-historically and in static rather than processual terms—the latter being a feature of some academic scholarship too. Indeed, within many academic accounts generally we also find somewhat limited explanations offered for specific developments. Historians, perhaps the most prolific discipline when it comes to published research on both Gaelic games and the GAA, tend to provide explanations from the 'big man' perspective. Here the assumed power of the single individual is accentuated while broader social changes, while recognised, tend to take on the position more reminiscent of a background choreography. Certainly, in some instances the social is given greater credence. But it often takes the form of locating changes as a reflex of a change in society. One of the problems with this mode of explanation, and the thinking and observation it reflects, is that it encourages 'the impression that society is made up of structures external to oneself, the individual, and that the individual is at one and the same time surrounded by society yet cut off from it by some invisible wall' (Elias, 2012b, p. 10). Indeed, a central focus of Elias's work, and the theoretical approach he developed, was dismantling the assumption that society is something abstracted from individual people. His concept of figuration is central to overcoming this view of individuals and groups as substantially different (a point we will return to below). Figurations are fluid networks of interdependent people with different and shifting power balances between the people comprising them: 'Individuals always come in figurations and figurations are always formed by individuals' (Elias & Dunning, 2008, p. 197).

Other historical explanations are often economic in their base. For example, Rouse (2015, p. 195), in attempting to explain amateurism in the GAA, suggests, 'The idea of a broad-based sports organisation spread across the island was entirely at odds with the scale of population and economy required to sustain a professional sport'. While our explanations of developments in Gaelic games and the GAA recognise growing commercialism and the expansion of economic interdependences, they are not treated as either isolated processes or as a 'cause-effect' dynamic, but rather as processes interwoven with other dynamic social and psychological processes.

It is important to stress that while we use historical evidence in our examination of Gaelic games and the GAA, we do not adopt a traditional historiographic strategy: 'The sociologist's history is not the historian's history' (Elias, 2008a, p. 152). By this we mean that we are less concerned with the imagined inventors and creators of the GAA—the big man perspective. This is not to say that such people were not important in the development and popularisation of the sports. Rather their actions and orientations were framed and enabled in the complex network of social relations which they formed with others. This figuration included not just those they interacted with face-to-face but also distant others, and also previous generations who inherited, upheld and modified the traditions of Irishness, and in particular the ideal of cultural distinction. It is only in this social context that leaders of the new sports movement (that led to the formal establishment of the GAA) could even conceive of the need for sports distinct from British sports that were proving to be enormously successful across the social classes in Britain, Ireland and beyond.

So while historians of Gaelic games in Ireland have tended to focus on origins, narrative and key individuals, in this book we focus on the changing structure of relations between Irish and British social groups. Figurational sociologists do not dismiss the significance of important historical figures, but they are placed in the fluid context of power relations between and within groups, including social classes and ethnic groups. Such individuals are formed in the fluid intersections between many social processes and relations over time. For instance, the specific actions of Michael Cusack (usually recognised as the key founder of the GAA) become less important than shifting power relations within Ireland and between Irish and British groups. This does not diminish his uniqueness in that the complex, changing figurations comprising millions of people allow for the formation of differentiated people.

We treat historical figures as occupants of particular social positions within the broader organisational figuration of the GAA, which itself exists within national and international figurations. This does not mean that such figures are inactive, passive instruments of inexorable structures colliding with other structures. They have been enabled through their habitus formation and relate to others according to particular sets of emotional dispositions and strategising capabilities. These resources are afforded by their nodal positions and their trajectory within the social networks they form with others. Of course individuals are not entirely coherent and consistent in their wishes and deeds, as their locations in figurations at different levels of integration produce contradictions and dilemmas.

Our critique of historians primarily concerns differences in how we explain social change and the relationship between individuals and society, not the importance of historical work *per se*. Indeed, we (and other process sociologists) are very reliant on historians and on the secondary historiographic literature they produce, as was the case for this book. This too is an example of social interdependence in the research process. We exist in a network of interdependences with other researchers, in this case historians who have collected and analysed primary documents concerning organisational formation and change, at the level of both states and sporting organisations. Consequently, this book is a synthesis of sociology and history, whereby existing historical studies, combined with empirical data, have been guided by a central sociological theory (for an expanded discussion of these issues, see Dolan & Connolly, 2014a).

NORBERT ELIAS AND FIGURATIONAL SOCIOLOGY

Since the publication of Elias and Dunning's seminal text *Quest for Excitement* in 1986, interest in the sociology of sport has grown enormously; this includes a significant number of studies drawing from a figurational approach. In that sense, it is fair to say it remains one of the few enclaves where figurational sociology retains a foothold on a par with other theoretical perspectives. Yet while 'Sport', from a sociological perspective, is no longer on the periphery, its status as a subject of importance lags behind those deemed as 'more' serious objects of sociological study—politics, globalisation, gender. Furthermore, the increased focus on the sociology of sport has run in tandem with its further compartmentalisation—both in relation to other disciplines addressing sport (further academic specialisation) and in their seclusion from sociological enquires of human relations more generally, as if an impermeable boundary existed between those involved in a sport and wider society.

While a detailed exposition of Elias's theoretical approach is outside the scope of this text, we will briefly outline some of the main concepts; an understanding of these concepts can also be derived from the synthesis in the chapters of this book. The key principle of Elias's figurational perspective is that all social life is in motion, or in process. This includes social structures, attitudes, values, norms, identities and even what might be loosely termed as mentalities (or social habitus). Therefore, to understand and explain any aspect of social life adequately, we must refrain from reducing social processes to states or substances; we must think processually rather than substantively; the concept of figuration itself coveys this.

Elias's concept of power (a structural characteristic of all human relations or figurations) is relational rather than absolute—no one is ever completely powerful or powerless because of the function each provides for the other. The balance of power between people is basically the balance of dependences between them—those who are more dependent on others than vice versa occupy less powerful positions, though these relationships are prone to change. Certainly there can be extreme power differentials with the power ratio lying greatly in favour of one individual or group over another. Another important concept in Elias's opus, which we mentioned above, is his concept of social habitus—meaning simply a second nature way of thinking, feeling and acting.

The phrase 'civilising processes', which partly constitutes the subtitle of this book, is very much associated with Elias and refers to some of his main theoretical contentions. In Elias's hands the concept (and phrase) is devoid of value connotations—it is a technical concept referring, primarily, to a change in the balance between social and self-restraint in the direction of the latter. Elias (2012a) argued, based on empirical examination of people living in West European territories over the centuries, that 'a civilising process' had occurred; people came to exert greater self-restraint over their behaviour and emotions through the compulsion of increasing dependencies between people. He illustrated how standards of social and self-control were transformed, particularly in relation to violence. The threshold of repugnance towards violence and its display advanced, and the balance between social and self-restraint shifted in favour of the latter as people came to exercise more even and all-round self-control over their behaviour and emotions. Elias illustrated and explained how the twin processes of a developing stable 'state' monopoly for the control of violence and taxation facilitate more extensive and interwoven functional differentiation and specialisation—that is lengthening chains of social interdependence (figurations). Both these processes, the state monopolisation of violence and increasing interdependence, facilitate civilising pressures. The greater state monopolisation over violence generates a more pacified social space by restricting non-state permitted violence and generally punishing those who engage in such violence. Lengthening chains of social interdependence can also exert a civilising effect through the process of functional democratisation (power balances become more equal between social groups). As groups become more interdependent (more equal power relations), they must increasingly and reciprocally adjust and adapt their behaviour to a greater extent and employ greater levels of all-round self-restraint in their daily lives. In effect, a pressure develops for people of more varied class and ethnic dispositions to exercise greater reciprocal control over their emotions and actions in social relations. This movement from social constraint towards greater self-restraint means the individual's conscience becomes more important as a regulator of behaviour (Sheard, 1999).

So while particular social standards become established and take on a level of solidity, these standards are always in process—evolving until newly emerging or competing forms become the dominant and established norm of emotional and behavioural self-restraint. Hence, what was once considered 'civilised' conduct becomes, in a later period, or generation, perceived and characterised as uncontrolled or disgraceful behaviour. This process of social development, which is neither even, unilinear or teleological, is reflected in different aspects of all social relations, such as in sport, for 'no sport can be insulated from the wider society in which it is played' (Dunning & Sheard, 1979, p. 175).

Following Elias, it is imperative to understand that although dominant or established social standards do emerge and take hold, they are always in process. Change is ongoing rather than a case of moving from one steady state to another. Elias (2012a, p. 500) was particularly critical of Talcott Parsons on this front: 'the concept of social change refers here [according to Parsons] to a transitional state between two normal states of changelessness, brought about by malfunction'. The dynamic of change consists of the unstable tensions between contending groups and individuals constituting any particular social unit, and indeed tensions between such units at higher levels of integration or interdependence. As actions have unforeseen and unintended consequences, the order of change is largely unplanned, but the relative contribution of planned and unplanned aspects of social change depends upon the power balances between the various groups and individuals.

DATA SOURCES, ANALYSIS AND SYNTHESIS

We relied mainly on historical documents in varying forms. They included existing historical monographs of the GAA and Gaelic games covering national, provincial, county and club level, as well as those pertaining to the overall history of Ireland. Given the relational aspect of the figurational approach, we were also concerned about developments in other sports and several historical monographs covering either a specific sport or several sports were used in our analysis. We also accessed newspaper reports. For instance, we used these for accounts of matches in order to get access to player and spectator behaviour. We also examined referee reports, organisational minutes of meetings, rule books, organisational reports, manuals and promotional magazines. Combining these sources allowed us to reconstruct practices, events and moral standards of earlier periods. For example, referee reports (accessed at the GAA archives) were used to supplement newspaper reports and an analysis of rule books was carried out to get a sense of changing 'shame thresholds' in relation to violence (Chap. 2). The minutes of meetings at various levels of the GAA were used to build models of the organisational figuration and changes in organising (see Chap. 4).

While we treated documents as fragments and legacies of events that really happened, it does not mean we acted as naïve empiricists gullible to every journalist's or administrator's written word. Such accounts were treated critically and sceptically in the light of other evidence available. The question of time periods is a difficult one when drawing on historical evidence. While social processes can initially appear to be going in a more or less consistent direction, closer inspection often revealed qualifications, exceptions, reverses and at the very least uneven diffusion and acceptance of newer standards of conduct. This is why we have been reluctant to fix change to any particular date. This is consistent with Elias's own periodisation of social change. While there are occasional spurts (even civilising spurts) in one direction, change tends to be gradual and uneven. There is a succession of events, but no single great event that serves as an imagined watershed of historical change.

Both data generation and synthesis are theory guided. And while we followed and applied Elias's overall approach we were also cognisant of not treating theoretical concepts and ideas with 'too much respect', to use a sporting analogy. So, as we suggested earlier, while we used figurational theory as a resource to explain developments in Gaelic games in Ireland, we simultaneously endeavoured to interrogate these theories and concepts against found and emerging evidence. Indeed, Elias (1987) himself continually stressed the importance of developing 'testable' models and explanations; in other words, data from other social contexts and situations could be used to revise the prevailing models as long as such revisions accounted for the evidence (facts) in such diverse contexts. And, while our findings largely parallel explanations developed by Elias and Dunning (2008) and Dunning and colleagues (see Dunning, Murphy, & Williams, 1988; Dunning & Sheard, 1979) concerning developments in sports such as soccer and rugby in Britain, there are some distinct differences in our explanation for similar developments in Gaelic games in Ireland. For instance, as we illustrate in Chaps. 2 and 3, our data and synthesis suggests that the relationship between violence in Gaelic games (both player and spectator) and state legitimacy in Ireland is particularly significant. In that sense, there are some distinct theoretical differences in how we explain some developments in relation to violence in Gaelic games in Ireland from figurational studies explaining changes in violence connected with soccer and rugby in Britain.

INVOLVED DETACHMENT

As we outlined in previous work (Dolan & Connolly, 2014a), one of the main arguments in Elias's (2007) *Involvement and Detachment* is that the development of more reality-congruent knowledge develops in a spiral process with greater capacity for detachment on the part of people towards objects, events, and processes that they encounter in life. Involvement and detachment are not polar opposites, nor are people predisposed to one inclination or the other: 'One cannot say of a person's outlook in any absolute sense that it is detached or involved ... Normally adult behaviour lies on a scale somewhere between these two extremes' (Elias, 2007, pp. 68–69). Kilminster (2007, pp. 122–124) argues that sociological research entails involved detachment, in that a passionate commitment to scientific discovery is required, not a diffident, indifferent emotional stale-ness to the process. However, detachment does mean distancing oneself from the preferred outcomes of research and ensuring that the political or moral perspectives of the researcher do not prejudice the findings. This is a considerable challenge; as sociologists participate in the 'objects' of their investigations, they are highly susceptible to feelings of danger, anger or outrage (Elias, 2007, p. 13). Yet it is also this participation which is neces-sary to generate understanding:

> [social scientists] cannot cease to take part in, and to be affected by, the social and political affairs of their groups and their time. Their own partici-pation and involvement, moreover, are themselves conditions for compre-hending the problems they try to solve as scientists. For while, in order to understand the structure of molecules, one need not know what it feels like to be one of its atoms, in order to understand the functioning of human groups one needs to know, as it were, from the inside how human beings experience their own and other groups, and one cannot know without active participation and involvement. (Elias, 2007, p. 84)

In our research of developments in Gaelic games and the GAA it has of course been difficult to access the experience of administrators, players and spectators over time. We have attempted this through the historical documents examined. It is important to empathise with those participants in terms of a kind of sociological and methodological imagination whereby one's developing knowledge of immediate and broader figurations, the dynamics of organisations and matches themselves, affords an understanding of participants' perspectives. This of course does not mean that researchers can experience the exact emotions and calculations of historical figures, but one can, so to speak, imagine themselves in their fluid positions within dynamic figurations. Indeed, Kilminster claims that Elias's method of writing allows 'the reader to experience, or perhaps to *re-experience* to a degree, the dominant behavioural codes of the different historical stages, from the unavoidable point of view of the current one' (Kilminster, 2007, p. 86, original emphasis). Through analysing historical documents, it is possible for researchers to imagine the prevailing standards and social situations of particular historical periods.

Doing figurational research can also produce what Elias (2007, p. 40) called 'secondary forms of involvement', in that finding connections between processes and structures produces its own enjoyment. Discovering the strangeness of historical events and practices from a modern perspective is an early form of involvement, not without its pleasures for the researcher, but a detour via detachment requires reducing the distance between past and present by locating such events and practices within the figurations, standards of conduct, and traditions of the past. Much of the early figurational work on sport by Elias and Dunning (2008) focussed on violence—by players and spectators in particular (Dunning and colleagues at the University of Leicester also examined violence by hooligan groups with tenuous connections to actual sports; see Dunning (1994), Dunning et al. (1988), Dunning and Sheard (1979)). Similarly, we found relatively high levels of violence in the early development of Gaelic games in Ireland, and also different forms or structures of violent events over time. This can be particularly challenging from the perspective of maintaining 'involved detachment' in the scientific sense described above. As will be illustrated in Chaps. 2 and 3 we came across accounts of death and severe bodily assault in the early decades of the GAA. However, it is important to eschew a moralising perspective on those involved in such violence. This is not to excuse it, but simply to acknowledge that moralising can interfere with developing explanations of the dynamics of violent encounters and of the formation of a social habitus quick to anger and violent assault. Remaining relatively detached involves focussing on the actions of participants in context rather than the painful and humiliating effects on victims. It also means avoiding blame attribution, at least initially. For us, part of the relative detachment process involved a degree of de-personalising of the various sports participants. We analysed people as spectators, players, referees, officials, administrators, and so on, but not as individual life stories. If researchers can view themselves as part of intergenerational links of knowledge development, then the emotional pressure of imagining what impact the research outcomes mean for the individual researcher him or herself can recede to some extent.

Chapter Overview

Chapter 2 examines the issue of player violence in Gaelic games and the changes that have occurred in respect of this since the 1880s. Though a recurring feature of contemporary commentary on Gaelic games, to our knowledge no study aside from our own previous work (Connolly & Dolan, 2010; Dolan & Connolly, 2009) has sought to sociologically theorise the changes that have occurred. Drawing extensively from our earlier work we illustrate and explain how players over time have come to adjust their conduct, gradually exercising a higher degree of self-restraint in the playing of Gaelic games. Certainly occasional transgressions of narrowing limits of permissible physical confrontation continued to occur, but they became subject to increasing social scrutiny and reprimand. We explain how these changing thresholds of violence have occurred within the context of the standardisation of the written rules of the game, and within a broader context of increasing social interdependences beyond the field of play. The chapter shows various aspects of these intertwined social processes—the convergence of rules; increasing social coordination around the scheduling and completion of match fixtures; the advancing threshold of repugnance concerning overt displays of violence; the shifting power ratios between players and governing officials; and relationships within the shifting figurations comprising people in Ireland.

Chapter 3 also examines the issue of violence but in relation to spectators rather than players. Given that spectator violence in relation to Gaelic games has tended not to fall within the category of 'football hooliganism' (often attributed to spectator violence associated with soccer), there is perhaps an assumption that spectator violence did not occur within Gaelic games. That is certainly not the case. In this chapter we outline how spectator violence has diminished in the context of greater emotional control and differentiation as part of a general civilising process. More significantly the nature of violent encounters shifted from a collective form based on local solidarity and a reciprocal code of honour, through a transitional collective form based on deferred emotional satisfaction and group pride, towards increasing individualisation of spectator violence. This occurs due to shifting objects of emotional involvement as functional specialisation proceeds and is partially accepted by spectators, as collective symbols of we-identity supersede interpersonal honour, and as 'mutually expected self-restraint' proceeds.

Chapter 4 begins by explaining the formation of the GAA sociologically. We then illustrate and explain the ensuing oscillations in the direction of greater centralisation or decentralisation and how this dynamic was connected to the changing structure of intra- and inter-organisational interdependences and social interdependences at a higher tier of social integration. The expansion in intra-interdependences, particularly from the early twentieth century, provided the momentum for greater mutual identification between disparate units of the GAA. It also facilitated processes of centralisation, though decentralising tensions remained. The further intensification of interdependences from the 1960s onwards and the resultant expansion in functional differentiation generated a compelling pressure for coordinating units at higher levels of orientation. However, the overlapping nature in the functional composition of many of the GAA's organisational units and the stronger identification of members towards we-images such as club or county, at different levels of intensity, mean divisions over, and pressures against, greater centralisation continue to surface.

Both Chaps. 5 and 6 deal with the interrelated issues of amateurism and professionalism. Chapter 5 explains how and why the initial organising ethos of the GAA was formulated around amateurism and why, from the outset, it was never 'pristine' amateurism due to the social class make-up of the GAA. In the decades that followed, players and other functionaries came to take a more serious approach to Gaelic games. Preparations for matches, coaching, tactical intellectualisation and scientisation of Gaelic games advanced. One consequence of this heightened achievement orientation and increasing stress on the seriousness of involvement has been the erosion of amateur principles and their replacement with more professional structures. This has also occurred at the administrative level with the expansion of paid professional staff. This is not an absolute movement from amateurism to professionalism but a tilting in the balance between amateurism and professionalism in the direction of the latter. We explain how this was connected with the changing structure of Irish society and how the sport took on increasing emotional and meaning functions for Irish people.

In Chap. 6 we explain how and why the amplification and stigmatisation of professionalism and amateurism has changed and oscillated since the foundation of the GAA. In the years following the formation of the GAA, through to the late 1920s, the discourse of amateurism was largely de-amplified by GAA activists and administrators. In the decades that followed, the concept of amateurism is increasingly amplified and mobilised, as is the discourse of professionalism. While, as we explain in Chap. 5, these developments are connected with the tide of growing seriousness of involvement and an achievement orientation from the 1960s, it was also interwoven with a further tilting in the balance of power between administrators and 'elite' players in the direction of the latter. It is partly this last dynamic which has given rise to the amplification of the phrase 'player power', often deployed by contemporary journalists and administrators alike. While this development is very much perceived as a recent phenomenon, a more long-term perspective illustrates how changes in the structure of society in Ireland in the 1960s were a crucial process in explaining what is a much longer and more complex process than is often understood. New we-feelings and identifications emerged and strengthened amongst specific groups of players, and contests for control of functions and resources intensified.

In Chap. 7 we trace and explain the changes in how GAA administrators and activists sought to attract and integrate Irish people—mainly young people—into the association over the decades. From the early years following its foundation through to the 1960s, the primary mechanisms through which GAA administrators and activists sought to achieve this were a mix of social constraints and processes of blame and praise gossip around sporting identification and the expression of 'true' national identity. From the 1960s significant changes are perceptible. The emphasis on social constraints as a means to integrate people subsides relative to self-restraints. One manifestation of this was the encouragement of a culture of focussing on individual needs and motivations. It was also reflected in diminishing displays of superiority by GAA administrators towards other sports. This evolved into greater tolerance of other sports and greater cooperation with competing sporting organisations. While a non-linear process, overall the stigmatising of other sports, and those who partook in them, as 'less Irish' by GAA activists and administrators declined, while expressions of superiority relative to other sports were increasingly 'pushed behind the scenes'. We explain how these changes were impelled by changing social and psychological processes concerning people in Ireland more broadly.

Chapter 8 looks at the problems and complexities in the development of the hybrid sport of International Rules football, a composite of Gaelic football and Australian Rules football. Early versions of this new hybrid sport initially emerged in the late 1960s and became more formally established as an occasional series of international games between Ireland and Australia from 1984. The social function of the international series agreed between the sporting organisations responsible for governing the two national codes concerned the provision of playing opportunities for elite players at an international level. Both sports are nationally distinctive in that no other country plays them, and so they function as symbols of national identity. However, players, and others associated with the sports, forgo the feelings of pride of representing the national group in sporting prowess. This requires the establishment of a common sporting code standardised across more than one nation. Problems of developing a hybrid sport are due to the relative power balance between the ruling bodies of the original sports, in terms of the contribution of each sport's rules towards the new code, and the irregular performance and lack of socialisation opportunities for the hybrid sport.

In Chap. 9, our concluding chapter, we reflect on various contemporary issues and developments concerning the GAA and Gaelic games pertaining to gender relations, inter-organisational cooperation, and intra-organisational tensions. Drawing from earlier chapters we illustrate how a long-term developmental approach can help better comprehend and explain contemporary issues.

Although the focus of each chapter is somewhat discrete, it would be a misrepresentation to suggest they are of a stand-alone nature. They are, in both an empirical and theoretical sense, utterly interconnected. For instance, the advances in centralisation and integration processes referred to in Chap. 4 served to facilitate the gradual acceptance and legitimacy of national rule making units noted in Chaps. 2 and 3, which in turn contributed to sportisation processes. Equally, centralisation processes and the development of a national GAA we-identity contributed to the tentative efforts to establish 'international' competition in what would become International Rules football, explained in Chap. 8. The motor of all these developments are social processes such as the growing social significance of sport, advancing thresholds of repugnance towards violence, power balances, expanding and changing social interdependences, and individualisation processes. And while these theoretical concepts and the processes they refer to are explained in detail within individual chapters they transcend all chapters in that they underpin the changes and developments in Gaelic games and the GAA. Changes in the structure of Irish society find expression and are manifest in changes in how Gaelic games are played, viewed and organised. For example, the expansion in social interdependences and the related change in the social habitus of Irish people documented in Chap. 2 are the very same processes that explain changes in displays of superiority towards other sports discussed in Chap. 7. Consequently, the descriptions and explanation of change provided within an individual chapter is enriched and widened as the reader cumulatively progresses through each of the following chapters.

NOTES

1. This study covers the time period from the 1880s to the present. During this time the territory of Ireland (which consists of 32 counties) formed part of the United Kingdom of Great Britain and Ireland until 1921, when it was partitioned and 26 counties attained independence. This new state was called the Irish Free State and later the Republic of Ireland from 1949. Six counties remained under the jurisdiction of Britain forming part of the United Kingdom of Great Britain and Northern Ireland. The GAA was established before partition and remains a 32 county all-Ireland organisation both in an organisational and playing sense. Consequently, we use the term Ireland to refer to the territory of the 32 counties, up to and including the present. We use the Republic of Ireland and Northern Ireland where we wish to specifically identify a development in these particular jurisdictions.
2. This is not a comprehensive list and those cited are for illustrative purposes only. An extensive range of academic articles, books, book chapters and other manuscripts dealing with the GAA and Gaelic games exists. Indeed, many of these are cited throughout this book.

REFERENCES

Connolly, J., & Dolan, P. (2010). The civilizing and sportization of Gaelic football in Ireland: 1884–2008. *Journal of Historical Sociology, 23*(4), 570–598.
Connolly, J., & Dolan, P. (2011). Organizational centralization as figurational dynamics: Movements and counter-movements in the Gaelic Athletic Association. *Management & Organization History, 6*(1), 37–58.

Connolly, J., & Dolan, P. (2012). Sport, media and the Gaelic Athletic Association: The quest for the 'youth' of Ireland. *Media, Culture & Society, 34*(4), 407–423.

Connolly, J., & Dolan, P. (2013a). The amplification and de-amplification of amateurism and professionalism in the Gaelic Athletic Association. *The International Journal of the History of Sport, 30*(8), 853–870.

Connolly, J., & Dolan, P. (2013b). Re-theorizing the 'structure–agency' relationship: Figurational theory, organizational change and the Gaelic Athletic Association. *Organization, 20*(4), 491–511.

Corry, E. (1989). *Catch and kick*. Swords, Co. Dublin: Poolbeg.

Corry, E. (2005). *An illustrated history of the GAA*. Dublin: Gill & Macmillan.

Cronin, M., Duncan, M., & Rouse, P. (2009). *The GAA: A people's history*. Cork: The Collins Press.

Cronin, M., Murphy, W., & Rouse, P. (Eds.). (2009). *The Gaelic Athletic Association 1884–2009*. Dublin: Irish Academic Press.

De Búrca, M. (1989). *Michael Cusack and the GAA*. Dublin: Anvil Books.

De Búrca, M. (1999). *The GAA: A history* (2nd ed.). Dublin: Gill & Macmillan.

Dolan, P., & Connolly, J. (2009). The civilizing of hurling in Ireland. *Sport in Society, 12*(2), 196–211.

Dolan, P., & Connolly, J. (2014a). Documents and detachment in the figurational sociology of sport. *Empiria, 30*, 33–52.

Dolan, P., & Connolly, J. (2014b). Emotions, violence and social belonging: An Eliasian analysis of sports spectatorship. *Sociology, 48*(2), 284–299.

Dunning, E. (1994). The social roots of football hooliganism: A reply to the critics of the 'Leicester School'. In R. Giulianotti, N. Bonney, & M. Hepworth (Eds.), *Football violence and social identity* (pp. 128–157). London: Routledge.

Dunning, E., Murphy, P., & Williams, J. (1988). *The roots of football hooliganism: An historical and sociological study*. London: Routledge.

Dunning, E., & Sheard, K. (1979). *Barbarians, gentlemen & players. A sociological study of the development of rugby football*. Canberra: Australian National University Press.

Elias, N. (1987). The retreat of sociologists into the present. *Theory, Culture & Society, 4*(2–3), 223–247.

Elias, N. (2007). *Involvement and detachment* (Rev. ed.). Dublin: University College Dublin Press.

Elias, N. (2008a). An essay on sport and violence. In N. Elias & E. Dunning (Eds.), *Quest for excitement: Sport and leisure in the civilising process* (Rev. ed., pp. 150–173). Dublin: University College Dublin Press.

Elias, N. (2008b). Introduction. In N. Elias & E. Dunning (Eds.), *Quest for excitement: Sport and leisure in the civilising process* (Rev. ed., pp. 3–43). Dublin: University College Dublin Press.

Elias, N. (2010). *The society of individuals* (Rev. ed.). Dublin: University College Dublin Press.

Elias, N. (2012a). *On the process of civilisation* (Rev. ed.). Dublin: University College Dublin Press.

Elias, N. (2012b). *What is sociology?* (Rev. ed.). Dublin: University College Dublin Press.

Elias, N., & Dunning, E. (1986). *Quest for excitement: Sport and leisure in the civilising process.* Oxford: Basil Blackwell.

Elias, N., & Dunning, E. (2008). Dynamics of sports groups with special reference to football. In N. Elias & E. Dunning (Eds.) *Quest for excitement: Sport and leisure in the civilising process* (Rev. ed., pp. 189–202). Dublin: University College Dublin Press.

Fullam, B. (1999). *Off the field and on.* Dublin: Wolfhound Press Ltd.

Kilminster, R. (2007). *Norbert Elias. Post-philosophical sociology.* London: Routledge.

Mandle, W. F. (1987). *The Gaelic Athletic Association and Irish nationalist politics, 1884–1924.* Dublin: Gill & Macmillan.

McAnallen, D., Hassan, D., & Hegarty, R. (Eds.). (2009). *The evolution of the GAA: Ulaidh, Éire agus eile.* Belfast: Stair Uladh.

Mullan, M. (1995). Opposition, social closure, and sport: The Gaelic Athletic Association in the 19th century. *Sociology of Sport Journal, 12*(3), 268–289.

Rouse, P. (2015). *Sport & Ireland.* Oxford: Oxford University Press.

Sheard, K. (1999). A twitch in time saves nine: Birdwatching, sport, and civilizing processes. *Sociology of Sport Journal, 16,* 181–205.

CHAPTER 2

Gaelic Games and Player Violence

Rule Convergence and Game Standardisation

In this chapter we examine the development of the games of hurling and Gaelic football primarily since their codification following the establishment of the GAA in 1884. Though games existed before then, they lacked the standardised rule structure that facilitated playing across wider geographical areas beyond local parishes or townlands. The GAA provided an organisational context for the promotion and imposition of common rules for playing games. Rules also reflected changing norms and values regarding the permissible displays of violence in Irish society.

With the establishment of the GAA in 1884 came the organisational impetus and capacity to standardise the playing of Gaelic games throughout the country (see De Búrca, 1989, pp. 71–99). The variability in playing traditions and the rudimentary nature of rules meant games between teams from different areas of the country were difficult to organise. Rules for both hurling and Gaelic football were published in 1885, with 10 rules for football and 12 for hurling. The mere publication of new rules did not ensure compliance or uniformity of play, but gradually people learned and applied the rules of play in order to enable matches across broader territories, and also to avoid penalties for transgression. While games resembling hurling and Gaelic football had existed long before the standardisation of rules, these games were, in structure and scope, functionally equivalent to folk games in Britain prior to the codification of rugby and association

© The Author(s) 2020
J. Connolly, P. Dolan, *Gaelic Games in Society*, Palgrave Studies
on Norbert Elias, https://doi.org/10.1007/978-3-030-31699-0_2

football in the nineteenth century (see Elias & Dunning, 2008). In both Ireland and Britain local games were occasionally organised as challenge matches between adjacent parishes or districts, or between different social groups or categories of the same town. There were few rules, and games were played according to local custom. Matches could occur on a temporary pitch or 'played' in areas with little sense of fixed boundaries.

The GAA rules of 1885 were not the first instance of written rules for hurling, as the Killimor rules of 1869 for a club based in Ballinasloe, County Galway, in the West of Ireland seem to represent the earliest evidence of such written rules (Lennon, 1997, p. 1). These rules attempted to ensure clearer distinctions between teams through colours worn, and also to legislate for a minimum number of players before a match could proceed: 'That for the future that not less than thirty be accepted to hurl a challenge match' (Lennon, 1997, p. 1); 'That to avoid mistakes our hurling colours for the future be green and gold' (Lennon, 1997, p. 3). The clearer distinction between teams probably allowed for more coordinated team play, or a more structured flow of interactions between players. But rules were still agreed in advance between sides in terms of how the game would conclude—for example, through a specified time duration or the first to reach an agreed score. So matches still involved local and immediate contingency and negotiation, similar to games played without written rules.

In the 1880s, prior to the establishment of the GAA, there were some attempts at forming new hurling clubs in Dublin (Mandle, 1987, p. 3). In April 1884, Michael Cusack organised a match between his Metropolitan Club from Dublin and the Killimor club. The match was played in Ballinasloe, and though both teams agreed on the rules before the commencement of the match, it was soon abandoned due to spectator encroachment and interference, as well as 'rough' play (Mandle, 1987, p. 3). Confusion over rules became increasingly apparent as teams from more distant areas tried to play matches: 'Not until teams from different areas met would differences in rules become apparent' (Mandle, 1987, p. 3).

The sport of Gaelic football followed a similar trajectory to hurling. Folk games of football were played in Ireland prior to the establishment and dissemination of more standardised rules (Mahon, 2000), and in this respect the folk football games of Ireland resembled those of Britain (see Dunning, 1999, pp. 83–88). The folk football played in Ireland was known as 'caid' in the Irish language and involved play within parish boundaries throughout the day (Guiney, 1976). Like earlier forms of hurling, football was played differently from place to place, dependent on local customs for some semblance of stability and structure (see Hunt, 2008, p. 154). Even after the establishment of the GAA, Gaelic football was sometimes played alongside soccer and rugby. Indeed some clubs who played these other codes constituted the basis for the formation of Gaelic football teams. These teams continued for a time to play a variety of football codes. For example, a County Waterford Gaelic football team, C.J. Kickhams, held 'an unbeaten record under the Gaelic, Rugby, and Association rules' (*Celtic Times*, 16 April 1887). So from the beginning leaders of the GAA existed in a competitive figuration with advocates of other sports, which initially tended to heighten animosity between followers of the different codes. This hostility was exacerbated by the ethnic and national connotations that were amplified by those aligned with the GAA who sought to advance Gaelic games partly through the condemnation of other sports (see also Chaps. 6 and 7). Before we return in greater detail to this process, we first address the refinement of rules which were an attempt at creating greater distinction between Gaelic football and other footballing codes.

The 1889 Gaelic football rules emphasised that the ball should not be carried or thrown (Lennon, 1997, p. 33), in a clear move to distinguish Gaelic football from rugby. The rule was refined in 1896 by defining carrying as taking more than four steps (Lennon, 1997, p. 52). As is often the case, the attempts of administrators to change the conduct of those actually participating did not meet with immediate success. Sometimes games were played according to a mixture of rugby and Gaelic football rules (see Hunt, 2008, p. 154). Furthermore, games often involved tripping, wrestling, scrummages and the carrying of the ball (*Celtic Times*, 29 October 1887). The multiplicity of local customs and emergent rules oriented towards standardisation led to considerable confusion among players, which in turn often contributed to the breakdown of matches and their abandonment (*Celtic Times*, 21 May 1887, 4 June 1887). The continued use of wrestling in Gaelic football matches during the late 1880s is evident from the following match report:

> The match was played under the G.A.A. Rules, but wrestling was allowed. Many of the members of the home team committed fouls, but no notice was taken of them. It would be much better if the rules were strictly adhered to, both on this and other points. (*Celtic Times*, 5 March 1887, p. 3)

Furthermore, referees experienced difficulties in imposing rules and discipline on players as they challenged their interpretation of rules. Sometimes players abandoned matches due to such disagreements (*Celtic Times*, 21 May 1895; Hunt, 2008, p. 149). Rule changes in 1895 included suspension and loss of the match for teams abandoning the game in defiance of the referee (Lennon, 1997, p. 45). Even organising matches in the early years of the GAA proved difficult, as teams often arrived late. The fact that some players might not arrive in time, or at all, meant the first rules permitted a wide range in terms of the number of players per team; the GAA rules of 1884 allow for between 14 and 21 players on each side (Lennon, 1997, p. 11). Michael Cusack had founded *The Celtic Times* to advance the appeal of Gaelic games and the GAA, but in the early years he reported on the difficulties in attracting spectators and fully committed players: 'there were at times during the contest a half-dozen of the hurlers lying with their faces on the ground resting themselves, while the side-your-own system [play according to your own rules] was in full operation' (*Celtic Times*, 16 April 1887). A form of vicious circle may have developed in relation to players and spectators; confusion over the interpretation of rules amongst players probably induced confusion and apathy amongst spectators (and potential spectators) which in turn diminished the commitment and enthusiasm of players. The difficulty in completing the inter-county championship meant that games were not played in the actual designated year of the championship—this alignment did not occur until 1910 (Mandle, 1987, p. 150). Rules continued to be refined in order to standardise Gaelic games. A rule change in 1895 specified that the number of players must be 17 (Lennon, 1997, p. 46), thereby removing one element of game organisation from local determination. However, the continuing problem of ensuring the requisite number of players led to a change in the rules in 1909 to permit the commencement of a match with only 13 players on each side (Lennon, 1997, p. 72). Greater precision regarding the scheduling of events had advanced by the framing of the 1943 rules, when the postponement of matches seven days hence was prescribed (Lennon, 1997, p. 199).

THRESHOLDS OF VIOLENCE

The idea that violence has declined in any sport is always difficult to determine, because violent acts become more newsworthy the more violence is abhorred or denigrated. Thus an increase in news reports of player violence is not necessarily an indication of an increase in the frequency or severity of actual violent acts on the field. It is relatively easier to ascertain the moral reactions to acts of violence, as these are expressed in public denunciations, partly to restore a sense of moral order—the way things ought to be. In the context of table manners in the upper-class circles of European court society, Elias (2012, p. 104) identified 'an advance in the threshold of repugnance and the frontier of shame', meaning formerly acceptable conduct at table gradually became a source of shame. Elias also identified similar processes in sports participation and spectatorship, even in ostensibly violent sports such as boxing (Dolan, 2018; Elias, 2008, 2018). Similarly, here in the Irish sporting context former acts of aggression that were accepted as part of the game gradually became shameful. The sense of shame becomes stronger and more effective in shaping conduct the more social constraints have been embodied as comprehensive and all-embracing self-restraints (Elias, 2012, p. 458).

The advancing threshold of shame around displays of physical violence meant that players became subject to greater scrutiny and surveillance, and the principle of fair play became more embedded in the culture of Gaelic games. However, there is no zero point in self-control: 'No human being lacks the capacity for self-restraint' (Elias, 2007, p. 119). With the development of longer and denser links of social interdependence, self-control becomes more pervasive, even and uniform across more and more social situations. In early forms of hurling, for example, some degree of self-control on the part of players was expected, but compared to later periods the expected standards of control over aggressive impulses were modest. For example, the 1869 Killimor rules stipulated:

> Three umpires to be appointed on each side who have power to order any hurler to cease playing, who in their opinion is under the influence of strong drink, who loses his temper or strikes any of his opponents intentionally. (Lennon, 1997, p. 1)

The specific rule against striking assumes players might engage in violent conduct through loss of emotional control, rather than instrumentally to gain an advantage or further the prospects of victory. Dunning (2008) argues that while violent conduct by players has not disappeared, it has changed its form and function from affective to instrumental violence. The more violent nature of early forms of hurling, prior to its codification by the GAA, is evident from the Laws of Hurley (1870) which was played in Trinity College Dublin: 'No Hurl to be shod with iron, or hoped with wire in a dangerous manner' (Lennon, 1997, p. 2). The lack of reference to wire on the hurley stick in the GAA rules would indicate a relative pacification of the game, in that it was taken for granted that players would not modify sticks in this manner. However, the sport of hurling was compared to British sports on the basis of its more masculine character. Archbishop Croke wrote to Michael Cusack in 1884 accepting the offer to become patron of the GAA:

> We have got such foreign and fantastic field sports as lawn tennis, polo, croquet, cricket and the like—very excellent, I believe, and health-giving exercises in their way, still not racy of the soil, but rather alien, ... if we continue travelling ... putting on, with England's stuffs and broadcloths, her masher habits and such other effeminate follies as she may recommend, we had better, at once, and publicly abjure our nationality, clap hands for joy at sight of the Union Jack, and place 'England's bloody red' exultantly above the green. (Croke quoted in Fullam, 2004, pp. 44–45)

This conflation of emerging 'national' sports with Irish ethnicity and exceptionalism in contradistinction to the imagined more cultivated tastes of the English contributed to a somewhat ambivalent attitude towards violence and aggression in Gaelic games. While changing social pressures beyond the field of play oriented many Irish people towards growing sensitivities to displays of violence, the collective rise of some social groups in Ireland relative to elite groups historically associated with British rule led to feelings of pride in physical strength. The contradictory nature of these social changes can be seen in the symbolic comparison between players and soldiers in media reports. For example, a journalist described the scene before a county championship match as follows:

> Shortly before one o'clock, the vast army of Gaelic soldiers [players]—with their numerous sympathisers—assembled in the O'Connell Square, and with discipline that would do credit to experienced and well-trained men, formed themselves into battalions and marched in their picturesque costume and carrying their *camans* [sic; camán is Irish for hurley sticks] on their shoulders to the scene of action. Their sturdy and resolute appearance affrighted the timid knot of self-important disciples of the foreign faction who peered from behind the curtains at the steady step of their triumphant foes, who are ready to take up arms at a moment's notice to fight for the supremacy of their respective parishes. (*Celtic Times*, 7 May 1887)

Here the evocation of the hostility between 'native' men devoted to 'national' games and those loyal to the British-oriented establishment reflects the changing power relations between social groups in Ireland, which itself is connected to similar dynamics in Britain. The declining position of the nobility and gentry relative to the rising middle classes in Britain also affected the position of the landed ascendency in Ireland. As Elias (2013, p. 337) notes, 'human groups usually revolt against what they experience as oppression, not when the oppression is at its strongest but precisely when it begins to weaken'. The land agitation struggles of the 1880s reflected the changing power relation between tenant-farmers and landlords (Kee, 2000, pp. 364–375; Lee, 1989, pp. 65–96), and together with the overlapping of ethnic identities with these social tensions, this gave growing confidence to those advocating for nationalist orientations in cultural practices such as sport. While there were both violent and non-violent perspectives in Irish nationalism at the same time, and often intertwined (Curtis Jr., 1988), the acceptability and even imperative to show aggression in some social contexts shaped the dispositions of players on the field. Faction fights remained common in Ireland, and hostilities manifested through them also sometimes emerged in the playing of Gaelic games (see, e.g., Garnham, 2004, p. 76; *Irish Times*, 23 July 1890). Such conflicts could lead to serious assault and even death:

> During a Gaelic football tournament on Sunday William O Connor, aged 21, one of the players, was assaulted by some members of the opposing team, and knocked down. A man then stabbed him through the heart with a knife causing instant death. (*Irish Times*, 29 August 1893)

Such examples do not mean that violence was always acceptable—there were no doubt limits, rationalisations and justifications regarding such behaviour. But there was at this time a general ambivalence towards violence, in that the use of physical aggression to protect property, defend oneself or attack antagonists was considered understandable and necessary in certain circumstances. This encouraged the development of a habitus, social learning embodied as second nature (Elias, 2010, 2012), predisposed towards spontaneous aggression in situations of conflict, including sports matches. In this context, as well as the shifting context of antagonism between some Irish and British (or British-oriented) social groups, Gaelic games were lauded as manly and dangerous. For example, in response to the accusation of the dangers of playing hurling, Cusack wrote: 'It is the most dangerous game ever played on this planet. The game was invented by the most sublimely energetic and warlike race that the world has ever known' (*Celtic Times*, 26 February 1887).

Demonstrating the ambivalence towards physical aggression, referees were given greater capacities to exercise control on the field through the use of sanctions. The tolerance for player violence and indiscipline declined. The free kick was introduced in 1888 to punish teams whose players had transgressed a rule (Lennon, 1997, p. 26). The number of rules increased from 10 to 27 between 1884 and 1896, indicating an aspect of the sportisation process whereby folk games are transformed into sports in part through greater precision and refinement of the rules to standardise play (Elias & Dunning, 2008). The revised rules of 1896 also included suspensions of 12 months for players found to have verbally or physically assaulted a referee (Lennon, 1997, p. 51), further demonstrating an advancing threshold of repugnance towards violence in Gaelic games. This advancing threshold on the part of organisational administrators did not of course necessarily or immediately translate into the orientations of players. Indeed such rule changes may have initially heightened tensions between players and referees as both adjusted to new social expectations. The referee may have been seen as a barrier to spontaneous conduct that players considered natural, customary and inevitable.

The rules of 1897 stipulated that the entire team could be suspended following threats made by an individual player to the referee, and this sanction was extended to 'rough play' in the 1910 rules (Lennon, 1997, p. 86). From 1908 goalkeepers were afforded greater protection through the introduction of a parallelogram surrounding the front of the goal from which opposing players were excluded until the arrival of the ball during play (Lennon, 1997, p. 66). These rule changes are examples of the increasing social pressures on players to exercise greater self-restraint. Indeed, at the time of the 1908 rule changes, one GAA official considered the new rules to constitute 'a very considerable constraint on players as compared with former times' (*Gaelic Athletic Annual and County Directory*, 1910–1911, pp. 58–61). These pressures to limit physical aggression on the field of play towards members of one's own social group (Irish nationalist) could operate alongside other pressures to heighten aggression towards those groups deemed to be hostile. In 1911 a future president of the GAA stated: 'We want our men to train and to be physically strong so that when the time comes the hurlers will cast away the caman [sic] for the steal that will drive the Saxon from our land' (McCarthy quoted in Mandle, 1987, p. 162). As social tensions heightened, the mimetic functions of sport, which involved generating emotional excitement to mimic real battles but in a relatively safe enclave (Elias & Dunning, 2008), blurred with preparation for actual military conflict. As British state functionaries contended with their declining monopoly of the means of physical violence in Ireland, some nationalist groups seeking a degree of autonomy from British rule engaged in military training through the use of hurley sticks. Indeed the GAA and its followers became associated with the nationalist cause. In 1913 a GAA county branch endorsed a motion to establish rifle clubs to train an army (Mandle, 1987, p. 162). In 1920 British state forces opened fire on players and spectators at Croke Park (a Gaelic games stadium in Dublin), killing one player and 12 spectators, as a reprisal for the assassination of British intelligence agents by the Irish Republican Army (IRA) earlier that day (Kee, 2000, p. 693).

Around this time, player violence did sometimes lead to the abandonment of a match, as occurred in the 1915 Munster hurling semi-final (Mandle, 1987, p. 174). Spectators (discussed in greater detail in the next chapter) often reacted to player violence by engaging in violence themselves. Following fighting between players, including one player striking another with a hurley stick, during the 1933 Munster hurling final, there occurred 'a pitched battle with upraised hurleys, swinging dangerously at one another' (*Irish Press*, 7 August 1933). When one player was injured in a 'fracas' during the 1936 All-Ireland hurling semi-final, his team walked off the pitch (*Irish Press*, 17 August 1936). During the game, 'There was a penchant to draw wildly and players suffered minor injuries as a result. … **Even when the ball was not in their immediate vicinity players were often vigorously tackling each other unnecessarily**' (*Irish Press*, 17 August 1936, original emphasis). While the journalistic emphasis in this account may suggest that the match was considered exciting, the moral repugnance towards the actions of the players is quite mild. Rather, the journalist lamented the futility of their actions in terms of winning the match. During this period the word 'exciting' (or 'excitement') was often associated with the outbreak of violence on the field. The newspaper reporter for the 1933 game described it as 'unpleasant', but the players were not labelled a disgrace, in contrast to the spectators invading the pitch, whose behaviour was deemed 'disgraceful'. This indicates that by this time spectators were held to a higher standard of emotional self-control compared to players.

Player violence continued to be a problem into the 1930s; many newspaper reports at both local and national level describe physical assaults on referees (see *Connacht Tribune*, 10 October 1931; *Irish Times*, 13 April 1936). We identified two instances of players dying during Gaelic football matches between 1927 and 1929, due to injuries. Manslaughter charges against a player from the opposing teams followed in both cases (see *Irish Independent*, 17 May 1927; *Irish Times*, 13 July 1929). Despite these events, player conduct at matches was sometimes characterised as improving. One sports journalist, known as 'Carberry', suggested in the *Gaelic Annual* of 1927 that 'malpractices and displays of temper on the playing fields have disappeared' (p. 8). Other journalists also noted an improvement in player discipline and 'self-control' (see *Irish Times*, 28 April 1933), and the decline of indiscipline 'even in remote areas' (*Irish Times*, 22 January 1936). The then GAA president expressed similar sentiments (see *Irish Times*, 13 April 1936). While these views could be considered wishful thinking to some extent, it is evident that players were subject to greater observation by referees increasingly enabled to penalise transgressions of rules. This enhanced social observation in the context of more serious consequences encouraged greater self-observation (see Elias, 2006), which in turn facilitated the greater exercise of self-restraint on the field.

The advance in player discipline was also supported by the greater centralisation and integration of the GAA as an organisation (see Chap. 4). While every county committee was affiliated to the GAA Central Council by 1909 (Carey, 2007), the organisation remained somewhat fragile and the processes of integration and centralisation did not proceed smoothly. Between the 1920s and 1940s (see Devine, 2002, pp. 24–33), many sub-units within the GAA defied decisions made by central authorities and sought greater autonomy (see GAA, 1943). However, with increased centralisation over the long term came enhanced capacity to impose rules to encourage player discipline. Referees were accorded greater powers on the field and their decisions were supported through suspensions by others responsible for advancing fair play in Gaelic games. But these developments were both gradual and uneven and did not always prove effective. For example, the referee was assaulted by players and supporters of the defeated team (Moortown) following the 1944 Tyrone county football final. In his report he stated:

I was immediately surrounded by about 6 Moortown players. They held me firmly by the throat, and at least two of them hit me. At this moment a crowd rushed on the field, and with my throat still in this human vice I was beaten, kicked. (*Minutes of Tyrone Co. Committee*, 12 October 1944)

So even though physical assaults on players and referees continued, the moral repugnance towards such violence had advanced. The Moortown club was suspended for five years, with several of its members, including players and supporters, suspended for life. Similarly, the physical assaults on referees during the 1943 All-Ireland final led to one-year suspensions for several players and a life ban for another (*Anglo-Celt*, 30 October 1943; Courtney, 2005, p. 17). However, at this point the threshold of repugnance towards violence was not uniform and was often dependent upon the group allegiances of the observer. One journalist from the county affected by the suspensions following the 1943 final was indignant at their 'severity', declaring the one-year suspension as 'most unreasonable' (*Anglo-Celt*, 30 October 1943). The contradictory nature of habitus formation is not unusual in contexts of changing cultural and moral standards as people have to contend with interpreting new norms and values in light of their older cognitive and emotional frameworks. Some observers, like journalists, were also in networks of dependence with local audiences emotionally attuned to identifying with local players representing a common identity. When this local layer of identification remains strong, the pull of wider and newer standards of conduct may be resisted as an attempted imposition by distant, outsider groups.

The growing social expectation that players should exercise more consistent self-control was supported with attempts at expanding the apparatus of social control through observation and potential sanction. However, there was a recognition by some policymakers within the GAA that not all players had the even, stable self-restraint to cope with such an apparatus. For example, at the 1955 rulemaking congress a motion was debated which would allow linesmen and umpires to report serious rule breaches that the referee may have missed. One member of Congress suggested:

This is a dangerous motion I would not like to be the linesman in a serious Championship who would call over the referee when the ball was up the field. Suppose the referee did not see the signals of the linesman? There would be civil war on the grounds if you had such a rule. (GAA, 1955)

The motion was defeated on the understanding that match officials could be the target of the players' or spectators' anger should decisions go against them.

From 1973, however, the referee was required to consult with linesmen and umpires regarding breaches of rules, while players could be cautioned for striking the goalposts with the hurley (Lennon, 1997, p. 274). This latter rule placed a higher standard of socially expected emotional self-control on players, as even the symbolic suggestion of violence without actual harm to other players or officials became within the advancing threshold of repugnance. Rules became more refined and precise in relation to the degree of physical contact with other players. Also in 1973, 'Pushing in the back, even with the chest, is a foul', again indicating social pressure to exercise greater self-restraint, and also an assumption that by and large such demands were within the capacities of each player. From 1975, players not only had to refrain from the intentional striking of another player with the hurley, but also from bringing the hurley 'through careless play in contact with the person of another player'. Thus players were expected to exercise greater foresight in terms of the potential, unintended consequences of their actions, requiring pronounced self-awareness of field position not only in order to contribute to victory but also protect the health of opponents. The general pattern of play became less wild and spontaneous.

The rule changes reflect not only the limits of how Gaelic games should be played, but also the changing sensitivities towards displays of aggression and violence. Physical aggression remained an important aspect of the games, and vital in the pursuit of victory, but increasingly valued if manifested in a more controlled way. Initially this could make the games appear less exciting to spectators accustomed to 'rough' encounters, but new skills opened up other forms of appreciation. A journalist described the 1974 All-Ireland semi-final as 'lacking bite', but 'enjoyable for those who enjoy the spectacle of master craftsmen forging scores' (*Irish Press*, 5 August 1974).

The growing concern with 'rough play' meant the tackle between opposing players became a focus of attention. It is here of course where opposing players come into direct physical contact, where injuries are most likely to occur, and where the public's sensitivities towards violence are most likely to be threatened. Particularly through the 1960s the legislators for Gaelic games, and for football in particular, sought to provide greater precision in the definition of permissible tackles between players. More precise definitions of legitimate tackles would also reduce the scope of interpretation of both players and referees alike, and potentially reduce the occurrence of the outrage felt by players when a particular tackle was considered illegitimate. Players were expected to control their movements and physical interactions with others to a more demanding and precise standard. For example, a 'fair charge' was defined in 1966 as 'shoulder to shoulder' and by 1975 as 'side to side with at least one foot on the ground' (Lennon, 2001, pp. 269, 307).

Even with the refinement of rules concerning physical interaction on the pitch, aggressive play beyond acceptable limits still occasionally occurred. But apart from the observation by referees and umpires, offending players increasingly became subject to review by adjudication panels. This was aided by the growing television coverage of games, so observation could be retrospective as well as immediate. So players in certain games, as not all games were televised, had to think about not only surveillance on the pitch by the referee and umpires, which might be avoided through players observing the referee, but also by the prospective observation of experts reviewing video footage at a later date. Of course any player's behaviour could also be subject to examination by his own conscience, and no doubt this conscience formation could itself be challenged by the competitive pressure to win. An example of the outcome of adjudication panels includes the case of the 1998 Munster hurling final when two players were sent off 'for a serious exchange of blows' (*Irish Times*, 20 July 1998). Subsequently, a Games Administration Committee viewed video evidence of the incident, which punished other players involved in violent encounters just before the game started. The journalist reporting on the events considered the violence in part to have occurred because the referee had left the field of play. So in the absence of perceived social observation (as the prospect of subsequent video review had not it seems been successfully internalised by all the players), player self-control could still be fragile in the face of imminent physical conflict with group and individual pride at stake. Both hurling and Gaelic football retained a structure of interactions between specific opposing players in various positions on the field, so the tradition of standing up to one's direct opponent remained. However, the public and especially media commentators subjected players to greater moral condemnation in the face of unacceptable displays of violence over the course of the twentieth century. While in the 1930s journalists tended to refer to the offending team as a whole, in later decades journalists were more willing to identify specific players (see *City Tribune*, 24 December 1986; *Irish Times*, 22 July 1998). Earlier referee reports also tended to be more forgiving. The referee at a 1946 inter-county hurling match reported he had sent two players off for striking each other with their hurleys. In his report (viewed by GAA Central Council only), he stated: 'I sent them to the line but I will now ask the Central Council member to deal lightly with those boys. I think if they were warned to control themselves in future it would meet their case' (GAA Central Council minutes, 10 August 1946). During an interview in 2002 a hurling referee of the 1940s and 50s (Murphy quoted in O'Sullivan, 2002, p. 122) recalled: 'Hurling in those days was much tougher than it is now. ... There was far more aggression in the game then.'

Over the course of the twentieth century the function and expression of violence on the field also shifted in terms of the balance between affective and instrumental violence towards the latter. Of course both forms remain possible, but with increasing emotional self-control players became better able to deploy physical aggression for strategic advantage in a game. This development is consistent with Dunning's (2008) argument that as more uniform and even self-control advances, in tandem with growing competitive pressures in sport, players are more likely to use instrumental violence, or to deploy violence more strategically as a calculation for more likely success overall for the team. The increase in this form of violence or aggression was noted in some of the GAA's own policies. For example, the GAA's strategic review of 1971 claimed that a '"win-at-all-costs" outlook' contributed to indiscipline (GAA, 1971, p. 108). Reports of more strategic use of violence by players became more prominent in media reports (see *Irish Press*, 4 July 1977; *Irish Press*, 11 September 1980). In his report of the 1970 All-Ireland Under-21 football final, journalist Mick Dunne noted a 'tendency to pull down forwards when they approached within scoring range', and continued, 'This has now become such a commandment of present day football and one that pays dividends under the rules of football, that the under-21s and minors employ it as a strategy of their game' (*Irish Press*, 5 October 1970). The offence of 'Persistent Fouling' was added to the rules in 1974 (Lennon, 1997, p. 302) in order to curb these player strategies. Yet the instances of these practices continued, leading to regular calls to address the problem (see, for example, *Irish Times*, 20 July 1977; *Irish Times*, 30 September 2008). Persistent fouling was labelled the 'major evil' in Gaelic football by the GAA director-general in 1982 (*Irish Times*, 23 March 1982). In 2004, The GAA's Football Task Force recommended the introduction of a disciplinary experimental rule that would enable the referee to send a player off for a period of ten minutes (a sin bin) for specific offences. This was eventually abandoned in Spring 2005 due to player and manager opposition (see *Irish Times*, 23 February 2005; *Irish Times*, 4 January 2005).

It is important to note that we are not implying that impulsive violence between players, or indeed assaults on referees, no longer occur, but in the context of overall violence on the field of play the balance between affective and instrumental violence has shifted in the direction of the latter. Furthermore, all forms of violence have become subject to greater scrutiny and also more pronounced moral repugnance and disgrace.

FIGURATIONAL DYNAMICS IN IRELAND

We have of course already discussed figurations within Ireland. The network of players, spectators, coaches, managers, referees and GAA administrators all form a sporting figuration which shapes the conduct and emotions of the various people comprising this figuration. But this figuration is also part of wider figurational dynamics that refers to the changing dependences between people beyond sport. In particular the threshold of repugnance or the growing sensitivities of people towards displays of violence are related to the development of a denser social network involving over time more ties to more people of more diverse social positions. This has encouraged a more circumspect and careful sense of one's place and socially appropriate forms of interaction, that gradually become part of the national habitus. This social development of more extensive interdependent links is a gradual, uneven process, meaning changes can be more sudden in certain phases of history, producing feelings of dislocation, and also that not everyone experiences figurational changes in the same way. This depends on people's positions and trajectories in the wider, changing network.

As we are concerned with the development of Gaelic games, we will focus on the historical period from the second half of the nineteenth century. We are less concerned with the lives and decisions of prominent historical figures, and more with tracing, albeit briefly, the changes in the kind of social networks that both enabled and constrained Irish people generally. Also, changes in the structure of Irish society were closely connected with changes in British society. As industrialisation flourished in England in particular over the course of the nineteenth century, Irish society underwent greater commercialisation in the agricultural sector. The functional specialisation in the cultivation of specific crops or the breeding of specific animals brought small farmers into a more complex network of relationships (see Clark, 1978, p. 31; Ó Gráda, 1994, pp. 255–270). This was aided by the development of transport, as well as trade and distribution networks and the increased capacity of state institutions to provide security enabling the carriage of goods. The commercialisation of Irish agriculture both facilitated and depended upon the mechanisation of many farming practices. This too constituted an expanding network of social interdependences, but also the movement of many people from rural areas into towns and cities in Ireland and beyond. According to selected *Census of Population* statistics (1861–2002) the proportion of the male labour force engaged in agricultural occupations was between 50 and 60 per cent up to 1946. Between 1961 and 2002 this proportion declined from 43 to 8 per cent. More urbanised societies tend to involve more frequent, diverse and pressing dependences between people, though this varies according to the specific functions any individual fulfils for others within the network.

Those more central to any figuration are compelled to exert a more 'steady control of conduct' over themselves (Elias, 2012, p. 419), and are more likely to have been socialised with a greater emphasis on emotional self-control and the foreseeable consequences of actions on others. Although the increase in social interdependences may in general favour the development of a less volatile habitus, in Ireland's case an agrarian class transformation occurred (Clark, 1978, 1979) which facilitated the emergence of the GAA to promote more nationally distinctive games. In the first half of the nineteenth century there were many tensions between farmers, landholders and labourers, but this shifted towards a clearer division involving farmers and landlords. This social division also tended to overlap with religious and ethnic differences. Landlords tended towards a social and cultural identification with established groups in British society, though there were of course notable exceptions. Violence between the rural classes of farmers, landholders and labourers declined in part through the decreasing proportion of the rural population employed as labourers due to mechanisation, as well as the declining function of landholders as middlemen. The more 'native' games of hurling and Gaelic football (or their earlier folk versions) became associated with national distinctiveness. Other popular sports such as soccer, rugby and cricket became negative symbols of British rule and domination. The more Gaelic games were conflated with the 'true Gael', the more other groups who identified with the United Kingdom (UK) clung to rugby and other sports as symbols of their allegiance. Of course some people played particular sports out of custom and preference, but specific sports became increasingly politicised in an 'us' and 'them' spiral of group distinction. Violence continued to be a significant element of social tensions in Ireland well into the twentieth century, even after partial independence[1] due to contesting visions of Irish nationhood or perhaps the recognition of the gap between ideals and realities.

The achievement of partial Irish independence in part through violence led to a rather ambivalent attitude to violence among many Irish people. While Elias (2008) contends that 'parliamenterisation'—or the acceptance that social conflicts should be debated and resolved without resort to violence—facilitated the growth of organised sport through upper-class patronage in England, the social conditions were somewhat different in Ireland. The Catholic, nationally oriented rural population became more homogenous and within this broad group relations became more pacified. Relations between this group and the landlords became more hostile, and this enmity shaped and reflected ethnic and national divisions. Part of the symbolic distinction between Irish and British sports involved pride in aggression, and so Gaelic games tended to carry contradictions towards violence. But as Irish people became more and more enmeshed in global relations of interdependence, particularly from the 1960s onwards (Dolan, 2005, 2009a, 2009b), the historical legacy of ambivalence towards violence receded. Politicians sought to develop a social infrastructure attractive to foreign industrialists, and greater investment in education (O'Connor, 2014) encouraged a more future-oriented disposition anticipating dependence on a diversity of nation-states in the globalising economy. Only 16 per cent of manufacturing output was exported in 1951, but this had increased to 64 per cent by 1988 (O'Malley, 1992, pp. 33–34). By then, foreign firms comprised 44 per cent of manufacturing employment and 75 per cent of manufacturing exports (O'Malley, 1992, p. 39).

Over time, more and more Irish people became enmeshed in lengthening and more complex social interdependences, and this relatively successful integration into wider and denser figurations encouraged the development of a national habitus oriented towards more pacified conduct. While people still enjoy the excitement of playing or watching (see Chap. 3) Gaelic games involving physical conflict, sensitivities towards violence have heightened. However, this has not been a linear process, and indeed due to the national (32-county) focus of the GAA, there have been quite uneven contexts in terms of the monopolies of violence upheld by state authorities. Therefore, the process of habitus formation inimical to violence varied somewhat, and the potential remained for the use of violence by those less ashamed of it to provoke reactions that might ordinarily produce shame in others later or in other social situations. While some tolerance for wayward conduct was available to players in the emotional intensity of sporting conflict, the same cannot be said for spectators. It is to this group that we turn to next.

NOTE

1. By the phrase partial independence, we mean that only 26 counties had attained a level of independence from Britain. It does not refer to the legal-political structures that continued to bind the Free State to Britain, such as the Free State's membership of the British Commonwealth, which were part of Treaty with Britain in 1921.

REFERENCES

Carey, T. (2007). *Croke Park: A history.* Cork: The Collins Press.
Clark, S. (1978). The importance of agrarian classes: Agrarian class structure and collective action in nineteenth-century Ireland. *British Journal of Sociology, 29*(1), 22–40.
Clark, S. (1979). *Social origins of the Irish Land War.* Princeton, NJ: Princeton University Press.
Courtney, P. (Ed.). (2005). *Classic All-Ireland finals.* Galway: Leinster Leader Ltd.
Curtis Jr., L. P. (1988). Moral and physical force: The language of violence in Irish nationalism. *Journal of British Studies, 27*(2), 150–189.
De Búrca, M. (1989). *Michael Cusack and the GAA.* Dublin: Anvil Books.
Devine, L. (2002). The twenties. In T. Moran (Ed.), *Stair CLG Chonnacht 1902–2002* (pp. 23–36). Carrick-on-Shannon, Co. Leitrim: Carrick Print.
Dolan, P. (2005). *The development of consumer culture, subjectivity and national identity in Ireland, 1900–1980.* PhD thesis, Goldsmiths College, University of London, London.
Dolan, P. (2009a). Developing consumer subjectivity in Ireland: 1900–80. *Journal of Consumer Culture, 9*(1), 117–141.
Dolan, P. (2009b). Figurational dynamics and parliamentary discourses of living standards in Ireland. *British Journal of Sociology, 60*(4), 721–739.
Dolan, P. (2018). Class relations and the development of boxing: Norbert Elias on sportisation processes in England and France. In J. Haut, P. Dolan, D. Reicher, & R. Sánchez García (Eds.), *Excitement processes: Norbert Elias's unpublished works on sports, leisure, body, culture* (pp. 235–254). Wiesbaden: Springer.

Dunning, E. (1999). *Sport matters: Sociological studies of sport, violence and civilization*. London: Routledge.

Dunning, E. (2008). Social bonding and violence in sport. In N. Elias & E. Dunning (Eds.), *Quest for excitement: Sport and leisure in the civilising process* (Rev. ed., pp. 222–241). Dublin: University College Dublin Press.

Elias, N. (2006). *The court society* (Rev. ed.). Dublin: University College Dublin Press.

Elias, N. (2007). *An essay on time* (Rev. ed.). Dublin: University College Dublin Press.

Elias, N. (2008). Introduction. In N. Elias & E. Dunning (Eds.), *Quest for excitement: Sport and leisure in the civilising process* (Rev. ed., pp. 3–43). Dublin: University College Dublin Press.

Elias, N. (2010). *The society of individuals* (Rev. ed.). Dublin: University College Dublin Press.

Elias, N. (2012). *On the process of civilisation* (Rev. ed.). Dublin: University College Dublin Press.

Elias, N. (2013). *Studies on the Germans*. Dublin: University College Dublin Press.

Elias, N. (2018). Boxing and duelling. In J. Haut, P. Dolan, D. Reicher, & R. S. García (Eds.), *Excitement processes: Norbert Elias's unpublished works on sports, leisure, body, culture* (pp. 173–215). Wiesbaden: Springer.

Elias, N., & Dunning, E. (2008). *Quest for excitement: Sport and leisure in the civilising process* (Rev. ed.). Dublin: University College Dublin Press.

Fullam, B. (2004). *The throw-in: The GAA and the men who made it*. Dublin: Wolfhound Press.

GAA. (1943). *Minutes of annual congress*. Dublin: GAA.

GAA. (1955). *Minutes of annual congress*. Dublin: GAA.

GAA. (1971). *Report of the commission on the GAA*. Dublin: GAA.

Garnham, N. (2004). Accounting for the early success of the Gaelic Athletic Association. *Irish Historical Studies, 34*(133), 65–78.

Guiney, D. (1976). *Gaelic football*. Dublin: Gaelic Press.

Hunt, T. (2008). *Sport and society in Victorian Ireland: The case of Westmeath*. Cork: Cork University Press.

Kee, R. (2000). *The green flag: A history of Irish nationalism*. London: Penguin.

Lee, J. (1989). *The modernisation of Irish society: 1848–1918*. Dublin: Gill & Macmillan.

Lennon, J. (1997). *The playing rules of football and hurling, 1884–1995*. Gormanstown, Co. Meath: Northern Recreation Consultants.

Lennon, J. (2001). *The playing rules of hurling 1602–2010; Gaelic football 1884–2010; hurling–shinty internationals 1933–2000*. Gormanstown, Co. Meath: The Northern Recreation Consultants.

Mahon, J. (2000). *A history of Gaelic football*. Dublin: Gill & Macmillan.

Mandle, W. F. (1987). *The Gaelic Athletic Association and Irish nationalist politics, 1884–1924*. Dublin: Gill & Macmillan.

Ó Gráda, C. (1994). *Ireland: A new economic history.* Oxford: Oxford University Press.

O'Connor, M. (2014). Investment in edification: Reflections on Irish education policy since independence. *Irish Educational Studies, 33*(2), 193–212.

O'Malley, E. (1992). Problems of industrialisation in Ireland. In J. H. Goldthorpe & C. T. Whelan (Eds.), *The development of industrial society in Ireland* (pp. 31–52). Oxford: Oxford University Press.

O'Sullivan, J. (2002). *Men in black.* Dublin: Sliabh Bán Publications.

CHAPTER 3

Spectators, Emotions and the Individualisation of Violence

SPECTATOR VIOLENCE AND GAELIC GAMES

In this chapter we address the question of emotional self-control in the context of watching Gaelic games. We examine the complex and changing relations between emotional controls, watching sports games, aggressive conduct by spectators and the nature and extent of dependences between people comprising Irish society since the late nineteenth century. While there has been spectator violence at Gaelic games since the establishment of the GAA, there is no tradition of organised hooliganism (Bairner, 2002, p. 128). Soccer hooligans in England were attracted to the sport due to is oppositional, masculine character, and specifically because it facilitates opportunities for violent encounters (Dunning, Murphy, & Williams, 1988). Gaelic games have not been used in this way, and violence has tended to be more unplanned and more directly related to events on the pitch. Indeed, this was also the case in relation to soccer in England before the First World War (Dunning et al., 1988).

Spectator violence at Gaelic games evoked recurrent waves of moral repugnance, but these intensified from the 1970s in particular. Over the history of the sport since the foundation of the GAA, spectators, like players, became more self-controlled in their conduct attending matches, but this has been non-linear, uneven and fragile. Overall, however, the threshold of shame regarding displays of violence by spectators has advanced. This can be seen most clearly when events over long periods are compared.

© The Author(s) 2020
J. Connolly, P. Dolan, *Gaelic Games in Society*, Palgrave Studies on Norbert Elias, https://doi.org/10.1007/978-3-030-31699-0_3

Before examining the early forms of spectator conduct, the following recent example illustrates the relatively advanced sensitivity regarding displays of aggression by spectators.

Media coverage of the 2010 Leinster (one of Ireland's four provinces) senior football final at Croke Park (GAA headquarters and main stadium) between neighbouring counties Meath and Louth involved extensive comment across television and newspapers. Louth were leading by a single point and the game had gone 34 seconds beyond the three-minute injury time period when a Meath player threw the ball (a foul in Gaelic football) into the opposing goal. Subsequent television replays showed that several fouls had been committed by Meath players, yet the referee awarded the goal. Louth were about to claim their first provincial championship for over 60 years through the defeat of their far more successful local rivals. Significant emotional excitement and tension builds up in that spectating context, as hope and expectant joy blended with relief rapidly turns to despair. When the experience of defeat so quickly follows the evidence of unfairness then spectator anger can produce moral transgression concerning the interactions between interdependent people pursuing different functions—those watching and those regulating. Shortly after the final whistle was blown by the referee he was approached by several players from the losing team and then by several spectators. One of the spectators shoved the referee in the chest, whereupon some players, officials and spectators sought to protect the referee or remonstrate with the offending spectator. As the referee walked towards the stadium tunnel he was further questioned (or possibly verbally abused) by several players. Another spectator attempted to push him from behind but missed and fell, while two or three others followed the referee closely while wagging their fingers at him. By this point, several police officers surrounded the referee and walked alongside him towards the tunnel. He was also protected by the manager of the losing team who initially ran onto the pitch apparently to remonstrate with him. The following commentary on RTÉ (the state broadcaster in the Republic of Ireland) television demonstrates the moral repugnance at the unfolding scenes:

First commentator: Louth had it, Louth should have won the game, but they haven't. They go to the referee Martin Sludden to ask him to consider his... [as first spectator pushed the referee] Oh this shouldn't happen. That is disgraceful, that is disgraceful.

Second commentator:	This is outrageous actually. Yeah, there's been an attack on the referee there. That's totally uncalled for.
First commentator:	Disgraceful.

...

[As another spectator attempts to shoulder referee from behind]

First commentator:	Oh! this is disgraceful, that's disgraceful.
Second commentator:	This is all wrong, this is all wrong, that the referee is being interfered with.
First commentator:	And this is one of the reasons the GAA have been saying we've got to keep fans off the field, they've no business being out there, and this is ...
Second commentator:	This is thuggish, it's wrong, I don't care what the result is, this is absolutely wrong what is happening the referee.

...

First commentator:	I haven't seen anything happen like that in a match here, where we normally see such good sporting behaviour. That was outrageous. You can understand their anger and their frustration, but that kind of behaviour cannot be tolerated, and I'm sure the GAA will take serious action.

So the moral standards concerning emotional experience and conduct suggest that feelings of anger are permitted once they do not escalate into physical assault. It is important to note that the referee was not punched or kicked though television images show contorted facial expressions and a spectator holding his clenched fist by his side, as though struggling to control his impulse towards physical assault. One spectator who sought to protect the referee subsequently punched a player from the opposing team who was engaged in an altercation with a player from the team he supported (he was wearing a Louth replica shirt). We are not attempting here to moralise upon the conduct of spectators, but rather to explain the moral pronouncements of media commentators. Newspaper headlines on the following day included: 'Referee shoved in the chest after GAA final'; 'Dark clouds cast over Louth's big day in the sun' (*Irish Times*, 12 July

2010). The GAA president labelled the treatment of the referee as 'absolutely disgraceful' while journalists described the scenes as 'ugly and totally unacceptable'.

In the early twentieth century, journalists also sometimes commented on the scenes they observed, but the moral tone was less severe. A headline in 1927 referred to 'FREE FIGHTS AT LOUTH FOOTBALL MATCH: REFEREE AND PLAYERS ATTACKED' (*Irish Times*, 20 September 1927). This concerned a match between two clubs within the county of Louth. The scenes of violence at this match were described as 'remarkable'. The referee ordered a player off the field for striking an opponent. He refused to leave so the referee awarded the game to the opposing team, whereupon he was attacked by players and spectators. Police spent an hour 'quelling the disturbances' as fights spread from the field to the local village. Both the referee and players were assaulted by spectators, and opposing spectators fought each other. As we show below, spectator violence often had this socio-temporal structure from the late nineteenth century and only gradually, unevenly and incompletely, did this event and social structure transform from 'free fights' to more individual and more delayed violent displays with the referee increasingly both the sole target of both aggression and protection.

Civilising Processes, Emotions and Forward Panics

A fundamental aspect of Elias's (2012) theory of civilising processes concerns the moderation of emotions, and indeed their nuanced differentiation in the context of expanding social interdependences. Gradually over the course of many generations from the late Middle Ages patterns of conduct became less spontaneous and higher, more exacting standards of emotional management and self-presentation prevailed. The key point here is the relativity of these movements—there was no zero point, no origin and certainly no possibility of identifying natural emotions beyond social moulding. For Elias, the opposition between the biological and social, and so many others that have plagued the social sciences, was anathema. Another distinction that Elias avoided was that between micro situations and macro social structures. However, he is now associated mainly with such broad concepts as social change and broader social networks developing over centuries that the micro aspects are relatively underemphasised. Here we compare the figurational approach (including the work of Eric Dunning on sport) with the more recent micro-sociological treatment of violence by Randall Collins (2008). Collins introduces the concept of 'forward panic' to convey the phenomenon of people overcoming natural inclinations towards positive emotional 'entrainment' with the result that violent outbursts become uncontrolled; violent episodes assume a life of their own as individuals get caught up in a tunnel of anger and aggression.

Elias's central argument is that a more self-steering and self-restrained habitus develops in the context of lengthening and multiplying links of interdependence, which requires an increasing monopolisation of violence within a given territory. The two processes of increasing monopolisation and social interdependences propel each other. Elias developed the concept of figuration to connote the changing network of mutual dependencies bonding and linking people together. This network is not harmonious, but a shifting web of tensions placing multiple pressures, constraints and compulsions on individuals in various directions, producing contradictions, reversals and dilemmas (Elias, 2010). While Elias has often been accused of linear thinking, assuming a straight trajectory from barbarity to civilisation, close inspection reveals no such linearity or teleology (see Mennell, 1998, pp. 228–237). Indeed, Elias specifically highlights the preponderance of reversals, de-civilising trends and the unevenness of the process over time. However, it is perhaps accurate to conclude that he did emphasise the overarching arc of social development towards more even and uniform self-restraint and less oscillation in emotional displays depending on social situations and specific relationships. Alongside this process of the civilising of conduct came an increasing 'scope of identification' between people over broader social networks covering class, ethnic and even national groups (Elias, 2010, pp. 155–237).

Thus a feeling of belonging and caring for others is part of a general process of 'functional democratisation' or relative equalisation This sense of an emotional connection with particular groups, and a duty of care towards others, is part of the process of 'functional democratisation' or relative equalisation, particularly between social classes. No longer does the state belong to the monarchy or even the wider nobility, but initially to the bourgeoisie and eventually, through industrialisation and the growing power chances of the working classes, incorporating much of the population. The state becomes a nation-state. Here Elias follows Weber's classic characterisation of the state as the organisation maintaining a *'monopoly of the legitimate use of physical force* within a given territory' (Weber, 1991, p. 78, original emphasis), though Elias stresses the twin monopolies of violence and taxation in state formation processes rather than the significance of legitimacy. Elias focuses on the effectiveness of state control of the means of violence, which ultimately leads to pacification as an unintended outcome of elimination contests between rival warrior families and groups. While this is strictly speaking accurate in terms of long-term developments, there is something significant to Weber's concern regarding legitimacy, at least in our study here. This relates to the level of mutual identification between the state agents of violence control and the rest of the population; where certain groups do not recognise the monarch or government as their head of state, in other words they have little or no feelings of loyalty towards such people, this can diminish the respect and compliance of such groups towards state forces. Elias (2010, p. 160) notes that the emotional identification between the state and the population can be weak in the case of new states, but the allegiance between state agencies of violence and the population in terms of perceived legitimacy are not explicitly addressed. However, Elias does stress the conflicting loyalties experienced by people; as part of processes of social integration, we-identities become multilayered and potentially contradictory. In an Irish context of course, we-identities are multiple and contested, and the emergence of the GAA not only reflected processes of state disintegration but contributed to them in terms of symbolism, traditions and social practices.

The effective monopoly of physical violence as well as the associated development of more embracing self-steering capacities and inclinations are not treated as achievements by Elias but rather processes which are largely unplanned. The more even and less emotionally oscillating habitus is formed through adult–child relations and so are not inevitable, or determined by the requirements of the social system (an idea anathema to Elias), but subject to considerable variation and effectiveness depending on the position of such people in the figuration. Thus while Elias's work has been mistakenly criticised for assuming modern civility in social relations, and indeed unfettered, unstructured impulsiveness in medieval societies (Dunning, 1989; Robinson, 1987), he recognises social spaces where established standards of civility have not taken root and have even been actively resisted due to exclusionary practices by established groups (Elias & Scotson, 2008). Elias and Dunning (2008) examine the development of special enclaves (most notably, sporting arenas) where the 'controlled decontrolling of emotions' (Elias, 2008b, p. 27) can occur. Dunning and other colleagues have also extended this figurational approach into an examination of soccer hooliganism (Dunning, 1994a; Dunning, Murphy, Waddington, & Astrinakis, 2002; Dunning, Murphy, & Williams, 1986; Dunning et al., 1988).

Elias and Dunning's (2008) basic arguments in relation to sport and sportisation are that the need for leisure as a source of pleasurable excitement emerges with the increasing pacification and routinisation of life. This occurred predominantly in England from the eighteenth century (but especially the nineteenth century with the development of rugby and soccer) because that national society became both more pacified due to relatively stable power balances between the monarchy, nobility, gentry and bourgeoisie, and less centralised and bureaucratic compared to other European states (Dunning, 1994b). Over the course of the nineteenth and twentieth centuries these new sporting forms underwent a civilising process, in that greater social and self-control advanced in terms of player and spectator conduct. Games had to continue to serve the function of providing excitement and generating emotional tension (as well as release), but violent displays gradually became more repugnant and unacceptable. As this was a social process over generations, there were of course overlapping cultures of morality concerning the toleration of violence, which itself constituted a source of tension and sports development, for example, through the bifurcation of football into rugby and soccer and of rugby into union and league forms (Dunning & Sheard, 2005). This civilising process entailed a more even and stable self-restraint that became more automatic and less prone to extremes of emotional display. Elias used the term habitus to refer to this learnt capacity that seems like second nature, and it is this trans-situational disposition and capacity that primarily distinguishes the figurational approach from that of Randal Collins. The rules and practices of sport are designed and redesigned partly in accordance with the prevailing habitus of players, administrators and spectators. This is not strictly speaking intentional, as the framing of rules is a collective enterprise with unplanned dimensions; people innovate from existing rulebooks and through their habitus which feels 'natural'. For Elias and Dunning (2008, p. 53), sport and other leisure activities serve a 'compensatory function' where 'the propensities for the serious and threatening type of excitement have diminished'. We argue, however, that in the case of Ireland sport and leisure served multiple functions which delayed and shaped the civilising of Gaelic games. These included the function of national distinction during a period involving serious and threatening excitement.

Though Elias and Dunning (2008, p. 62) do emphasise the mimetic functions of modern sport, meaning the capacity of sport to arouse emotions related to other spheres though in a more pleasurable and less threatening form, they also acknowledge the potential for excited spectators to lose control. Indeed Dunning (in Elias & Dunning, 2008, p. 62fn) states that sports events can lose their mimetic functions during revolutions. Also, while sporting events can produce violence in the midst of a violent society, the relative autonomy of sport can itself sustain violence despite the increasing pacification of social relations. Dunning (2008, pp. 230–231) argues that violence in sport has declined over generations since the nineteenth century as local ties have decreased in importance relative to social and occupational dependences far beyond the local. Dunning sees this as similar to Durkheim's famous distinction between mechanical and organic solidarity.

In subsequent work on spectator violence, Dunning et al. (1986, 1988) argue that since the late nineteenth century the working classes have to a large extent been incorporated into norms and ideals of the established groups in British society. However, some segments remained unincorporated and, according to Dunning et al., football hooligan gangs that emerged from the 1960s mainly came from this social group. Of more relevance to our research is their finding that spectator violence before World War I tended to be more match-related and assaults were directed at players and officials rather than rival fan groups. They also argue that aggressive masculinity is a norm that displays some continuity over time, even though the performance of this norm is recognised as limited to defence rather than attack; this latter modification does not extend to football hooligans, a fact which demonstrates the unevenness of civilising processes. Dunning (1994a, p. 152) also contends that in part the limited incorporation of some groups within the working classes into dominant norms regarding displays of violence relates to their interactions with the police, the state agents of violence control. Members of such groups often receive inadequate protection and so resort to violence to protect themselves, and indeed are more likely to experience state violence. Before the incorporation of the majority of the working class, the police were often attacked, and so referees could be seen by such groups as examples of resented authority (Dunning et al., 1988, pp. 89–90). Dunning does not address the connection with legitimacy, but whether any state authority is seen as right or just is related to either the procedures for selecting such authorities, or the fairness of their decisions in distributing resources

(Rothstein, 2009). Where some groups in any jurisdiction believe that state agencies, including the police and defence forces, act in the interests of particular groups (e.g., based on ethnicity, religion or class), then trust in such state authorities may be limited.

There is some commonality between the figurational approach to emotions and violence and Collins' (2008, 2009) interactional perspective. Both Dunning and Collins eschew the notion that violence is somehow contagious, though both accept that as tensions build up involving opposing groups then violence can occur. Elias recognises the relative ease of violence at a distance compared to face-to-face combat as the civilising process unfolds. Both approaches highlight emotions as central processes in human conduct, and actions are not assumed to be the outcome of individual intentions. Collins (2008, p. 128) writes of the crowd amplifying the emotion and both Collins (2008, pp. 285, 308) and Dunning (1999, p. 7) refer to the 'collective effervescence' of sports spectatorship. Collins, however, focuses, like Goffman, on immediate fact-to-face interactions. Here people face considerable difficulty in overcoming the natural inclination towards positive emotional entrainment. In order to inflict injury, they must go beyond the confrontational tension of the conflict situation. For Collins, interpersonal violence is unusual, and most people are incompetent in displays of violence. Social encounters involving conflict and aggression normally fade into verbal bluster and retreat rituals. However, if people do overcome the confrontational tension, then they can get lost in a tunnel of forward panic, and extreme violence can result. As one opponent gains the upper hand, the other diminishes, becoming immobilised by fear. This in turn encourages the winning participant to pile on further blows and attacks; a vicious circle of victory and defeat is predicated upon the related emotional energies between the fighters. The difficulty with Collins' analysis is that this micro orientation cannot explain the changing moral order regarding displays of violence, and also the historical variability in the tendency to resort to violence, to overcome confrontational tension. Collins does not adequately address the changing degree and forms of violence across time and space (Cooney, 2009). Also, as Felson (2009, p. 578) states, there is a tendency towards an opposition between normal and abnormal (violent) situations in Collins's work. The figurational approach does not assume a norm of harmony in social life.

Collins (2008, pp. 91, 475n2) does refer to a violent incident in 1912 between the baseball player Ty Cobb and a verbally aggressive spectator who worked in dangerous manual labour as a 'type of individual'. This reliance on the individual characteristics of the spectator as part of the explanation of conduct comes close to Elias's use of habitus, but Elias clearly connects habitus as a process to other social processes far beyond the immediate situation and interactions—the shifting structure of inter-dependent ties and links over generations. A social habitus formed in more conflictual and violent societies or social groups tends towards more volatile emotional dispositions. The socially generated tensions produce aggressive impulses which are enacted before self-control mechanisms moderate such emotions and impulses in situations involving conflict.

In the sections below we organise our analysis and synthesis of violent episodes and their media treatment into several themes, which demon-strate both continuities and some discontinuities. While there is a ten-dency towards the individualisation of violence from the 1980s in particular, collective violence does not disappear entirely. However, con-sistent with a more general increase in functional specialisation in Irish society (see Chap. 2), and indeed in Gaelic games themselves, the targets of violence become more focussed on the referee as the specialist of rule enforcement and social order within the flow of games themselves. There has also been an advancing 'threshold of shame' regarding displays of vio-lence within media accounts of matches. Again, there is no zero point. Journalists and commentators of the late nineteenth and early twentieth centuries did not revel in a voyeurism of violence, but 'rough' play and spectator participation did not evoke the same degree of odium compared to the late twentieth and early twenty first centuries.

COLLECTIVE IMPULSES AND VIOLENT ACTIONS

An important factor in the propensity for social conflict in leisure activities is the time required for people to adjust to both game standardisation and functional specialisation. According to Elias, lengthening chains of inter-dependences produce greater foresight, more even and extensive emo-tional controls and a less volatile habitus. However, Mennell (2007, p. 214) argues that in the short term, conflict may initially rise as groups engage in 'integration struggles'. Similarly, an emotional habitus formed in one set of social conditions can feel resentment towards people occupy-ing new interdependent functions.

In the Killimor hurling rules of 1869 (see Chap. 2), spectators were expected to adhere to their role of watching rather than participating in the play:

Bystanders to have no voice in any decision, and should they interfere with the hurlers in any way, that may be considered by the umpires and judges as preventing the game being fairly played, the aggrieved hurlers may claim the prise. (quoted in Lennon, 1997, p. 1)

The mere presence of the rule obviously indicates that spectator involvement was a concern for the organisers of these matches. Indeed when Killimor played Michael Cusack's Metropolitans (discussed also in Chap. 2), repeated pitch invasions by spectators occurred (De Búrca, 1989, p. 83). The 1886 GAA rules empowered the referee to award a score if a shot bound for the goal 'had not struck a bystander' (quoted in Lennon, 1997, p. 20), suggesting that spectators were prone to interfering with play. Cusack's praise of spectators indicates that correct conduct could not always be expected:

The spectators behaved splendidly. They, to a man, kept behind the ropes, and never in the least interfered with the hurlers. This is certainly to be commended, and the spectators in the other places at which I have been present might, with advantage, follow the example of these orderly, and, at the same time, highly enthusiastic crowd of 15,000 people. (*Celtic Times*, 7 May 1887)

The 1897 GAA rules allowed the referee to terminate the game due to 'interference of spectators', and clubs were expected 'to prevent spectators threatening or assaulting referees, officials, or players, during or after matches' (quoted in Lennon, 1997, p. 52). During the 1903 All-Ireland final (though played in 1905) the referee disallowed a goal because a spectator was involved in the play; this decision resulted in a pitch invasion and the match was subsequently abandoned (Mandle, 1987, p. 146).

When Gaelic games became more standardised across the country following the establishment of the GAA, not only players but also spectators had to adjust to new ways of playing. The existing habitus was still attuned to the conditions of its formation, namely the local community. The relatively incomplete state monopoly of violence control, in the context of local ambivalence or even hostility towards the legitimacy of the state, meant that local people often depended on each other rather than state agents for protection. This felt obligation was conducive to collective violence against outsiders deemed to have harmed one's fellow community members.

The following example relates to a match between two districts less than 10 miles apart (*Southern Star*, 14 May 1892). During the game spectators participated in the play by entering the field and attempting to score points for their team. The journalist argued that 'roughness by the players or encroachments on the field of play by the crowd may frequently be overlooked,' but some transgressions warrant censure. He gives an account of two players falling during play, and one struck the other as he got back on his knees:

> The spectators in the vicinity witnessed the action, and with loud shouts a number of them surrounded the two men; two or three sticks were raised, and while Neagle [the offending player] was still on his knees, he received a violent blow of a stick from a respectable-looking man, whose hat was off, and who seemed filled with passion and excitement.

According to the journalist, but for the interference of four priests, 'a serious disturbance might have ensued'. The police arrived but the 'crowd were now all over the field, and the greatest disorder prevailed'. Though the match occurred nearly a decade after the establishment of the GAA, spectators found it difficult to adhere to the division of functions between those present at the match. Some of them tried to interfere with play, assuming the role of player, and also inflicted their own idea of punishment rather than leave that function to the person officially responsible to penalise rule transgressions. The existing habitus did not as yet align with the required social differentiation of the standardised game.

Control of the game according to standard rules was not performed through the detachment of a neutral regulator but the highly charged emotional involvement associated with a common social belonging or solidarity. The game represents a phase in the development of the sport when media observers did not expect norm compliance and expressed moral condemnation at the sight of extreme violence with weapons. Similarly a game in 1893 (*Irish Times*, 7 March 1893) quickly escalated from a fight between two spectators to a 'free fight' involving 'a large section of the spectators'. Again weapons such as sticks and stones were used and the journalist noted the 'political element' as the fight corresponded to conflict between opposing camps of Irish nationalism.

The functional specialisation and social differentiation associated with players, spectators, referees, managers and other roles, also involves a degree of spatial specialisation in that certain parts of the ground are designated for the performance of certain roles. In the early stages of the sportisation process however, these spatial boundaries were often ignored. During a game in 1905 (*Westmeath Examiner*, 25 February 1905), spectators began 'loudly protesting' against two players. The spectators invaded the pitch 'and a free fight ensued, about a hundred taking part, and sticks being used.' The police 'tried in vain to calm the troubled waters, and in the wind up one of the [players] was carried home on a stretcher.' The journalistic tone is far less moralising than the reaction to a referee being shoved in the 2010 game described above. The use of weapons at games by spectators seems to have subsided by the foundation of the Irish Free State in the 1920s.

The recurring and shifting social conflicts from the late nineteenth century and into the 1930s, and much later in the case of the territory that became Northern Ireland, are connected with the prevalence and even tolerance of some forms of interpersonal violence. As discussed in the previous chapter, conflicts between landowners and tenant farmers (increasingly conflated with ethnic and national conflicts) succeeded earlier, more dispersed and fragmented conflicts between groups within a more differentiated class structure (Clark, 1978, 1979). The growing national dimension of conflicts produced internal conflict within national groups based on different ideals and strategies of nationalism, as well as conflicts between emerging nationalists and unionists, and social conflicts developed between urban industrial classes as power relations shifted due to commercialisation (Dolan, 2005, 2009). Though the state which later became the Republic of Ireland gradually gained legitimacy following partition, the same cannot be said for Northern Ireland, at least from the perspective of the mainly Catholic nationalist population (nationalist in terms of Ireland rather than the UK). Gaelic games in Northern Ireland were largely supported by this nationalist group, which led to attacks on GAA supporters and premises there (Hassan & O'Kane, 2012).

Recurring, though changing, social conflicts favour the formation of a habitus predisposed towards greater social distances between 'them' and 'us'. Of course a series of challenge matches between neighbouring districts constitutes a form of conflict in itself, but these were not intentionally organised as sites of spectator violence. That they often became such was due to the continuing rural tradition of collective violence sustained through obvious social cleavages, and the consequent emotional habitus formation with less moral repugnance towards aggression compared to modern sensibilities. Class conflicts intertwined with the international conflict between Ireland and Britain, and of course, once again, intragroup divisions and emotional hostilities based on the course of this international conflict. This proceeded well into the twentieth century through the Civil War (1922–1923) and various splits in political parties. Ireland of course was partitioned and many people with an emotional belonging to a distinct national we-group formation found themselves remaining in a jurisdiction with a state monopolisation of violence perceived as lacking legitimacy.

From the 1920s to the 1950s displays of violence tended to be labelled as sources of excitement by journalists, but increasingly they conferred feelings of disgrace upon transgressors, and displayed feelings of contempt for their violent conduct. Supporting Elias, there seems to be an advancing threshold of shame concerning physical violence, but collective violence during games still occurred up to the 1980s at least.

The structure of the 'free fight' continued to be a common form of violent encounter at matches after the partition of Ireland; collective spectator violence quickly followed inter-player violence, and the referee was the object of both player and spectator violence. For example, in 1928, after one player struck another there was an immediate pitch invasion by the crowd (*Irish Times*, 13 October 1928). The referee was assaulted by a spectator, then by a player, and 'a prominent official' then struck the offending spectator. The match was abandoned as the crowd could not be dispersed from the pitch. The journalist praised the performance of the referee during the game and noted that his treatment 'was roundly condemned' though he did not engage in any moralising himself. A report in 1931 (*Irish Times*, 21 July 1931) included the headline 'Wild Scenes at a Football Match' and noted the abandonment of the game. Here the referee decided to end the game following a 'dispute' between the referee and one set of supporters. He was immediately pursued 'by an angry crowd' over the field and was repeatedly struck. Some 'onlookers and Civic Guards' tried to protect him and he eventually found refuge in a house in the local village. When offending spectators were arrested and subsequently prosecuted, they did not always demonstrate remorse for their actions. According to Elias, as civilising processes unfold people still transgress thresholds of shame on occasion, but such episodes are accompanied by lingering feelings of guilt. During a court case in 1932 (*Irish Times*, 23 November 1932), a referee gave evidence that he was warned by spectators that if the opposing team won he 'would not go home alive'. He was about to award a free when 'the crowd rushed on to the field' and he was struck by a spectator. The accused admitted the offence but blamed the referee 'as he was "no good of a referee"'. The judge stated that no action would be taken as long as the three accused men made a public apology, but they refused to do so.

The referee of the 1933 Munster hurling final finished the match early, awarding the game to one of the teams when a 'melee' amongst the players led to a pitch invasion 'with [the] crowd from the sidelines joined in the encounter, camáns [hurleys] and fists being used. The row was soon stopped, but the pitch could not be cleared of the crowds' (*Irish Press*, 7 August 1933). A journalist referred to 'the most disgraceful and unsporting action of a certain section of the crowd ... attempting to stave off inevitable defeat'. During the 1936 All-Ireland hurling semi-final spectators invaded the pitch following an injury to a player (*Irish Press*, 17 August 1936). Once the pitch was cleared of spectators, one of the teams walked off when the player deemed responsible for inflicting the injury was not sent off by the referee. The remaining team cheered, which prompted another immediate pitch invasion. The emotional involvement and more or less spontaneous actions of teams and their supporters represented a 'vicious circle' or 'double bind' (Elias, 2007) between the sides, from which each group had difficulty escaping. GAA administrators recognised that excitement levels needed to be maintained for spectators; from 1945 referees were instructed, 'Always keep the game going by prompt decisions—the spectators enjoy such' (quoted in Lennon, 1997, p. 220). It was thought that prompt decisions would reduce the likelihood of the crowd 'taking the law into their own hands'. But more civilised behaviour did not immediately follow rule changes. Before the 1950 Munster hurling final drew to a close, some supporters ran on to the pitch to celebrate (*Irish Press*, 24 July 1950). At the final whistle, a large-scale pitch invasion occurred, and the referee was escorted from the pitch by police. There had been fighting in the crowd between opposing supporters, and during the game one spectator attacked a player.

From the 1960s the degree of direct spectator involvement at inter-county matches declined. There have been occasional exceptions, such as some spectators throwing plastic bottles and tin cans onto the pitch following a player being booked during the 1989 Munster hurling final between Waterford and Tipperary (*Irish Times*, 3 July 1989). But throwing missiles is more detached than directly assaulting players or officials, and reduces the chances of detection and also injury through player retaliation.

Increasingly media commentaries highlighted breaches of social standards of conduct and self-control. This in turn placed further pressure on administrators and officials within the GAA to exercise greater control of spectators and players. The growth in media coverage accelerated with the advent of television in 1961 (see Chap. 7; also Connolly & Dolan, 2012), and the developing competition between various media organisations led to the amplification of moral panics concerning the conduct of spectators (see Murphy, Dunning, & Williams, 1988). The intensified media observation of games and spectator conduct in the context of competition for audiences encouraged GAA administrators to encourage members to monitor their own conduct and avoid moral transgressions. Spectator emotional displays of anger and aggression would serve only to later bring feelings of shame, especially to those fulfilling the control and coordination functions of the organisation. The Ulster GAA annual convention included the following appeal:

> Always remember any lapse in conduct will be seized upon immediately and noised abroad to bring shame on the organisation and delight to its opponents. Let your conduct as officials of club or county committee, as players and spectators at all times show that courtesy and Christian forbearance which will avoid angry words and regrettable scenes. (GAA Ulster annual convention minutes, 2 March 1963)

Collective violence occasionally occurred during the 1970s. For example, a spectator kicked a player in the head as he lay on the ground (*Irish Independent*, 11 August 1976). The county board chairman described the game as a disgrace. As the match was abandoned a replay was ordered, but the wives and mothers of one of the teams sought to have the match postponed. This led to embarrassment among players and GAA administrators (*Sunday Independent*, 22 August 1976), but it also indicates the social pressure on players and organisational functionaries through their dependency on media journalists and editors. The newspaper report (*Irish Independent*, 11 August 1976) also included a photograph of two players from the opposing teams shaking hands prior to the county board meeting. This suggests that certain emotions of anger and bitterness should be removed from public presentations and the media offered the opportunity to restore the moral reputation of the sport and organisation to some extent.

In 1977, a spectator died following a pitch invasion during a football game between two County Tyrone (situated within the jurisdiction of Northern Ireland) clubs (*Irish Times*, 10 August 1977). Matches between the clubs had a history of trouble (Grimes, 2009), and as discussed above the lack of legitimacy concerning Northern Ireland may have been conducive to a more volatile habitus at this time. Though there is no clear boundary between phases of forms of spectator violence, particularly as processes of civilisation had been so uneven, we argue that violence based on deferred satisfaction became more prominent.

DEFERRED SATISFACTION AND SOCIAL PROTECTION

From the 1950s, the dependences between the types of participants in Gaelic games shifted. Referees were more likely to be protected by players from spectators. Also, pitch invasions or other forms of attack by spectators on players and referees became more prominent at the end of matches. In other words, spectators learnt to defer their satisfaction, in terms of seeking retribution for perceived injustice or insult (see Elias, 2013). In part this can be seen as less impulsive behaviour, as spectators waited to see the outcome of the game and did not want to jeopardise the chances of their team winning. But the shift also relates to the acceptance to some extent of spatial and functional specialisation. While spectators experience anger at the decisions and actions of interdependent others, this is also combined with hope and anticipation until the play comes to the end at the discretion of the referee. This particular role in the game figuration continues to be the object of spectator anger because the specialised function involves controlling the flow of player movements more or less following rule transgressions. Players are stopped in their movements once fouls have been committed and seen, provided the referee is performing his functions without fear or favour from either side or their representatives. Unlike some sports, life golf, players are not expected to call attention to their own transgressions. In the emotional intensity of fast play and close bodily movement this is not socially expected, and so there is a certain 'division of labour'. Unlike Durkheim's (1984) model, however, this is not a division of tasks based upon a shared desired outcome. Though the various functional specialists are interdependent they pursue distinct ends. The players and spectators seek victory, which is structurally impossible for both sides as both teams cannot win, while the referee and umpires ideally seek the completion of the game according to the current rules. Beyond the specific match itself, their interests are more convergent, as the good reputation of Gaelic games, and hence their players and supporters, is desired by all participants.

Players and spectators gradually learnt to accept their roles and functions within the developing GAA figuration. As discussed in the previous chapter, players came under greater scrutiny by administrators, and as spectators' emotions and impulses were in part dependent on those of players, they too became less likely to react spontaneously to felt injustice. Spectators also came under greater surveillance by police, stewards, and journalists. Indeed journalists and referees called for increased control over spectators (e.g., *Nenagh Guardian*, 12 May 1951; *Irish Times*, 23 January 1952; GAA Central Council minutes, 2 December 1955, 9 November 1962). With this growing acceptance of functional specialisation, there is also a degree of social fragmentation between players and spectators, as players increasingly seek to protect referees. Spectators' sense of duty to protect players declines somewhat, as the anticipated group pride in victory tends to move to the foreground. Spectators become more emotionally focussed on the referee as functional specialisation is accepted, as spectators develop heightened expectations of referee competence, impartiality and fairness (though through their partial lens), and as they refrain from exacting their own perceived justice on opposition players. So in this context, functional specialisation can lead to a shift in the target of anger and violence, rather than necessarily decreasing violence.

This transitional phase itself did not proceed evenly, and there is overlap between forms of violence. For example, there was some spectator encroachment on the pitch during a 1955 inter-county football match, and an umpire was also assaulted. At the end of the match, some spectators struck the referee and umpire. The referee reports that 'Due to the intervention of members and officials of both teams—to whom I am grateful—the incident did not reach more serious proportions' (GAA Central Council minutes, 2 December 1955). The referee also notes that the match 'was played in a very sporting manner, the conduct of both teams was exemplary and they did not in any way contribute to the actions of the spectators mentioned'. Another referee's report in 1958 described how 'a mob of cowards made several attempts to assault me' after the game ended, and he appealed to the county board to 'take drastic action to put a stop to such acts of hooliganism' (*Meath Chronicle*, 12 July 1958). This represented an early use of this term that became so popular in the British media in relation to violent soccer supporters, but it attracted limited use among Irish referees and journalists. In 1966 Longford county players 'appealed to the supporters to leave the field' after a national league final against New York (effectively a team of Irish emigrants), when spectators attempted to attack the referee as well as some New York players (*Irish Independent*, 10 October 1966). The emerging norm of players protecting referees represented another type of interdependence, and the functional distance between players and spectators grew further. Of course players and spectators remained interdependent, but their emotional experience did not always align at the same time. Players increasingly tried to control the anger of supporters, based on their common group belonging.

Another national league match between Derry (located in the jurisdiction of Northern Ireland) and Kerry in 1973 produced 'disgraceful scenes' when 'a large group of young men and youths waged a pitch battle with gardai [police] on the field and under the Hogan stand. Regrettably, the brutal scene put sport, in the name of Gaelic football, to shame' (*Irish Times*, 9 April 1973). The journalist argued that should sport produce such violence, 'ordinary, civilised people' would shun it. At the end of the game, over 200 Derry supporters invaded the pitch and the referee suffered 'several blows' before he was protected by officials and police. Two Derry players had been sent off for violent conduct in the 43rd and 47th minutes but groups of spectators assembled and waited on the sideline until the end of the game before invading the pitch. The same journalist in the following day's newspaper attempted to understand the conduct of the Derry supporters in the context of their experience of injustice 'in other spheres' (*Irish Times*, 10 April 1973). It is significant that the propensity towards emotional control and violent conduct is theoretically related to the state monopolisation of the means of violence (Elias, 2012).

During the 1970s an effective demonopolisation of violence occurred in Northern Ireland. Spiralling processes of course meant that places and groups could not be entirely insulated from violence, but escalating social conflicts in a jurisdiction deemed by some outsider groups to be favourable to politically established groups often translated into a declining dependence on state agencies of violence control, and subsequent reliance on other groups. Elias and Dunning (2008) argue that civilising processes in the context of sport (or sportisation processes) depend in part upon a broader process of state pacification. In the Irish case, this process underwent a partial reversal, but within a territory over which the police already had an incomplete legitimacy along ethnic and religious divisions. Following partition, Gaelic games often became a national symbol across the border, but this solidarity was fragile and ambivalent due to different experiences and expectations regarding the common national ideal and its fulfilment. In 1998, an under sixteen schools match involving teams from both jurisdictions, but played in the Irish Republic, culminated in the referee being 'kicked, punched and spat upon' after he blew the final whistle. He was protected from officials from both teams and stayed in the dressing room for nearly an hour until a policeman dispersed a small group of supporters. A supporter declared to the policeman, 'You abandoned us in 1922 and now you are at it again' (*Irish Times*, 28 March 1998). Though Gaelic games are organised on an all-Ireland basis, social divisions remained on the basis of divergent narratives of belonging and betrayal to the national group.

The collective, deferred forms of collective violence based on emotional allegiance to representative teams declined in significance without entirely disappearing. It occasionally re-emerged, and especially in social conditions lacking legitimacy, or through the emotional intensification of regular opposition between local rivals. But from the 1980s in particular, there tended to be more individualised reactions to events on the pitch.

INDIVIDUALISATION OF VIOLENCE

The earlier predominance of collective violence followed a social structure where people were more strongly bound to local groups, particularly those organised along kinship and residential boundaries. Formerly, each person's existence and sense of identity was tied to these local groups across the life course. As stated above, this argument of course echoes Durkheim's (1984) analysis of the transition from mechanical to organic solidarity. Dunning (2008, pp. 229–230) does acknowledge the similarities between the idea of lengthening chains of interdependence and that of the movement towards organic solidarity. Indeed, Durkheim attributes the growth of individualism to this latter transformation, as does Elias in relation to the former process. Elias though places more emphasis on the actual social processes of transformation rather than static polarities (Mennell, 1998, pp. 293–294), and does not conflate greater interdependence with harmonious social relations (Dunning, 1999, p. 16). Dunning (2008, pp. 222–241) contrasts the segmental bonding of local self-sufficient communities corresponding to pre-industrial society and indeed some sections of the British working classes, to the functional bonding characteristic of highly specialised and differentiated societies integrated at the national level. This contrast also relates to the propensity for affective or rational forms of violence (see Chap. 2).

As we have seen, in the case of Gaelic games, the collective forms of violence become imbued with rational dimensions but still retain their affectivity. The more individualised form of spectator violence emerges due to a general civilising direction, so that spectators become less likely to act in unison in response to perceived wrongdoing against a fellow member of the group. This weakening emotional homogeneity within the spectating crowd, as well as a more rational form of interpersonal relations within the crowd, mean that those that do become emotionally overwhelmed and submit to aggressive impulses generated through the contest between teams are less likely to face social constraints from other people in the crowd. The social constraint towards self-constraint becomes established so that others in the crowd are less likely to see it as their place to intervene in the conduct of others. This social function is increasingly seen as the proper specialised role of parents and educators, and failing that, a police force that has attained greater legitimacy in the course of the state's integration. Of course to the extent that any individual engages in violent conduct contravenes the established norms of this society, but this, as Elias and Dunning maintain, demonstrates the contingent nature of the various inter-related social processes that produce more exacting forms of self-control and non-violent social interactions. There is nothing inevitable about these outcomes, as it depends on each person's initial position and subsequent social trajectory as part of the dynamic social figuration. Dunning argues that rational forms of violence dominate within societies characterised by functional bonding, but he refers mainly to players in this regard. Spectators have little scope for rational violence as part of an achievement orientation, in order to affect the course of a contest in their favour.

Though the immediate situational dynamics generate emotional experiences, these are anchored by the more individualised habitus, permitting a variety of emotional experiences that are not solely shaped by the immediate situation. As the moral repugnance towards violence advances, and as the state monopoly of violence becomes more secure and legitimate, people become less willing to directly restrain others. The 'mutually-expected self restraint' (Goudsblom cited in Wouters, 2007, p. 188) characteristic of more individualised societies may ironically reduce the likelihood of immediate face-to-face social constraint, partly in the expectation that others have acquired emotional self-control and also that functional specialists are responsible for such constraint.

From the 1980s, individual assaults on players and referees became more prominent. Though this spectator violence was still connected to events on the pitch, the collective actions of the earlier period subsided. Sometimes lone spectators attacked individual players at the end of games (*Irish Times*, 1 August 1983; *Irish Times*, 4 December 1984).

Violence directed at referees tended to be more extreme compared to players. For example, in 1987 during a club football match the referee 'was beaten about the head and kicked in the groin' and later hospitalised (*Irish Times*, 19 August 1987). At the time of the assault the referee was speaking to one player in relation to an injury to another (*Irish Times*, 16 October 1987). After the 1988 All-Ireland football final replay, during a brief 'scuffle' between two opposing players, a lone spectator assaulted one of the players (*Irish Times*, 11 October 1988; *Irish Times*, 13 October 1988; *Irish Times*, 21 October 1988). These events attracted comprehensive and sustained moral condemnation by both journalists and senior administrators within the GAA. Indeed from the 1980s there was been a recurring debate in media commentary and GAA officialdom regarding the acceptability of spectators invading the pitch after games in celebration. This eventually led to the prohibition of this spectator tradition at Croke Park[1] during the 2010 championship (a decision unrelated to the events after the Leinster final detailed at the start of this chapter).

Cooney (2003, pp. 1392–1393) argues that Elias does not provide an adequate explanation for the individualisation and privatisation of violence, on the grounds that 'although uncivilized individuals are uncivilized all the time, they are violent only occasionally' (p. 1392). Elias of course never claimed anybody was uncivilised, simply because civilisation is a process without absolute origins. But we can construct such an explanation based on Elias's (2010) examination of the we–I balance and the related development of *homo clausus* (closed person) conceptions of the person. As figurations become more extensive and complex, people develop bonds over longer links and more varied and multiple types of interdependences based on the functions people perform or fulfil for one another. With wider interdependences, new sources of meaning and purpose develop, new types of identity constituting multilayered we-identities (Elias, 2010, p. 181). Some people can find emotional meaning and fulfilment across diverse planes of social integration, while others resent new ties because they are experienced as unequal or oppressive. Longer, denser and more diverse interdependences generate varieties of emotions that inhibit the capacity for collective action on behalf of a specific locality. But this diversity of emotional experiences enables individual transgression, even if such transgression is retrospectively a source of moral condemnation by others or remorse for the offender.

CONCLUSION

Spectator conduct has undergone a non-linear, uneven and incomplete civilising process since the late nineteenth century. We argue that this is mainly due to the uneven process of state pacification in the jurisdictions where these social practices were performed. Gaelic games were organised on a national level in Ireland in 1884, but unlike the case in England this was not primarily as a counterbalance to the increasing routinisation of social life. Indeed Finnane (1997, p. 54) describes the 1880s as one of the nineteenth century's most violent periods primarily due to social struggles over control of land. Violence was not limited to rural areas; in the largest city Dublin, there was a 'long-running feud between the Dublin Metropolitan Police ... and the city's "lower classes"' from the 1830s to 1914 (Griffin cited in Finnane, 1997, p. 62).

Elias (2010, p. 151) argues that as groups become part of a new stage of social integration, their scope of identification also increases. For Elias, this higher level of integration forms due to lengthening chains of interdependence. As people depend more and more on each other over greater distances and multiple connections, strong pressure emerges towards greater social coordination and regulation. The establishment of the United Kingdom of Great Britain and Ireland in 1801 is an example of such a new stage of social integration. But this integration was an offensive managed by social elites in both Britain and Ireland. The social distance between social classes in Ireland meant that this project did not attain the emotional belonging characteristic of a nation. The increasing economic interdependences between Irish and British people led to the expansion of middle-class social functions increasingly accessible to rising groups. This interdependence did not eradicate a concurrent but contradictory function of Britain as a symbol of empire and power for these rising groups in Ireland to oppose. Indeed this sense of within-group identification was strongly dependent on out-group exclusion, which ironically strengthened in the context of economic interdependences advancing. This process was uneven in that some Irish groups did develop an emotional sense of identification with the United Kingdom (UK). This very heterogeneity was itself a source of continued social conflict and division that relates to the recurrent escalation of violence. The GAA was established in response to the advance of English sports in Ireland during the second half of the nineteenth century. So routinisation was less a factor than the volatile emotions associated with nationalist projects of self-determination. Such projects produce conflict between oppositional groups, but also within groups due to contested notions of the nation and strategies for its fulfilment. The state monopolisation of the means of physical violence was also incomplete, and crucially did not enjoy legitimacy with large sections of the population. O'Donnell (2005, p. 683) notes that non-political interpersonal violence was common in Ireland before 1922 (when the Irish Free State was founded); legal remedies were not available to much of the population, so disputes were resolved directly between opponents. Although effective state monopolisation is a necessary condition for the pacification of social relations, it is not a sufficient condition for the continued and stable internalisation of norms prohibiting violence. For this, the state in question must be legitimate in the sense of being seen as representative of a more or less coherent group. Lack of legitimacy encourages rival units claiming the right to monopolise violence, which in turn undermines the state's effective monopoly. This lack of legitimacy does not by itself produce violent interpersonal encounters. Conflict must also generate emotions such as anger which develop as part of the total physiological, symbolic and action sequence (see Elias, 1987). Violent outcomes become more likely in social situations of conflict where the habitus of protagonists have not previously been formed in socialising conditions prohibiting violent acts. Where state agents of violence control are not trusted or not relied upon, people learn to rely on themselves or other groups for defence and attack (Dunning et al., 1988).

Collins (2008) emphasises the social situation rather than background variables or the individual personality, but some variables such as gender or class coincide with the preponderance of certain types of situations and certain positions within social figurations which over time affect the emotional impulsiveness of participants. In other words, each individual's habitus is formed through numerous, successive face-to-face interactions and situations which are partly shaped by values and norms generated by shifting interdependences beyond the immediate situation. When Gaelic games were first organised by the GAA as spectator events, people could not leave their habitual mode of emotional conduct in conflict situations at the gate. While sport ostensibly recreates the exciting mimetic tension of violent encounters (Elias & Dunning, 2008), the multiple purposes of Gaelic games organisation in Ireland included national distinction, partly on the basis of a dependent reaction to the success of some English sports. These more organised sporting encounters were introduced following a phase of acute social conflict between tenant farmers and landlords, which escalated to an almost national level of recurrent violence. Since then political violence has increased and receded, so continuous and even values of non-violent conflict resolution failed to dominate until the second half of the twentieth century. Of course, violence increased strongly again in parts of Ireland from the 1960s; such 'warfare' tends to legitimise interpersonal violence (Gurr cited in Mennell, 2007, p. 128). Also, the relative lack of effective and legitimate state monopolisation of violence is often part of a generally weak level of social integration at the state level. This in part reflects a limited scope of emotional identification (a sense of social belonging in a cohesive and coherent survival unit) between people within the state's jurisdiction. For Elias (2012), one of the conditions of nation-state formation is the transfer of the state from private to public ownership, but this can be an incomplete and partial process in that 'the public' is socially divided in terms of commitment to the state as it has developed through broader processes and conflicts. This lack of 'we-feeling' can produce dimensions of the habitus ill-disposed not only towards individual state functionaries, but other positions specialising (albeit temporarily) in the function of social control and rule compliance.

During the early phase of GAA organisation, most people were interdependent on the basis of 'segmental bonding' rather than the 'functional bonding' characteristic of an advanced division of labour (Dunning, 2008, pp. 222–241). Local interdependences predominated based on a structural pattern whereby most people earned their living as tenant farmers, agricultural labourers and domestic servants. Also of course sons were highly dependent on fathers for inheritance purposes, and guarded zealously their land claims, for, as part of this social structure, control of land (and ownership if possible) constituted not only economic survival but social status and marriage prospects (all these being interdependent themselves). Social conflicts with landlords, land agents, employers and police tended to heighten the emotional dimensions of social interdependences as people placed pressure on each other to observe boycotts or vote in accordance with sectional interests. In this context, sporting contests between teams (even local parishes and towns) constituted occasions for displays of group pride. Players and spectators came from the same parish or town and through recurring cooperation and conflicts beyond the field of play were prepared to defend members of the 'we-group' against attack by other groups, or even to attack fellow group members who failed to comply with group norms. The lack of state legitimacy heightens this mutual dependence as defence units. This propensity for impulsive defence recedes as both the state acquires greater legitimacy with partial national independence (this partiality accounts for subsequent violent conflicts within the national we-group and thus the unevenness of the state pacification process), and as forms of interdependence extend far beyond local communities. This broadening scope of identification and acceptance of rule compliance specialists does however contain inherent contradictions. As referees and umpires are increasingly seen as neutral functional specialists, they become the focus of anger when perceived injustice occurs during play. Spectators increasingly expect referees to enforce rules (which also change over time) and even expect players to transgress rules due to competitive pressure from potential replacements and the hopes generated by supporters themselves. The we-identification with the sporting unit as a symbol supersedes the felt need to physically avenge attacks on players (though this does not disappear in that some spectators remain strongly bonded to local people, including to the players themselves). There is some rationalisation of emotional impulses in that collective responses become postponed until the end of the match and, rather than a cathartic release of tension (Elias, 2008a, p. 158), an escalation of rage occurs similar to a 'collective effervescence' (Durkheim, 2001, see also Dunning, 1999, p. 7) in violent form.

This partial rationalisation (but temporally non-linear in that delayed satisfaction of emotional impulses generated by game conflict can produce violent collective responses) also corresponds to an increased acceptance of functional specialisation as well as spatial and social differentiation. Players play, spectators watch and referees adjudicate and penalise. There are different spaces for these activities and gradually the impulse to transgress these boundaries is brought under greater psychic control. This remains a fragile process, and some individual spectators, bonded more strongly to local communities or to particular players through kinship, do occasionally transgress non-participation and non-violent norms. The increase in 'mutually expected self-restraint' (Goudsblom cited in Wouters, 2007, p. 188) also involves an implicit reticence in directly and bodily restraining the moral transgressions of immediate others. Thus while collective forms of violence recede, more individual forms come into the foreground.

But although the general, non-linear and uneven trajectory towards state pacification has encouraged a less violent habitus, sporting contests constitute a figuration within broader figurations and have a relative autonomy. To the extent that occupational life had become more routinised for many people, the enclave represented by sport can take on more emotional and social meaning (see Dunning, Murphy, & Waddington, 2002, p. 220). In that context, sports fandom and attachment to a particular team (and opposition to rival teams) becomes an oscillating emotional narrative depending on the fortunes of the team. Successive failures over decades lowers expectations prior to matches, but unexpected anticipations of victory heighten emotions as the match draws to a close. So the long-term emotional career of the fan shapes the emotional experience of specific spectating situations. Local rivalries also tend to produce sustained emotional narratives because they tend to play more regularly. For many sports supporters disappointment remains contained because of hopes for the future—other days or even other sports teams to follow. Gaelic football is not played on an international basis (there are occasional 'compromise rules' games between Ireland and Australia, based on a hybrid between Gaelic and Australian Rules football—see Chap. 8), so in the sporting sphere the highest plane of integration remains at the inter-county level (see also Chaps. 5 and 6), despite the fact that these Gaelic games were first standardised on a national level to counteract the appeal of British sports. This aspect of the nation-building project contained the inherent contradiction of promoting regional emotional attachments.

NOTE

1. It still persists and/or is permitted at other GAA grounds.

REFERENCES

Bairner, A. (2002). The dog that didn't bark? Football hooliganism in Ireland. In E. Dunning, P. Murphy, I. Waddington, & A. Astrinakis (Eds.), *Fighting fans: Football hooliganism as a world phenomenon* (pp. 118–130). Dublin: University College Dublin Press.

Clark, S. (1978). The importance of agrarian classes: Agrarian class structure and collective action in nineteenth-century Ireland. *British Journal of Sociology, 29*(1), 22–40.

Clark, S. (1979). *Social origins of the Irish Land War.* Princeton, NJ: Princeton University Press.

Collins, R. (2008). *Violence: A micro-sociological theory.* Princeton, NJ: Princeton University Press.

Collins, R. (2009). The micro sociology of violence. *British Journal of Sociology, 60*(3), 566–576.

Connolly, J., & Dolan, P. (2012). Sport, media and the Gaelic Athletic Association: The quest for the 'youth' of Ireland. *Media, Culture & Society, 34*(4), 407–423.

Cooney, M. (2003). The privatization of violence. *Criminology, 41*(4), 1377–1406.

Cooney, M. (2009). The scientific significance of Collins's *Violence. British Journal of Sociology, 60*(3), 586–594.

De Búrca, M. (1989). *Michael Cusack and the GAA*. Dublin: Anvil Books.

Dolan, P. (2005). *The development of consumer culture, subjectivity and national identity in Ireland, 1900–1980*. PhD thesis, Goldsmiths College, University of London, London.

Dolan, P. (2009). Figurational dynamics and parliamentary discourses of living standards in Ireland. *British Journal of Sociology, 60*(4), 721–739.

Dunning, E. (1989). A response to R. J. Robinson's 'The "civilizing process": Some remarks on Elias's social history'. *Sociology, 23*(2), 299–307.

Dunning, E. (1994a). The social roots of football hooliganism: A reply to the critics of the "Leicester School". In R. Giulianotti, N. Bonney, & M. Hepworth (Eds.), *Football violence and social identity* (pp. 128–157). London and New York: Routledge.

Dunning, E. (1994b). Sport in space and time: "Civilizing processes", trajectories of state-formation and the development of modern sport. *International Review for the Sociology of Sport, 29*(4), 331–347.

Dunning, E. (1999). *Sport matters: Sociological studies of sport, violence and civilization*. London: Routledge.

Dunning, E. (2008). Social bonding and violence in sport. In N. Elias & E. Dunning (Eds.), *Quest for excitement: Sport and leisure in the civilising process* (Rev. ed., pp. 222–241). Dublin: University College Dublin Press.

Dunning, E., Murphy, P., & Waddington, I. (2002). Towards a global programme of research into fighting and disorder at football. In E. Dunning, P. Murphy, I. Waddington, & A. Astrinakis (Eds.), *Fighting fans: Football hooliganism as a world phenomenon* (pp. 218–224). Dublin: University College Dublin Press.

Dunning, E., Murphy, P., Waddington, I., & Astrinakis, A. (Eds.). (2002). *Fighting fans: Football hooliganism as a world phenomenon*. Dublin: University College Dublin Press.

Dunning, E., Murphy, P., & Williams, J. (1986). Spectator violence at football matches—Towards a sociological explanation. *British Journal of Sociology, 37*(2), 221–244.

Dunning, E., Murphy, P., & Williams, J. (1988). *The roots of football hooliganism: An historical and sociological study*. London and New York: Routledge.

Dunning, E., & Sheard, K. (2005). *Barbarians, gentlemen and players: A sociological study of the development of rugby football* (2nd ed.). London: Routledge.

Durkheim, É. (1984). *The division of labour in society* (W. D. Halls, Trans.). Hampshire: Macmillan.

Durkheim, É. (2001). *The elementary forms of religious life* (C. Cosman, Trans.). Oxford and New York: Oxford University Press.

Elias, N. (1987). On human beings and their emotions: A process-sociological essay. *Theory, Culture & Society, 4*(2–3), 339–361.

Elias, N. (2007). *Involvement and detachment* (Rev. ed.). Dublin: University College Dublin Press.

Elias, N. (2008a). An essay on sport and violence. In N. Elias & E. Dunning (Eds.), *Quest for excitement: Sport and leisure in the civilising process* (Rev. ed., pp. 150–173). Dublin: University College Dublin Press.

Elias, N. (2008b). Introduction. In N. Elias & E. Dunning (Eds.), *Quest for excitement: Sport and leisure in the civilising process* (Rev. ed., pp. 3–43). Dublin: University College Dublin Press.

Elias, N. (2010). *The society of individuals* (Rev. ed.). Dublin: University College Dublin Press.

Elias, N. (2012). *On the process of civilisation* (Rev. ed.). Dublin: University College Dublin Press.

Elias, N. (2013). *Studies on the Germans* (Rev. ed.). Dublin: University College Dublin Press.

Elias, N., & Dunning, E. (2008). *Quest for excitement: Sport and leisure in the civilising process* (Rev. ed.). Dublin: University College Dublin Press.

Elias, N., & Scotson, J. L. (2008). *The established and the outsiders* (Rev. ed.). Dublin: University College Dublin Press.

Felson, R. B. (2009). Is violence natural, unnatural, or rational? *British Journal of Sociology, 60*(3), 577–585.

Finnane, M. (1997). A decline in violence in Ireland? Crime, policing and social relations, 1860–1914. *Crime, Histoire & Sociétés/Crime, History & Societies, 1*(1), 51–70.

Grimes, P. (2009). *The Moortown story*. Moortown, Co. Tyrone: St. Malachy's GAA Club.

Hassan, D., & O'Kane, P. (2012). Terrorism and the abnormality of sport in Northern Ireland. *International Review for the Sociology of Sport, 47*(3), 397–413.

Lennon, J. (1997). *The playing rules of football and hurling, 1884–1995*. Northern Recreation Consultants: Gormanstown, Co. Meath.

Mandle, W. F. (1987). *The Gaelic Athletic Association and Irish nationalist politics, 1884–1924*. Dublin: Gill & Macmillan.

Mennell, S. (1998). *Norbert Elias: An introduction*. Dublin: University College Dublin Press.

Mennell, S. (2007). *The American civilizing process*. Cambridge: Polity.

Murphy, P., Dunning, E., & Williams, J. (1988). Soccer crowd disorder and the press: Processes of amplification and de-amplification in historical perspective. *Theory Culture & Society, 5*(3), 645–673.

O'Donnell, I. (2005). Lethal violence in Ireland, 1841 to 2003. *British Journal of Criminology, 45*(5), 671–695.

Robinson, R. J. (1987). The civilizing process: Some remarks on Elias's social history. *Sociology, 21*(1), 1–17.

Rothstein, B. (2009). Creating political legitimacy: Electoral democracy versus quality of government. *American Behavioral Scientist, 53*(3), 311–330.

Weber, M. (1991). *From Max Weber: Essays in sociology*. London: Routledge.

Wouters, C. (2007). *Informalization: Manners and emotions since 1890*. London: Sage.

CHAPTER 4

The Sociogensis and Development of the GAA: Centralising and Decentralising Tensions

THE SOCIOGENESIS OF THE GAA

We begin this chapter by looking at the social context in which the GAA came to be established. By the mid to late 1800s pursuits and leisure activities such as athletics, hurling, cycling, cricket and various types of football were common in Ireland (Rouse, 2015). National, central, organising bodies were also beginning to be established. In 1874, the Irish Football Union[1] was formed with eight rugby playing clubs affiliated, while a few years later in 1880 three clubs in Belfast came together to form the Irish Football Association (IFA) to regulate a game of football (soccer) under the Scottish association rules (Garnham, 1999).

This too was a period of increasing tension between Irish middle-class groups and a declining, yet established, Anglo-Irish-dominated upper class. Ireland had become part of the United Kingdom of Great Britain and Ireland following the Act of Union in 1801, though the territory had been subject to control by groups from Britain for several centuries prior to that. Over this time an Anglo-Irish elite closely aligned with British representatives in Ireland had become the leading social group in Irish society. However, by the late nineteenth century a significant and socially ascending native Irish middle class had emerged. Their social position vis-à-vis the British-inclined Anglo-Irish elite had strengthened following a series of land acts which gave greater 'economic' security, and increased power chances, to middle-and lower-middle-class farmers in Ireland

© The Author(s) 2020
J. Connolly, P. Dolan, *Gaelic Games in Society*, Palgrave Studies on Norbert Elias, https://doi.org/10.1007/978-3-030-31699-0_4

(Dolan, 2005). Similarly, in urban areas, the expansion of trade networks with Britain facilitated the growth and increased social power of an Irish commercial middle class. Commercialisation processes also propelled the growth in numbers of the lower middle classes as new functions emerged and migration to towns and cities intensified as people sought the social opportunities and employment (see also Chap. 2) connected with this (Dolan, 2005, 2009a, 2009b).

While the Anglo-Irish elite were in relative decline, they were at this point still able to sustain their social position due to their greater power sources, which stemmed largely from their allegiance and identification with the British establishment. Neither the Irish middle classes nor the Anglo-Irish were unified and homogenous social groups. Both social stratums comprised a complex mix of diverse social class subgroups and were bound to each other through both cooperative and hostile interdependences. For instance, a small minority of the Anglo-Irish came to identify more strongly with the native Irish—later playing a central role in the Gaelic literary revival (Dolan, 2009b, p. 728). Similarly, the native Irish middle class comprised various subclass groups ranging from upper middle to lower middle. Other social divisions and identifications also existed along political, religious and agrarian lines. Some of the upper middle classes aligned themselves more decisively with the established Anglo-Irish and British social groups (Dolan, 2009b, p. 729).

And, while hostilities had re-emerged between landlords (mainly drawn from the Anglo-Irish elite) and tenant farmers, tensions also existed between small holding farmers and large graziers (Maguire, 2011) and between landless labourers and farmers.

Notwithstanding these differences and tensions amongst the native Irish, it was from this structure of interdependences through which a social habitus in which 'Gaelic' ways and mores of the past came to be valued and elevated in status as a form of national distinction developed. By the 1880s the social rising attained by Irish middle-class strata, and simultaneously the ceiling which their aspirations and hopes met, crystallised into the development and espousal of a 'Gaelic' culture, which served to legitimatise and self-justify the belief that the native Irish middle classes were the authentic and true heirs of political and social power in Ireland. Gaelic culture was developed as the antithesis of Anglo-Irish (and British) upper-class norms and values and found expression in various social practices. This included the revival of many 'native' Irish cultural activities such as the promotion of the Irish language (McDevitt,

1997) as well as the formation of literary and political debating clubs like The Young Ireland Society (McGee, 2005). This crystallisation of native middle-class frustration and aspiration from which Gaelic culture sprung was also the social soil from which the impetus for a native Irish sports organisation emerged. Many of the lower middle classes were blocked from further career progression and further social advancement, generating frustration and resentment. Indeed, as Garvin (1986, p. 73) notes, 'Sinn Féin and the I.R.B. enjoyed membership booms partly because of the career frustration of the over-equipped and ill-regarded'. It was from this social stratum that a large membership of the GAA would be drawn (Mullan, 1995).

Several efforts had already been made to establish an organisation prior to the meeting of 1 October 1884 in which the GAA was proclaimed with the intention of resisting the Anglicisation of sport in Ireland by reviving 'native' Irish games and bringing athletics under the control of nationalist-minded Irishmen (De Búrca, 1989, p. 8). Many athletic clubs at the time competed under the rules of the English Amateur Athletic Association (AAA) (Ó Riain, 1994, pp. 22–27). The membership of these clubs was mainly drawn from the Irish middle classes and Anglo-Irish upper middle classes (Ó Riain, 1994); the working classes and some sections of the lower middle classes were debarred from competing under the rules of the AAA. The establishment of the GAA, with the stated aim of taking over the function of governing athletics, both embodied and symbolised the felt threat to those then governing athletics and the social position of the wider established group from which they were drawn. Competitive tensions escalated as several of the founding members of the GAA sought to garner support from existing athletic and football clubs (Ó Riain, 1994, p. 76). In response, those opposed to the GAA began to organise themselves. The Irish Amateur Athletic Association (IAAA) was founded by several of those representing existing athletics clubs opposed to the GAA. This new sporting organisation also claimed to be the representative body for athletics in Ireland (De Búrca, 1999, p. 19). In this struggle for greater control over Irish sports, representatives of the GAA drew on cultural narratives of 'ancient Ireland' and emphasised the GAA's nationalist and Gaelic-Irish credentials, as opposed to Anglo-Irish. Simultaneously, they began labelling not only the IAAA as English and anti-nationalist, but also the clubs who competed in sports under English rules (e.g., see *Celtic Times*, 5 March 1887).

In this spiral of competitive tensions, the leadership of the competing sports organisations sought to enhance their legitimacy by increasing their respective membership and club affiliation. Many sports clubs at the time were organised around place associations (towns or townlands), specific institutions, or the division of labour (occupations) (Mullan, 1995; Nolan, 2005). The GAA leadership and its wider body of activists appealed to existing clubs to switch allegiance to the GAA while also encouraging the formation of new clubs often with emotional entreaties based around national and ethnic identity. Perhaps indicative of the success of this was the repertoire of names based on then contemporary and past militant nationalist groupings, nationalist leaders, ancient Gaelic warriors and images of 'Gaelic' Ireland under which clubs now affiliated to the GAA. Indeed, by 1886 the number of affiliated clubs to the GAA reached about 400 (Mandle, 1987, p. 31).

The expansion in membership of the GAA was underpinned by several processes. At a wider level it was facilitated by the increasing desire of people to participate in sport and in the process of club formation. Both developments were connected to the broader social transformation in which sport was becoming a central outlet through which emotional excitement could be aroused (Elias & Dunning, 2008). In addition, aside from facilitating the opportunity for mimetic release, sports clubs or similar types of social gatherings provided the opportunity for sociability. Neither of these processes of course meant that people would necessarily gravitate towards the GAA. Other processes, combined with those above, would aid that. The GAA was less exclusionary than many of the existing sporting organisations of the time. They enabled greater membership through the organisation of games on Sundays, unlike rugby, soccer and cricket. The organisation of Sunday sports permitted those drawn from the lower classes, including the lower middle classes, to participate as they generally worked six days including Saturdays. Participation fees, both affiliation and spectator, were also lower than competing sports (Garnham, 2004). Administrative positions in local sports clubs also provided an outlet for the members of the rising Catholic middle classes motivated by the desire for social prestige to give expression to their feelings (Hunt, 2008, 2009; O'Donoghue, 1987). In that vein, the aligning of Gaelic games with nationalism at a time of rising national sentiment ensured that many aspiring young men looked to the GAA rather than other sports bodies to fulfil their desires. The conflation of the GAA with nationalism provided a social impetus on several levels. More militant nationalists were drawn to it too. In particular members of the Irish Republican

Brotherhood (IRB) who felt their interests—support for an independent Irish republic—could be advanced through expanding the GAA (Mandle, 1987).

Centralising and Decentralising Tensions and County Committees

Despite the relatively rapid growth in club affiliation, several factors hindered more substantial progress on this front. The ephemeral nature of many clubs or 'combinations' meant formally constituted clubs did not exist for long enough to affiliate in the first place, or if they did affiliate to continue to do so. The intra-club nature of sporting contests meant many clubs felt no significant need for, or functional dependence upon, a national organisation, instead playing by locally agreed rules in ad hoc arrangements (Hunt, 2008; Mulvey, 2002b). Furthermore, many combinations or clubs did not confine themselves to a specific sport or code exclusively; they played different sports or codes at different times of the year (see Hunt, 2008). This structure also, as we suggested, weakened the functional dependency on the central executive of the GAA.

The nascent organisational structure for the management and administration of the GAA consisted of a central executive (or council), which included 'two representatives from each affiliated club' (O'Sullivan, 1916, p. 29). A general committee (what would later be known as congress) with representatives from affiliated clubs would meet once yearly to elect a central executive and agree rules for governing the organisation. As the number of clubs affiliating to the GAA grew the pressure for regional coordinating bodies advanced to coordinate fixtures beyond contiguous local regions (Hunt, 2008, pp. 145–147; Mulvey, 2002b, p. 5). Consequently, GAA county committees[2] were established under the 1886 constitution and comprised a chairman, secretary and five other members. All were to be elected by representatives from clubs within a county boundary. Their functions included the organisation of championships, and the formation of clubs and affiliation. This organisational structure based around counties mapped on to the existing state administrative one. The structuring of the territory of Ireland into spatial entities known as counties for administration purposes had occurred several centuries earlier as part of the colonisation process undertaken by English monarchs (Daly, 2001). Over time, given the interdependences between people within a county, a level of county we-identification (Elias, 2010) had emerged as a form of social identification.

The rise in affiliated clubs to over 600 by 1887 (Mandle, 1987, p. 45) also impelled a change in the structure of the central executive. The number of club representatives on the central executive was changed to four elected members from the general committee (*Celtic Times*, 18 June 1887, p. 136). The previous structure was unworkable owing to the number now affiliated. The formation of county committees, in an unplanned way, enhanced the functions and related power chances of those constituting clubs. County committees now had authority over the organisation of intra-county fixtures and the formation and affiliation of clubs within the county. The formal establishment of intra-county championships enhanced the functions (and power) of county committees as they were now the coordinating and regulating entity at the local level. Furthermore, the structure of financial interdependence favoured clubs and county committees rather than the central executive. The primary source of income for the central council was affiliation fees from clubs and to a lesser degree gate receipts from centrally sanctioned inter-club sports competitions and fixtures (Mandle, 1987, p. 95). For example, in 1888 affiliation fees accounted for one-third of all income despite the fact that many clubs failed to submit their fees (O'Sullivan, 1916, p. 74). The reluctance to submit affiliation fees stemmed from the fact that many clubs were financially strapped from the need to provide medals, cups and prizes for various tournaments and competitions, which they funded through affiliation fees, competition entry fees and gate receipts (Hunt, 2008; McElligott, 2013). Consequently, it appears that many clubs and county committees were unable, or refused, to submit affiliation fees to the central council (De Búrca, 1999, p. 36; Nolan, 2005, p. 8), thereby further constraining the financial resources available to the central council.

By 1887 the IRB faction had attained relative control within the central executive of the GAA. Several members of the central executive were leading members of the IRB as were various members of clubs and county committees. For instance, by 1886 the four vice-presidents, the treasurer and the three secretaries of the GAA, all of whom were on the central executive, were also members of the IRB (Mandle, 1987, p. 31), while IRB activists across the country played significant roles in encouraging club affiliation to the GAA. They sought to enhance this level of influence by extending the powers of the central executive as they felt it would allow them to further direct the organisation in their own interests (McGee, 2005, p. 165). Meanwhile, those opposed to all secret societies (the clergy and constitutional nationalists) sought to subvert this through the various clubs and county committees of which they were members (De Búrca, 1999; Mandle, 1987; McGee, 2005). The IRB's challenge to the clergy's social influence locally throughout parts of Ireland had existed since the 1860s and now resurfaced with renewed vigour in the contest for control of GAA units (Maguire, 2011).

As we suggested above, the relative balance of power between the central executive and the clubs and committees lay in favour of the clubs and county committees. Not only was the central executive dependent on clubs for finance, but clubs held the function of rule-making for the association. The GAA's constitution of 1887 stated that no new rule could be introduced 'nor any of the foregoing altered except at a meeting of the general committee [national congress] called for the purpose' and where 'two thirds of affiliated clubs must be represented, and three-fourths of those present at the meeting must agree on the question' (*Celtic Times*, 18 June 1887). Essentially, annual congress, which included two members from each affiliated club, retained the function for amending rules for the governance and regulation of the association. So when the IRB-controlled central council attempted to garner greater control it was by attempting to make the central council *ex officio* members of every affiliated county committee. This would permit them to exercise considerable control over county committees by potentially outvoting them; county committees comprised seven members as opposed to thirteen on central council (Mandle, 1987, p. 38). And while the power balance between county committees and clubs on the one hand and central council on the other was asymmetrical, clubs and county committees were in several ways dependent on the central executive. First, the central council provided an emotional function for those comprising clubs. Central council functioned as a medium through which club members could display their allegiance to Gaelic nationalist ideals through affiliation to the GAA. Second, the formation of inter-club competitions involving clubs from different counties ensured a need for central coordinating and standardising functions, all the more so given the lack of national game-forms in both hurling and football at the time (see Chap. 2). Furthermore, and, interrelated with the organisation of sport contests, the frequency of acrimonious disputes involving individual competitors and club teams meant a need for third-party regulating and adjudicating functions. Consequently, the central executive provided not only an organisational structure for inter-club activities, but also functioned as third-party regulators.

Notwithstanding this, the functional dependences of clubs and county committees on central council were moderated somewhat by the fact that although a structural shift from localism was taking place towards more advanced levels of regional interdependence this process was at an early stage. For instance, club involvement in national competitions was limited (Mandle, 1987, p. 76) and so too was the standardisation of game-forms at national level.

The efforts of the IRB-controlled central executive to seek greater central control were opposed by many comprising clubs and county committees, though for different reasons (see *Celtic Times*, 3 September 1887; 19 November; 26 November; Mandle, 1987, pp. 39–44, 59). Certainly, as has been well documented (Mandle, 1987), clerical opposition was fomented through some clubs but there were other reasons too. County committees offered clubs, as county committees were comprised of club representatives, the opportunity to exert influence over local affairs—the management and organisation of match fixtures within the county, control over player and club suspensions, and the appointment of third-party controllers (*Celtic Times*, 19 November 1887). Furthermore, and interdependent with this, was the need by these subunits to maintain the financial and social power of the units they comprised. For instance, the Wicklow County committee passed a resolution that 'affiliation fees and other moneys received by the County Committees should be devoted to furthering Gaelic pastimes in the county in which the money was subscribed' (O'Sullivan, 1916, p. 82). Indicative of the power balance was the fact that clubs were able to force the devolution of more functions to county committees, including 'power to suspend, disqualify, or expel clubs' in 1888 (O'Sullivan, 1916, p. 64).

WE-IDENTIFICATIONS AND INTRA-ORGANISATIONAL TENSION

As we said, the divisions between those favouring greater centralisation and those opposed to it were interdependent with and overlapped by the factional hostilities emerging between the IRB and the clergy in particular (Mandle, 1987, pp. 39–44, 59). But the divisions and animosities were more complex than this binary opposition. While the divisions of this time are often presented as a contest between the IRB and a coalition of opposed interests including the clergy, other we-identifications could generate animosities even between those who identified with the IRB. Indicative of the different social interdependences and layers of we-identification, divisions stemming from the emotional charge generated by more local identifications also found expression. Some representatives of the central executive at times identified more closely with their respective county and/or club, and central executive meetings were often a site of antipathy and sectional struggles (see *Sport*, 31 January 1891, p. 9; 7 February, p. 7; 21 February, p. 2; 7 March, p. 7; 21 November, p. 8; 5 December, p. 8). For instance, in a letter to the newspaper *Sport*, Maurice Moynihan, the then general secretary of the GAA and member of its central council, and GAA secretary of the Kerry County committee (his native county) and a leading member of the IRB (secretary for the IRB in County Kerry) (McElligott, 2013), wrote:

> [I]f Dublin is the natural headquarters and the Dublin Gaels the pioneers of the association, how is it they could not hold their county convention in time ...We who live at the back of God speed down here in Kerry managed to have all our arrangements made. (*Sport*, 7 February 1891, p. 7)

A further example of the intensity of the emotional charge generated by the we-identification of the county at this time can be seen from a dispute which arose in 1895 over a match between teams representing the counties of Cork and Dublin. At a subsequent central council meeting in which the contest was discussed, Michael Deering (County Cork representative on central executive) and Patrick Tobin (County Dublin representative on central executive) had to be prevented from coming to blows. Both men were in fact also members of the IRB (Mandle, 1987, p. 105). This again exemplifies the layers of we-identification and the conflicting emotional pulls generated by different interdependences. We emphasise this because the decline of the GAA in the early 1890s has been largely presented as a reflex of the Parnell split in Irish society more generally. Yet, it was interwoven with other conflicts and tensions generated by different social identifications and related emotional charges, which were also contributing processes in the disintegration dynamic that afflicted the GAA in the 1890s. Indeed, when the tensions between the different political groups in Ireland escalated following the death of the leader of the Irish Parliamentary Party, Charles Stewart Parnell, it led to both direct and indirect disintegrating pressures (McGee, 2005, pp. 164–165). As the GAA split along similar lines, the internecine disputes arising from this, at both club and county committee level, resulted in many clubs and county committees disbanding or disaffiliating from the GAA (De Búrca, 1999; Mandle, 1987). This also led to the breakdown in sporting competitions with few county committees entering a team in the national championships (O'Sullivan, 1916, p. 111), decreasing further the functional dependence of the subunits on the central executive. By 1892 the number of clubs affiliated had fallen to 122 from over 770 in 1889 (Mandle, 1987, pp. 77, 99). Where the central council's functional value for its subunits declined, so did its power and control over the subunits. An already weakened central council saw its social power diminish even further. For instance, although financially dependent on clubs it was forced in 1896 to allow clubs retain two thirds of the affiliation fees collected (O'Sullivan, 1916, p. 122). Indeed, where clubs and county committees continued to function many acted autonomously with county committees amending and creating new rules; levying affiliation fees; all without any reference to the central executive and the formalised procedures in place (Lennon, 1999, p. 647; 2000, p. 118) and without fear of any significant rapprochement. In some cases, they even established a rival organisation (De Búrca, 1999, p. 56; Mandle, 1987, p. 105). However, the divisions that emerged over Parnell have perhaps masked the other decentralising pressures we alluded to.

A Decentralising Spurt: The Formation of Provincial Councils

Tendencies towards re-integration came to the fore again by the latter half of the 1890s reflected by a rise in the number of clubs affiliating. This was driven in part by developments in other interconnected figurations. Many of the GAA's leading members and activists were still members of organisations such as the IRB; divisions within the IRB (McGee, 2005) saw the various factions involved seeking to enhance their position by fostering the formation of, and controlling, GAA clubs (Mandle, 1987, p. 108). The rise in clubs and related inter-club activities strengthened the functional requirement on the GAA's central committee as clubs enmeshed in interdependent relationships required coordination. Tensions stemming from other social interdependences such as disputes between county committees arising from sporting contests were still commonplace, adding to the need for third-party adjudicating functions. Testimony to this can be drawn from central council meetings in the late 1890s which were primarily given over to addressing disputes between county committees (O'Sullivan, 1916, pp. 129, 133, 140).

Despite this centralising dynamic it was far from comprehensive and other social interdependences and decentralising pressures existed simultaneously. For those comprising clubs and county committees, and even central council, they experienced conflicting interdependences being both partners and opponents. Significantly, it was these interdependences, of both a cooperative and conflictual nature, that actually sustained the requirement for coordinating and adjudicating functions at a higher level of orientation. Despite their dependence on each other and on some form of coordinating and rule-making body, many representatives of county committees (and clubs) sought to not only retain their functions but enhance them by seeking even greater autonomy for their units. As before, the balance of power lay in the direction of county committees and clubs rather than the central executive. Most of the affiliated county committees and clubs, at this time, came from the provinces of Munster and Leinster and the struggle by county committees for greater functional control and influence took place under the guise of these regional blocs. Indicative of this, and of the power balance which lay in favour of the clubs, were several changes instituted at the 1896 annual convention. The number of vice-presidents was increased 'from one to eight – three for Leinster, three for Munster, and one each for Connaught and Ulster', while county committees were only required to send forward one-third of their affiliation fees to the central council (O'Sullivan, 1916, p. 122).

This interdependence structure, and the balance of tensions within it, provided the context in which the creation of a further tier of coordination emerged between 1899 and 1903—the provincial councils. By the turn of the twentieth century the tensions between various county committees had escalated. Many sought to maintain their status and social power. Simultaneously though they feared any advance in the social power of other county committees. In some cases, the desire for greater functional control involved attempts to subsume the functions still held by the central council. In 1901 the representatives of some county committees sought to disband the social institution of central council and replace it with regional councils (O'Sullivan, 1916, p. 149), in which county committees within specific regions would have greater authority. However, the requirement for a unit to coordinate inter-county activities meant the need for higher-tier coordinating functions persisted. It was this ambivalent situation and the related structure of power and interdependence between the central executive and the county committees which resulted in the creation of a new tier of coordination which were known as provincial councils. These 'new' units (provincial councils) comprised representatives from each affiliated county committee within each of the four provinces of Ireland. Many of the functions at central council level were now decentralised to these new units (De Búrca, 1984, pp. 8–9)—central executive was still required for national coordination. This demonstrates the social power of county committees at the time as many more of the functions of the central executive were devolved to the provincial councils. For instance, in 1903, county committees succeeded in changing the allocation of revenue model then in existence. Instead of revenues from the inter-county competition within each province going to the central council, half would go to the provincial council, a quarter to the counties involved and a quarter to the central council (Mandle, 1987, p. 135). By 1907 the GAA constitution stated provincial councils could 'exercise all the powers previously held' by the central council (GAA, 1907, p. 37). The power structure had become more multipolar with the formation of the provincial councils. This was essentially a decentralising spurt as the central council lost function to these 'lower' tier units.

ADVANCES IN PROCESSES OF INTEGRATION AND MUTUAL IDENTIFICATION

By the early 1900s the number of clubs and county committees affiliating grew even more rapidly (De Búrca, 1984, p. 7; Nolan, 2005, pp. 78, 81)—over 700 clubs and 23 county committees had been affiliated by 1906. This was facilitated, to an extent, by the healing of a rift within the IRB (Mandle, 1987, pp. 118–123), and by rising nationalist sentiment and greater identification of more social groups with the Gaelic-Ireland movement (De Búrca, 1999, p. 67). This was reflected by, and further propelled, the increasing association between membership of the GAA, anti-Britishness and a 'true' Gaelic Ireland. The symbolism and conceptual repertoire of this alignment was increasingly mobilised by GAA activists at all levels in the struggle to maintain and enhance membership.

The expansion in membership included greater diversity in the age profile of those joining which in turn partly facilitated the creation of more differentiated and specialised competitions (Mandle, 1987, p. 133; Nolan, 2005, pp. 75–86). The expanding web of interdependences was a driving force in the advance in functional specialisation occurring at different levels within the organisation. This created a greater requirement for more integrated coordinating functions and a central authority to oversee this; the functions provided by the central executive and central administrators increased. The expansion in the number of clubs and related sporting contests and in the overall scale of interdependences that these activities reflected also exacerbated tensions at inter-club and inter-county level. An analysis of the minute books of various county committees, provincial councils and the central executive during this period reveals an extensive array of appeals and protests by clubs over on- and off-field transgressions or perceived transgressions. In cases where clubs or county committees were dissatisfied with the result of the decision they often appealed to a higher-tier unit. The social prestige and emotional satisfaction obtained from success in competitions, which at one level advanced integration, also led clubs and county committees to use various methods and approaches to seek to either advance their own cause or impair the chances of their opponents. Significantly, these disputes and the antipathies precipitating or following them had the effect of partly cementing the status and authority of units at higher levels of coordination as their function of third part adjudicator took on increasing importance. As such, both clubs and county committees became more dependent on provincial and central councils for their regulatory and administrative functions. As the interdependences between each unit, club, county committee, provincial council and central council expanded, the functions they provided for each increasingly interlocked. This brought with it a compelling pressure for coordinating functions at a higher level of orientation and upon which the other 'lower tier' units were more functionally dependent. A movement in the power ratio in the direction of the central coordinating unit (central executive) was taking place.

At one level the web of interdependences in which all units were enmeshed propelled an advance in integration processes and in the 'national' GAA we-identity experienced by many members. This was helped also by the widening division between those aligning themselves with greater independence for Ireland (through either a Republic or Home Rule) and those identifying more closely with the Union with Britain. This advance in integration towards a more national and unified GAA was exactly that, an advance from a less developed one. It did not mean decentralising or disintegrating tensions had dissipated. Many GAA members felt a stronger 'local' GAA we-identity and this found expression in both lower-tier and higher-tier units. The composition of provincial and central council involved representatives of county committees. The we-identification of some members of these higher-tier units was more strongly orientated towards their county or club. This often manifested itself in disputes arising from sporting competition and in respect of the very structure of the units they comprised. For example, by 1909 the number of affiliated county committees had increased to 32 (De Búrca, 1999, p. 75), an illustration of the integration advance we referred to. This now meant that the central executive comprised over 40 members—including a representative of each county committee. Some now felt that to achieve more effective coordination the number of county committee representatives on central executive should be restricted to three delegates from each of the four provinces (*Freemans Journal*, 28 March 1910, p. 9; *Sport*, 10 April 1910, p. 2). Indeed, such a proposal was duly accepted. However, within a year of this resolution being passed, attempts were made to revert to the previous structure of central executive as some county committees felt they had lost influence (GAA, 1911, 1913).

In part, this demonstrated the sense of meaning obtained from county identification and how this had also grown with the expansion and intensification of interdependences within and between counties, and in conjunction with a national we-identification. Indeed, the strength of local we-identifications combined with the structure of functional interdependence between county committees and the central organs then pertaining meant some units were still inclined to disaffiliate from the GAA over disputes. Indeed, inter-club and inter-county wrangles could still lead units to not only disaffiliate from the GAA (Looney, 2008, p. 71), but seek to set up a new county committee (Mulvey, 2002a, p. 18), or even a rival organisation independent of the central council (Looney, 2008, p. 61). For instance, in 1915 a Dublin club, Kickhams, as result of a dispute with the Dublin County committee, formed a rival National Association of Gaelic and Athletic Clubs (Nolan, 2005, p. 100), and a number of clubs from across Ireland affiliated to this new organisation (Mandle, 1987, pp. 173–174). Despite these counter pressures integration processes remained.

The strengthening of we-images (Elias, 2010) at GAA county committee level had advanced alongside a growing sense of a national we-image. This was facilitated by the intensification of interdependences involving units from disparate regions. It was also impelled too at a higher level of integration and competition by the escalation in tensions between those seeking an independent Ireland and those seeking to maintain the Union of Ireland and Great Britain which took a more militant and violent turn from 1916. The interweaving processes of rising nationalist sentiment, and competition between the rival sports organisations, led to the conflating, though contested, of specific sports and sporting organisations with Irish nationalism or British imperialism. This facilitated and contributed to an advance in the national we-image of the GAA and in smoothing the path towards greater national unification of the organisation as a whole. As before, this we-image of a national organisation and the emotions and feelings it aroused existed simultaneously with other 'we' feelings towards club and/or county. Sporting processes also contributed to the strengthening of we-identifications. In 1887 the GAA had created a championship competition for Gaelic football and hurling where a club, which had won a championship within its county boundaries, went on to represent that county in the national championship (what became known as the All-Ireland championship) against the champion clubs from the other counties. As this inter-county competition became more competitive, clubs began to supplement their team with players from other clubs within their own county boundary (Mandle, 1987, p. 106), a feature which was legalised within the rules in 1892 (O'Sullivan, 1916, p. 98). This development eventually led to the formation of representative county teams containing players from several clubs, even though the champion club in a county had the official authority to represent the county in inter-county competition until 1923. With the formation of county teams, mutual identification around county allegiance developed and advanced this we-image (and the they-image of opposing counties in national competitions). As more counties took part, and the status and meaning of these championships for people throughout Ireland grew—the rise in attendances and in media coverage were indicative of this—the functions of central council were strengthened; for inter-regional fixtures of this nature to take place it requires centralised coordinating functions.

THE ADVANCE IN THE POWER SOURCES OF THE CENTRAL UNITS

Both the War of Independence and Civil War led to a breakdown in the organisation of sporting contests while also exacerbating disintegrating tensions. The animosities of the Civil War led to significant divisions within the GAA organisation in some parts of the country. For instance, two county committees functioned in County Clare. As a more pacified social space emerged the organisation of sporting contests and related interdependences re-emerged and expanded. Between 1924 and 1937 the number of clubs affiliated increased from 1051 to 1671 (GAA, 1947). This involved and further propelled an expansion in interdependences between units across all tiers. More units came to be engaged in different and more varied relationships of a cooperative and conflictual nature.

The interdependences which brought the units together or separated them—animosities generated by previous sporting encounters, and which often provided the seed for further hostilities—were equally important in cementing the different layers of we- and they-identities and maintaining their durability. Such we- and they-feelings in conjunction with an intensification in functional interdependence often exacerbated tensions. Disagreements emerged between clubs, between county committees, between provincial councils, and between county committees and provincial councils. These disputes had the unplanned effect of increasing the functional importance of the central council as they were the last arbiters of disputes. Combined with the expansion in other intra-organisational interdependences, this sustained the need for more centralised functions despite persisting decentralising pressures. As before, the strengthening and enhanced status of GAA's intercountry championships, reflected in their popularity, also contributed to an increase in the functional importance of central council. It was the coordinating unit for national champions and it also controlled much of the gate receipts derived from these competitions, which had grown significantly.

A further reflection of the enhanced functional power of the central council was that it was increasingly perceived by various units to be the primary social organ in which more and more decisions were being determined. Indicative of this were the efforts by county committees for permanent representation on central council. These became more frequent from the late 1920s onward with repeated attempts by representatives of county committees (and clubs) to amend the GAA constitution to allow for an individual representative from each county to become a member of central council (GAA, 1929, 1935, 1936, 1939, 1940). For instance, one delegate from County Meath speaking in support of such a motion in 1939 claimed:

> Some counties felt they had not a fair chance of representation…all counties should have a voice in the control of the Association. It was not fair that three men should represent twelve counties [the province of Leinster] when the interests of the counties may clash. This might occur in the making of fixtures. (GAA, 1939, p. 10)

Another delegate at the 1939 congress, supporting the proposal for individual county representation, suggested, 'A county representative could keep his county in touch with the working of Council', while an opposing delegate countered 'that if the motion was adopted a province with twelve counties could dominate the Central Council. It would be a lop-sided council' (GAA, 1939).

The repeated attempts to attain individual representation finally came to fruition in 1946, when a motion was passed at national congress. However, the expanded scale and nature of the interdependences, and the related speed of coordination and decision-making connected with them, in which GAA functionaries were enmeshed, meant the pressure for a unit to accommodate this was strong. Consequently, in parallel with the expansion of the central council to include a representative of each county committee, an 'executive committee' of twelve to 'deal with the routine matters' between central executive meetings was formed (GAA, 1946). The desire for such a unit was clearly advocated by GAA functionaries positioned at the highest level of orientation and coordination—the senior administrators. They had previously sought a smaller 'executive committee' which would subsume some of functions up to then the preserve of central council (GAA, 1942).

Indicative of the competitive tensions and rivalries pervading the GAA figuration there were still demands for individual county representation on this new committee (GAA, 1946). The representatives of county committees were expected, by some members of the social groups they represented, to maintain or enhance the status and social power of their county, while simultaneously fulfilling their function as the main coordinating unit for the national organisation. The addition of the management committee further extended the complexity of the overall GAA figuration, generating new tensions and pressures. The we-identity of the county for some was far stronger than their national GAA we-feeling and their primary focus was on maintaining the position of their county. For others, the national we-image was stronger and they looked beyond individual representation. In the years that followed, the division between those who increasingly espoused a more national outlook towards the organisation and those who identified more closely with local or provincial interests manifested itself in motions to amend the structure of the central executive and reduce its size (GAA, 1951, 1952, 1953)—single county representation was maintained, however.

CENTRALISING SPURTS

From the 1960s the scale and nature of interdependences enmeshing functionaries within all GAA units expanded and intensified. The number of clubs affiliated grew to over 3000 (GAA, 1962). This involved an expansion in interdependences impelling further functional specialisation. For example, more tasks were devolved to subcommittees at central level (GAA, 1963). Alongside these cooperative interdependences were intra-organisational tensions and hostilities—stemming from both sporting and resource interdependences. Many administrators continued to be shaped by county we-feeling which generated a greater emotional charge than any other we-image.

The competitive pressures facing those occupying positions of organisational direction and coordination including those comprising its central units intensified in the late 1960s and 1970s. The competitive pressures from competing sports and related pressures emanating from changes in the structure of Irish society more broadly (see Chaps. 2 and 7) generated a renewed pressure for both greater functional specialisation and relatedly on coordinating and organising functions. The longer and denser structure of interdependences, and growing awareness of these interdependences, meant more individuals at different levels within the organisation now felt the need for higher levels of coordination. Some members, as was reflected in a special report for the GAA published in 1971, called for a smaller unit with 'more authority and freedom of action' (GAA, 1971):

> It is a fairly widely held view that many of the Association's ruling bodies, including the Central Council and Congress, are too large and too cumbersome to do effective work and that control of the association should be given to a much smaller body. It is accepted that a small committee can usually reach decisions faster than a larger one and so get through a larger amount of work.

Again tensions emerged between those more closely identifying with their county or club and those with a wider national outlook towards the organisation (De Búrca, 1984). Nonetheless, the decision to add a management committee was passed by delegates at a special national congress in 1972 (GAA, 1972). However, this decision still reflected the intra-organisational tensions based on regionalism, and the power relations connected with this—the new management committee had to contain one elected member from each of the provinces (GAA, 1972). Given the structure of the dependence relationships, and consequently the power balance, which existed between the GAA's subunits, clubs and county committees were still capable of extracting concessions. The demand for one member from each province reflected a fear of dominance by other provincial units. Illustrative of the power ratio, the representatives of some clubs and county committees were able to defeat attempts to further decrease the function of county committees and clubs by rejecting a proposal to reduce the size of the national congress, which was also recommended at the time (GAA, 1972). Some within the central executive deeply resented the new structure, and attempts were made in subsequent years to overturn the decision (GAA, 1974). The perceived, and indeed real, loss of function was lamented by one delegate, who stated: 'Central Council [executive] today is nothing but a glorified fireside chat without a fire. It has no effect, good, bad or indifferent' (GAA, 1974, p. 40).

Functional differentiation and specialisation continued to expand in the following decades. The subcommittee system, which had intermittently been affected at various times by the central units up to the 1960s, became a structural requirement at central level so as to enable the operation of an expanding number of functions. This form of specialisation—subcommittees deal with specific tasks and/or activities—gradually became a feature of other coordinating units. By the 1990s they were considered necessary for county committee level (GAA, 1991). Almost two decades later in 2008 the Ulster provincial council operated 24 separate committees (GAA Ulster Council, 2008). An expanded and differentiated professional bureaucracy developed (see Chap. 5), further lengthening the chain of interdependences. The overall expansion in interdependences between the social units comprising the GAA intensified integration processes and led to a compelling pressure to maintain, and indeed enhance, the power of coordinating units at higher levels of orientation. In this regard the functional dependence on the central authorities of the organisation for coordination advanced and with it the social power of the central authorities, as social power corresponds, solely, 'to the degree of dependence of the various interdependent functions on one another' (Elias, 2012, p. 350). Just as the functional importance of the central organs (central executive and management committee) of the organisation advanced, so too has the social power of these units. For, from a specific degree of functional differentiation onward, the complex web of intertwining activities cannot grow or function without coordinating organs at a correspondingly high level of organisation (Elias, 2012).

Notwithstanding, the overlapping nature of these units (central executive and the management committee contain representatives from subunits in the organisational tiers below them) and the identification of members with other we-images at different levels of intensity means divisions surface around sectional and/or provincial interests and indeed emotional attachments (see for instance Kelly, 2007, pp. 234–235). That many individuals simultaneously comprised the different organisational units of the GAA underpins the problem of conceiving of these as separate interacting entities. The concepts of figuration and we-identification help to better capture the complex and contradictory nature of this process.

CONCLUSION

Centralising and decentralising processes have interwoven since the establishment of the GAA. While the overall trajectory of the GAA has been towards increased integration and centralisation this has not been an even and linear development with movements towards and away from centralisation, depending on the shifting balances of power between different social groups and units at interconnected levels of organisational and social integration.

As the network of interdependences became longer and denser (functional differentiation and specialisation advanced), the requirement for a higher-tier coordinating function for the GAA increased, and over time, particularly in the latter half of the twentieth century, the power chances of the central units of the organisation became greater. This dynamic is also reflected in changes concerning the process of legislation development, and in the channels used to achieve this. Between 1889 and 1997, motions for changing or amending the rules and constitution of the GAA could solely be proposed, and thereby voted upon, by the representatives of county committees and clubs at the national congress. In the 1940s attempts were made to change this process and also permit central council this function (GAA, 1945; Lennon, 2000, p. 129). Perceived by some as an attempt by those in more central functions to exert more comprehensive control, it was rejected by national congress (comprised by club/county representatives). Repeated attempts were made in respect of this function in 1974, 1980, 1993, and 1995 until finally it was agreed by the national congress in 1997 (Lennon, 2000, pp. 130, 135). This struggle for control over power chances and functions is a persistent feature of the GAA as it is of all social organisations. For example, in 2002 the *GAA's*

Strategic Review suggested some of the activities of national congress, 'could, and should, be devolved to Central Council, which in turn, could and should, devolve some of its activities to' the management committee (GAA, 2002, p. 23). Another example concerns the repeated attempts by some to reduce the size of congress, and, with it, some of its social power, but these were rejected by congress in 1972 (GAA, 1972, p. 24) and also in 2002 when the GAA's *Strategic Review* (GAA, 2002, p. 236) sought such a change. This issue was raised again in 2011 and in 2018 but so far the majority of representatives on national congress have resisted it. Despite the overall trend of a shift in the power balance in the direction of the central units, the interdependences which bound, and continue to bind, the central units of the organisation to the lower-tier units exert considerable constraints. The functional dependence of the central units and related functionaries on national congress (and on county committees, and provincial councils) mean these units were (and are) able to exert some control over the actual configuration of the organisation and the central units comprising it. However, this overall dynamic has generated an organisational structure which was neither planned nor intended by any single individual.

NOTES

1. The Northern Football Union of Ireland was also formed by several clubs in some of the counties in the north of the country. These Unions amalgamated in 1878 (Garnham, 1999), becoming the Irish Rugby Football Union (IRFU) in 1880.
2. County committees are more commonly known as county boards nowadays. We use the term county committees rather than county boards as this was the term used in the early years.

REFERENCES

Daly, M. E. (Ed.). (2001). *County and town: One hundred years of local government*. Dublin: Institute of Public Administration.

De Búrca, M. (1984). *Gaelic games in Leinster*. Mullingar: Comhairle Laighean, CLG.

De Búrca, M. (1989). *Michael Cusack and the GAA*. Dublin: Anvil Books.

De Búrca, M. (1999). *The GAA: A history* (2nd ed.). Dublin: Gill & Macmillan.

Dolan, P. (2005). *The development of consumer culture, subjectivity and national identity in Ireland, 1900–1980*. PhD thesis, Goldsmiths College, University of London, London.

Dolan, P. (2009a). Developing consumer subjectivity in Ireland: 1900–1980. *Journal of Consumer Culture, 9*(1), 117–141.

Dolan, P. (2009b). Figurational dynamics and parliamentary discourses of living standards in Ireland. *British Journal of Sociology, 60*(4), 721–739.

Elias, N. (2010). *The society of individuals* (Rev. ed.). Dublin: University College Dublin Press.

Elias, N. (2012). *On the process of civilisation* (Rev. ed.). Dublin: University College Dublin Press.

Elias, N., & Dunning, E. (2008). *Quest for excitement: Sport and leisure in the civilising process* (Rev. ed.). Dublin: University College Dublin Press.

GAA. (1907). *Gaelic Athletic Association. Official guide, 1907-8-9.* Wexford: GAA.

GAA. (1911). *Minutes of annual congress.* Dublin: GAA.

GAA. (1913). *Minutes of annual congress.* Dublin: GAA.

GAA. (1929). *Minutes of special annual congress.* Dublin: GAA.

GAA. (1935). *Minutes of annual congress.* Dublin: GAA.

GAA. (1936). *Minutes of annual congress.* Dublin: GAA.

GAA. (1939). *Minutes of the annual congress.* Dublin: GAA.

GAA. (1940). *Minutes of the annual congress.* Dublin: GAA.

GAA. (1942). *Minutes of annual congress.* Dublin: GAA.

GAA. (1945). *Minutes of annual congress.* Dublin: GAA.

GAA. (1946). *Minutes of annual congress.* Dublin: GAA.

GAA. (1947). *An comhdháil bhliantúil.* Dublin: GAA.

GAA. (1951). *Minutes of the annual congress.* Dublin: GAA.

GAA. (1952). *Minutes of annual congress.* Dublin: GAA.

GAA. (1953). *Minutes of annual congress.* Dublin: GAA.

GAA. (1962). *An comhdháil bhliantúil.* Dublin: GAA.

GAA. (1963). *An comhdháil bhliantúil.* Dublin: GAA.

GAA. (1971). *Report of the commission on the GAA.* Dublin: Gaelic Athletic Association.

GAA. (1972). *Minutes of special congress 1972.* Dublin: GAA.

GAA. (1974). *Minutes of annual congress.* Dublin: GAA.

GAA. (1991). *An comhdháil bhliantúil.* Dublin: GAA.

GAA. (2002). *G.A.A. strategic review—Enhancing community identity.* Dublin: Gaelic Athletic Association.

GAA Ulster Council. (2008). Committees. Retrieved from http://ulster.gaa.ie/council/committees/

Garnham, N. (1999). Origins and development of Irish football. In N. Garnham (Ed.), *The origins and development of football in Ireland: Being a reprint of R.M. Peter's Irish Football Annual of 1880* (pp. 1–29). Belfast: Ulster Historical Foundation.

Garnham, N. (2004). Accounting for the early success of the Gaelic Athletic Association. *Irish Historical Studies, 34*(133), 65–78.

Garvin, T. (1986). Priests and patriots: Irish separatism and fear of the modern, 1890–1914. *Irish Historical Studies, 25*(97), 67–81.

Hunt, T. (2008). *Sport and society in Victorian Ireland: The case of Westmeath.* Cork: Cork University Press.

Hunt, T. (2009). Parish factions, parading bands and sumptuous repasts: The diverse origins and activities of early GAA clubs. In D. McAnallen, D. Hassan, & R. Hegarty (Eds.), *The evolution of the GAA: Ulaidh, Éire agus eile* (pp. 86–99). Belfast: Stair Uladh.

Kelly, S. (2007). *Rule 42 and all that.* Dublin: Gill & Macmillan.

Lennon, J. (1999). *A comparative analysis of the playing rules of football and hurling 1884–1999.* Gormanstown, Co. Meath: The Northern Recreation Consultants.

Lennon, J. (2000). *Towards a philosophy for legislation in Gaelic games.* Gormanstown, Co. Meath: The Northern Recreation Consultants.

Looney, T. (2008). *Dick Fitzgerald: King in a kingdom of kings.* Dublin: Currach Press.

Maguire, C. (2011). *Peasants into patriots: Instruments of radical politicisation in Clare 1800–1907.* PhD thesis, Mary Immaculate College, Limerick.

Mandle, W. F. (1987). *The Gaelic Athletic Association and Irish nationalist politics, 1884–1924.* Dublin: Gill & Macmillan.

McDevitt, P. F. (1997). Muscular Catholicism: Nationalism, masculinity and Gaelic team sports, 1884–1916. *Gender & History, 9*(2), 262–284.

McElligott, R. (2013). *Forging a kingdom: The GAA in Kerry 1884–1934.* Wilton, Cork: Collins Press.

McGee, O. (2005). *The IRB: The Irish Republican Brotherhood from the Land League to Sinn Fein.* Dublin: Four Courts Press.

Mullan, M. (1995). Opposition, social closure, and sport: The Gaelic Athletic Association in the 19th century. *Sociology of Sport Journal, 12*(3), 268–289.

Mulvey, J. (2002a). A new dawn. In T. Moran (Ed.), *Stair CLG Chonnacht 1902–2002* (pp. 11–22). Carrick-on-Shannon, Co. Leitrim: Carrick Print.

Mulvey, J. (2002b). Sowing the seed. In T. Moran (Ed.), *Stair CLG Chonnacht 1902–2002* (pp. 1–10). Carrick-on-Shannon, Co. Leitrim: Carrick Print.

Nolan, W. (Ed.). (2005). *The Gaelic Athletic Association in Dublin 1884–2000* (Vol. 1). Dublin: Geography Publications.

Ó Riain, S. (1994). *Maurice Davin (1842–1927): First president of the G.A.A.* Dublin: Geography Publications.

O'Donoghue, N. (1987). *Proud and upright men.* Indreabhán, Galway: Clódóirí Lurgan Teo.

O'Sullivan, T. F. (1916). *The story of the G.A.A.* Printed at 49 Middle Abbey Street, Dublin.

Rouse, P. (2015). *Sport & Ireland.* Oxford: Oxford University Press.

CHAPTER 5

The Amateur–Professional Tension Balance

THE AMATEUR IDEAL AND THE GAA

In Chap. 4 we explained how the structure of interdependence between those comprising rising Irish middle-class groups and the Anglo-Irish elite provided the social context through which the desire and motivation to establish the GAA was formed. It was also a specific structure of interdependence which shaped the form and meaning of amateurism that emerged and took hold in the GAA. By the 1880s in Ireland as in Britain, amateurism was the organisational ethos for most sports. However, it was already increasingly intertwined with social demarcation arising from escalating social tensions between the landed classes and rising middle- and lower-class groups in Britain at the time. As Dunning and Sheard (1979) have shown, professional sport became the subject of increasing stigmatisation by the British upper classes—the aristocracy and gentry[1]—as their power relative to middle classes (and working classes) declined, and their awareness of this grew. This process had been ongoing for well over a century due to industrialisation and urbanisation, which slowly eroded the power base of the landed classes. As their status insecurity grew, so did their efforts to exert barriers between them and rising middle- and lower-class groups. The stigmatising of professional sports was an element of this, as was the conflation of amateurism with 'gentlemanly' behaviour.

In Ireland similar tensions would soon find expression. It was however complicated further by the fact that the upper classes in Ireland were considered lower in social status than their British peers, and also because

© The Author(s) 2020
J. Connolly, P. Dolan, *Gaelic Games in Society*, Palgrave Studies
on Norbert Elias, https://doi.org/10.1007/978-3-030-31699-0_5

of the lower level of industrialisation, and the identification that emerged between middle-class groups, lower social groups and even elements of the gentry around an ethnic Gaelic nationalism (Dolan, 2005). Certainly, a majority of the established Anglo-Irish were closely aligned with the British upper classes, aspiring to, and mirroring, their standards of behaviour and mores—an indication also of their subordinate status. Consequently, they too sought to invoke the status of amateurism and associate it with the gentlemanly ideal. Athletics in Ireland during the early 1880s was governed by the rules of the English Amateur Athletic Association (AAA), which excluded many native Irish games and lower social class participation. The constitution and rules of the AAA, reflecting the class tensions in Britain, were based on the values and ethos of the British upper classes, with participation confined to 'amateur gentlemen':

> one who has never competed in an open competition or for public money or for admission money, or with professionals for prize money, and who has never at any period of his life taught, pursued or assisted in the pursuit of athletic exercises as a means of livelihood, nor as a mechanic, artisan or labourer. (cited in Ó Riain, 1994, p. 30)

Although the established Anglo-Irish ascendancy, who were closely aligned to the British establishment, were in decline, they continued to exhibit the social confidence that went with their position as the leading strata in Irish society. At a local level throughout Ireland, the gentry remained the dominant force. They retained a monopoly or controlling stake over the principal sources of power in Irish society and the social functions connected with these, including the ownership of property and positions of influence in relation to the police, military and judiciary. They also, to a large degree, retained the social function of gatekeeper for entry to and participation in many social activities. Their position allowed them to confer social prestige on specific practices, and on those who could partake in them. Concomitantly, they also retained the capacity to stigmatise particular practices, individuals or social groups. To that extent, they remained a model-setting group for many members of the socially ambitious middle classes in particular. Nonetheless, this was a complex social process with subordinate groups simultaneously ambivalent towards some aspects of these social standards, in part resisting and counter-posing alternatives (the Gaelic movement itself being an example of this). Certainly the power balance between Irish middle classes and established landed classes had narrowed, permitting the accommodation of more native middle-class interests and values. However, although having risen socially, even the elite of the Irish middle classes had not eclipsed the Anglo-Irish as the dominant social group in Ireland. Because of this, they remained somewhat subservient to them. And no more than those above them, the lower tiers of the middle classes were also forced to accommodate some of the values and mores associated with the landed classes. Sport was one domain in which this occurred. Thus, to organise in ways directly opposed to amateurism would have left them open to attack on the grounds that they were socially inferior in behaviour and standards.

So while the GAA was founded on the basis of resisting the Anglicisation of Irish sport, it was the British upper-class model of organised sport which was partly applied as the nascent organisational frame (Mandle, 1987). For instance, at the founding meeting of the GAA in November 1884, although amateurism was not explicitly referred to, Michael Cusack observed: 'he must confess that the code of the A.A. Association was a good one, and in the management of Irish athletics and games could not do better than adopt somewhat similar rules' (cited in *Cork Examiner*, 2 November 1884, p. 7). Notwithstanding, in the months that followed, the concept of amateurism would be increasingly invoked by those both aligned with and opposed to the GAA. In Britain a relatively pristine idea of amateurism (and its antonym professionalism) had crystallised and been increasingly deployed in the social struggle which enveloped sport there at this time. It soon found expression in Ireland too in the emerging contest between the GAA and the newly formed Irish Amateur Athletics Association (IAAA). The ethos of amateurism was increasingly deployed by those representing the IAAA as a means to stigmatise the GAA. For instance, a few months after its foundation, the first president of the GAA, Maurice Davin, in a letter to a national newspaper in response to allegations that the GAA's rules contravened the prevailing (English) rules on amateurism, claimed the GAA's rules were similar to those of the AAA: 'The A.A.A. have laws for the purposes of preventing men making a living by amateur athletics… The G.A.A. have similar laws' (*Freemans Journal*, 13 February 1885, p. 7). Indeed, the GAA's rules of 1885 on athletics reflected this, though they did permit money prizes to offset travelling expenses (McAnallen, 2009, p. 158). The latter appears to have contributed to criticism of the GAA in the press, and it seems it was subsequently expunged from the rules of 1886 (Ó Riain, 1994, p. 94).

It seems likely that the early founders of the GAA adopted amateurism partly on the grounds that a form of amateurism was the dominant
organisational basis for sport in Ireland. However, it also seems likely
that they were somewhat compelled to do so in order to distance themselves from the class-derived stigmatising labels attached to them by the
very group they opposed (the IAAA). The capacity of the IAAA membership to invoke such a stigmatisation was interconnected with the
higher tier figuration involving the upper classes and middle classes in
Ireland and the power structure pertaining within it. The IAAA leadership was primarily drawn from the Irish upper- and upper-middle classes.
We contend it was partly this higher tier structure of interdependence
which generated a compelling pressure on the GAA's founders to claim
and implement an amateur ethos. At the same time, for many of the
founding members of the GAA, and those they hoped would join the
GAA, the ethos of the 'pure' amateurism was in many ways incompati-
ble with their interests and social values—those of the Irish lower middle classes and labouring classes. Garnham (2004a, p. 72) has referred
to these groups as the 'leisureless' classes, for they tended to work long
days and at least a six-day week, leaving little opportunity for leisure. It
was from this group that many of the GAA's administrators, players and
spectators were drawn. Several historians have already noted the paltry
data on the social structure of the GAA membership—though there
have been some advances in recent times. The most informative work
emanates from Hunt (2008, 2009), McElligott (2013), Garnham
(2004a), Mandle (1987), Mullan (1995) and Curran (2015). Even
combined these studies give a relatively small sample in comparison to
the numbers of people who were players and administrators throughout
the country. However, this aside, and acknowledging differences
between the studies (McElligott and Hunt for instance), what is defini-
tive in a collective sense across these studies is that the GAA membership was almost exclusively drawn from the lower middle classes and
skilled working classes. We emphasise this social make-up of the GAA
because, as we now explain, it shaped the form of amateurism that
emerged and the lack of conflict over moderations to amateurism in the
subsequent years.

As we outlined above, the GAA leadership did declare that GAA competitions were amateur in status, and amateurism was the organisational
structure embodied in sporting contests. However, it was not, from the
very outset, the 'pristine' amateurism (see also Rouse, 2015) of the

AAA. The GAA's version of amateurism permitted and accommodated lower social class participation. Indeed, the desire and willingness to facilitate lower social class groups found expression in several other areas including Sunday play and lower admission fees. Club affiliation fees and individual membership fees, as well as admission fees for spectators to GAA contests were often lower than for many competing sports (Garnham, 2004a, p. 74). Furthermore, despite Davin's assertions concerning prize money to offset travelling expenses, the payment of expenses was permitted in places (McAnallen, 2009, p. 158). Competing for prizes and wagers had long been a feature of sport in Ireland pre-GAA (Rouse, 2015) and it had continued as the nascent codification of GAA sports was taking place. In addition, and though it varied across regions due to a lack of financial resources, some GAA clubs began covering the cost, or reimbursing their players, for transport to sporting contests in those early years (McAnallen, 2009). Similar accommodations were made at the administrative level with national secretaries and the official handicapper reimbursed for travelling expenses. Gate-taking was permitted from the start, as was commercial involvement through the provision of prizes and trophies. The issue of gate-taking here is important in considering the amateur–professional tension balance (between purely amateur principles and rules and more professionally orientated structures). While gate-taking is not directly a contravention of the amateur ethos, where it is used to pay administrators it is an early stage process of professionalisation for it means player performance has become subject to an economic exchange (Dunning & Sheard, 1979, p. 242). Indeed, there was a level of ambivalence towards paying administrators, indicative we would suggest of the fact that amateurism was not a strongly held value for some of those involved. For example, in 1887 Michael Cusack, writing on the need to fill the then vacant position of secretary, noted:

> The resignation of Mr. John Wyse Power has created a vacancy on the Executive. The remaining Dublin Secretary has to work in Messrs. Clery & Co.'s establishment from nine in the morning till six in the evening. The long hours leave him very little time to improve his mind and attend to the work of the Association [the GAA] …. That he needs assistance has been amply demonstrated …. Fresh young men, vehement, capable, and true, should be selected. If officers must be paid, it is better to pay young men. (*Celtic Times*, 26 March 1887)

Similarly, four years later in 1891, Maurice Moynihan, then national secretary of the GAA, in a letter to the national newspaper *Sport* observed:

> Whatever ability I possess, and whatever spare time I have on my hands, are of the service of the Gaelic Athletic Association but as long as the position of secretary remains an honorary [unpaid] one I am afraid that things must of necessity be conducted, to some extent at all events, in that happy-go-lucky eighteenth century fashion. (7 February 1891)

Moynihan wrote in a relatively disparaging way of organisational volunteerism suggesting it was old fashioned and rather haphazard. That the GAA's national secretary could make such a declaration in a national newspaper, and that it generated no internal conflict or dissent, illustrates how the invective around professionalism which was occurring within soccer and rugby, in particular, at the time had not infiltrated the GAA. Indeed, the GAA's annual congress agreed later that same year to award the national secretary a salary in the form of a percentage of the organisation's total receipts. And, two years later in 1893, a paid secretary was appointed to assist the national secretary (McAnallen, 2009, p. 276). As we noted already, both Moynihan's comments and the later changes on remuneration occurred without generating any conflict at a time of rising tension around amateurism and professionalism in sport more generally in Ireland (see Garnham, 2004b). We believe the relatively seamless inclusion of professional practices (or to phrase it differently, moderations to pure amateurism) stemmed from two interrelated processes both connected to the broadly lower middle-class make-up of the GAA. As we suggested earlier, based on the available evidence, most GAA clubs and other units were dominated by the lower middle classes[2]; those drawn from lower social class groups were also involved but it would seem to a lesser degree. It is this relatively homogeneous lower-middle-class make-up of the GAA which we contend was a factor in preventing any great anxiety or social pressure emerging around professionalism within the GAA. This was in marked contrast to what was occurring in soccer and rugby. Although they would diverge down opposite paths, within the representative associations for soccer and rugby the tension around professionalism aroused considerable and heated debate at this time (Garnham, 2004b; Rouse, 2015).

As we suggested, this does not appear to have occurred within the GAA. Certainly, as we explain in Chap. 6, professionalisation was amplified in later years as part of an inter-organisational blame-gossip, but at this period (from the early 1880s through to the early 1900s) no significant debates or conflicts arose within the ranks of the GAA on the issue. Unlike the GAA, the representative associations for soccer and rugby comprised a significant number of men drawn from the upper classes and middle classes at this time (Garnham, 2004b; O'Callaghan, 2011). It was elements of this social cohort who increasingly lauded amateurism and maligned professionalism in both soccer and rugby. We contend that it was the general absence of this social cohort from the GAA which meant little or no tension arose over amateurism or professionalism in the GAA in those early decades. The social anxieties experienced by the upper classes, which in turn lead them to extol amateurism, and for many to abandon soccer, were essentially absent from the GAA owing to the omission of the upper (upper-middle) classes from the ranks of the GAA.

BUREAUCRATISATION PROCESSES, ADVANCING SERIOUSNESS OF INVOLVEMENT AND THE EROSION OF AMATEUR STRUCTURES

The professionalisation of administrative functions in the GAA remained relatively limited in the early decades of the twentieth century with most positions filled on a voluntary basis. Nonetheless, tentative elements of professionalism were increasingly integrated and formalised. At a bureaucratic level, the increasing administrative workloads, due to the expansion of the association, led some county committees to award 'grants' to cover the work and/or expenses pertaining to the function of county secretary (McAnallen, 2009, p. 164). In 1914 the GAA's constitution was amended so that provincial councils were entitled to fix the provincial secretary's remuneration (GAA, 1914). Basically, some elements—however small—of the voluntary organisation of Gaelic games were being replaced by professional structures.

In several counties, players were awarded travel expenses and recompense for other costs incurred in playing. While this had been a feature of the GAA from the very early years such practices had been more ad hoc. Now it was being given more formal sanction in some counties (McElligott, 2013, p. 168). In parallel with this there were advances in what Dunning (2008) labelled seriousness of involvement and an achievement orientation. This concerned both players and administrators and it occurred more rapidly at what had become the elite level—the men's inter-county competitions. The competitive interdependences between units of the GAA led to an increased emphasis on pre-match preparation. Specialist training, including what were known as training camps, was initiated in some counties (McElligott, 2013, pp. 157, 192; Rouse, 2015, p. 196). Many working men (both lower middle class and working class) were unable to commit to such training camps, and also more localised training, without remuneration of some form. Consequently, GAA administrators arranged for various systems of compensation including the provision of broken-time payments. These were not 'under the counter' but openly declared practices. One example of this was in County Laois in 1914. Here the county committee appealed to the public to support a training fund to provide 'broken time' for players:

> The preparation of the team for the Leinster Championship was carried out at the personal expense of the members of the team. This has involved a serious drain on the means of the men, who, in many cases, had to provide substitutes to fill their places of employment during frequent special practices. It would be too much to expect them to bear the expenses of the extra special course of training which will be necessary for them to undergo for the playing of the All-Ireland Final. The team is mainly composed of working men to whom loss of a day's wages is a serious matter, and they have, as stated, already sacrificed a considerable sum in this way. (Higgins, 1914–1917)

This was a feature in other counties too, and the general public in the respective counties duly supported such funds (see Rouse, 2015, p. 196 for a description of the practice in County Clare). In a spiralling process of competition and emulation, teams, particularly at the inter-county level, sought to gain advantages over their rivals. Consequently, the practice of pre-match training and fundraising came to be perceived as essential:

> We relied on the fact that our men were born hurlers and natural athletes. These, of course, are qualities that should be inherent in any first-class team, but systematic training is necessary to develop these qualities. That is the object to which the County Board has now decided to address itself. A scheme has been prepared for the raising of funds to train our county team… Many counties now train their hurlers and footballers at the public expense. Then should not Limerick. (*Gaelic Athlete*, 27 March 1915)

We stress these examples because, while some references were made in newspapers about the practice, no conflicts or widespread tensions emerged at this point over the possible contravention of amateurism and a slide towards professionalism. Furthermore, as we outline in Chap. 6 this occurred at the same time as 'professionalism' in soccer became increasingly vilified by GAA activists and administrators (see also Chap. 7).

Gate-taking continued to be an important source of revenue for the association and the inter-county competitions attracted large 'paying' crowds, illustrating the growing dependence on spectators. Indeed, it was this income which generally paid the expenses/salaries/honorariums of administrators. The expansion of the GAA also had the unplanned effect of increasing the scale of interdependences in which GAA administrators were enmeshed. More clubs and inter-club activities increased the organisational tasks on 'volunteer' functions. For instance, the minutes of the Ulster Convention in 1920 noted:

> Regarding the Secretaryship the outgoing Secretary tendered his resignation on the grounds that the work of the secretary of the Ulster Council is becoming heavier + of increased responsibility every day + that his own private work which is also increasing prevented him giving sufficient time to the Ulster Council. The Convention would not accept the resignation + on the motion of Mr. Dobbin seconded by Mr. McFadden it was decided to call a special meeting of the Ulster Council to consider the question of providing assistance to the Secretary in his office work. Under these conditions the secretary agreed to continue in office. (GAA, 1920)

After the War of Independence and Civil War, the GAA continued to expand. Although not without tensions and fractures, a more integrated national framework of administration and affiliation developed (see Chap. 4). In tandem with this, national sporting competitions re-emerged, while new ones at different levels of competition were introduced. The inter-county championships in particular, and the meaning attached to them, added to the competitive interdependences between county teams and their respective administrative units. This fuelled a spiral dynamic of innovative and emulative processes in terms of both preparation and match play. These developments in pre-match preparations both reflected and further impelled a growing stress on seriousness of involvement and achievement-striving by players and administrators alike. The competitive relations between counties ensured a double-bind process (Elias & Dunning, 2008, p. 10) with each county trapped in a position of mutual fear that the other (county) was or could train more, or better, and thus achieve success. It was the pressures and compulsions generated by this figuration that impelled the spiral process of more intensive training regimes.

Certainly there were variances across the country. For some teams the structure of team training consisted primarily 'of local training' and 'challenge and test matches with other selections' (GAA, 1934b). For others, collective training camps were arranged. The question of costs associated with training and travel continued to be raised at annual congress and these debates also illustrated the pressures and demands on players. During one such debate in 1930 a delegate in seeking training grants stated that his county team 'had to play two semi-finals against Roscommon and Limerick, and had to bring men from their work three times a week for training' (GAA, 1930). As part of this competitive dynamic the phenomenon of 'wholetime collective training' also evolved. Caught in the double-bind structure of constraints, teams reciprocally modified and expanded training regimes. In 1946 one inter-county team completed seven 'collective' training camps over the Summer and Autumn (Conboy, 2002, p. 63). GAA teams and players were increasingly recognised as representing wider social units—parishes, villages and counties. In that way too, the pressures had increased for administrators who had the responsibility for organising the financial supports to sustain and enhance player preparation. One reflection of this was the increasing demands by the representatives of county committees for greater financial resources from the central (and higher tier) units of the GAA to support team preparations.

The process of professional bureaucratisation around specific functions also cemented. For instance, by the mid-1930s provincial secretaries were remunerated through either a fixed salary, an honorarium, commission or combination of salary and commission (GAA, 1936). Very occasionally the remuneration of administrators was opposed. However, this was on the grounds that alternative uses could be found for the money involved rather than any ideological opposition (GAA, 1930)—no narrative around amateurism or professionalism was invoked in such discussions. The GAA continued to expand; the number of affiliated clubs rising from 1671 in 1937 to 2048 by 1945 (GAA, 1947). This again increased the web of interdependences and the pressures on specific organisational and administrative functionaries.

The stress on seriousness of involvement and achievement orientation continued and manifested again in enhanced developments in training. Competitive interdependences at all levels of sporting competition intensified. In a spiralling process, players and other functionaries were increasingly compelled to dedicate more time, resources and commitment in pursuit of winning (see also Chap. 6). The central council of the GAA continued to award financial grants to support this. Collective training became lengthier and more widespread by the 1940s, and the practice of broken-time payments in conjunction with this continued (McAnallen, 2009). As we outline in the next chapter, amateurism and professionalism became increasingly amplified in discussions between administrators as tensions rose over the increasing seriousness of involvement and achievement orientation in relation to Gaelic games. Indeed, these concerns would lead to a ban on collective wholetime training being instigated in 1953 (GAA, 1954). Despite this, the stress on seriousness of involvement persisted. It found expression in both social and individual constraints on players who were required to dedicate increasing personal time to training and preparation.

Various tiers of administrative units came under pressure to allocate financial resources to cover the expenses associated with team preparation (Conboy, 2002). That the GAA's income came mainly from gate-taking meant this also reflected a growing dependency on gate-taking to subsidise team preparation. For example, in 1946 the two teams competing in a regional final were allocated one third of the gate to cover associated training costs (Conboy, 2002, p. 63). The annual congress of GAA—the rule making body—was regularly petitioned through motions to institutionalise financial aids for training. Such motions were a recurring feature from the early 1900s through to the 1940s (see for instance GAA, 1911, 1925, 1929, 1930, 1934a, 1946). The financial income to support this derived from gate-taking; aside from affiliation fees, income was essentially gate-taking. It was the revenue from this source which largely sustained the GAA's activities including: the compensation of administrators and players, whether salaries or expenses (and whatever the extent of this at the time); the rent, purchase and development of grounds; and grants to support training. For example, in 1947 the income of the GAA's central unit increased by £9,393; of this, £9,014 was due to increased gate receipts (GAA, 1947).

ADVANCES IN PROFESSIONALISATION: FROM THE 1960S ONWARDS

Despite efforts in 1953 to constrain the stress on seriousness of involvement and achievement orientation around Gaelic games by prohibiting collective training practices, such pressures soon manifested again (McAnallen, 2009, p. 175). Indeed, the dynamic of inter-county rivalry, which had partly led to the ban on wholetime collective training, was now ironically a driver in its re-emergence. Fearful of teams from counties of a smaller geographical size, or more urbanised counties, which could more easily bring players together regularly without needing to keep them overnight in a special training camp, some activists pushed to rescind the ban (see *Gaelic Sport*, 1958, pp. 29–33). Coupled with more advanced transport systems and the availability of cars, collective training returned in a renewed format and added seriousness. By the 1970s, the training commitments at the inter-county level advanced further. It was not only the frequency of training that changed; players became subject to increased external and internal pressures to regulate and discipline their behaviour so as to meet the increasing physical and psychological demands of training and match day performance.

The competitive tensions generated by the GAA inter-county competitions further escalated. This involved and propelled a further reciprocal spiral of innovations and emulations in relation to pre-match preparation, training and what can be described as the 'intellectualisation' of the games (Dunning & Sheard, 1979), as more time was given to thinking and planning around them. Training became more complex and comprehensive. Players and coaches became more sensitive to new innovations and developments in sports science (physiology and psychology), reflecting an advance in the intellectualisation of the games.

Since the 1970s players have sought and been awarded greater compensation for the time commitments involved—this of course involved power struggles which are discussed in the next chapter. Indeed, as we outline in the next chapter, it was tensions arising from the issue of player (and manager) compensation, both officially permitted and illegal forms, that led to the 'amateur ethos' to be increasingly affirmed and amplified from the 1970s. As the stress on seriousness of involvement continued to escalate through the 1980s and 1990s, and in parallel with their increased power chances, elite players were able to attain greater material rewards to compensate for the time commitments involved (GAA, 1997b). The increasing stress on seriousness of involvement can be seen from the fact that playing (and preparation for playing), at so many levels, now involved more of players', managers' and administrators' time, and in the case of players increased regulation of their time and bodies. At the elite level, the players involved have become in many ways what Dunning and Sheard (1979) call 'time professionals'. For example, by 2002, as a former GAA manager noted:

> [players had] to do some form of training either on the field or in the gym on six out of the seven days a week at certain times of the year...I spoke to one of the Galway players this morning at 8.15 am and he had already done his gym session before he headed off to work. (*Irish Times*, 30 December 2002, p. 28)

For some time, going back several decades, the sporting reputations of some players permitted them to be employed for commercial gain—commercial organisations saw a benefit in employing individuals given their 'sporting' reputation. It should be stressed though that this was a relatively small minority of GAA players. In more recent times inter-county players have received greater levels of direct and indirect compensation (see also Chap. 6). For example, a relatively small number of individual inter-country players have since 2000 agreed deals with commercial enterprises in which they were expected to earn €6,000 to €7,000 (split between cash and equipment) annually (*Sunday Business Post*, 1 June 2003).

A further feature of the increasing stress on serious involvement and achievement orientation is the emphasis placed on success at levels and tiers beyond the 'elite' inter-county competitions. The time and self-regulating commitments expected of inter-county players percolating down to other levels. Furthermore, the advance in seriousness of involvement and achievement orientation was not confined to players and coaches. An element of this dynamic was the felt compulsion on administrators to commit more and more financial resources to team preparation as the training requirements and related expenses provided to all grades of competition continued to increase through the 1970s and 1980s. By 2002 the average expenditure by county committees on their inter-county teams had reached €335,000 with some individual counties spending over €800,000 (*Irish Times*, 11 February 2003, p. 22). Linked with this too were advances in greater functional specialisation in team preparation and management. This too is both an example of increasing professionalisation as specialists in diet, nutrition and sports psychology tend to receive financial compensation for this work.

More broadly at an administrative level, the scale of interdependences in which GAA functionaries were enmeshed has grown considerably at both an intra- and inter-organisational level. Competitive interdependences intensified considerably since the 1960s, stemming from mediatisation and competition from rival sports, and advances in individualisation in Ireland (see also Chap. 7). This increased the pressures and anxieties experienced by GAA administrators at varying tiers. These pressures partly fuelled further bureaucratisation with the creation of a range of professional salaried positions—sports development, communications, accounting and managerial positions—to replace, or support, existing functions so as to compete with other sports. For instance, in 1958 the GAA's staff at its headquarters in Croke Park included the secretary general and four other staff members, two of whom were administrative secretaries; by 1969 the number of permanent staff employed had increased to eight (GAA, 1971) and to 24 by 1987 (*Irish Times*, 15 December 1987). This process also gradually percolated downward across other administrative units. Increased inter- and intra-organisational interdependences at regional (county committee) level increased workloads on county secretaries in particular, generating pressures to move towards more professionalised structures. By the early 1970s the GAA had appointed full-time professional administrators (country secretaries) to the counties of Dublin and Cork which comprised two of the largest urban conurbations in Ireland (GAA, 1971).

In the following decades, the expansion of intra- and inter-organisational interdependences continued to contribute to professionalisation pressures. One manifestation of this was the increasing work demands placed on voluntary administrators (GAA, 1978, 1985). Indeed by 1997 a 'full-time executive officer at every level' was suggested by the GAA President as a desirable situation (GAA, 1997a, p. 50). Within a few years the appointment of full-time secretaries became GAA national policy (GAA, 2002, p. 221), and more and more counties began to employ a professional full-time secretary. There is little doubt that many GAA administrators saw this as essential for competing with other sports and supporting the mostly voluntary structure of the organisation. Yet these developments, paradoxically as Dunning and Sheard (1979, p. 242) suggested in the case of rugby in England in the late 1970s, serve only to undermine amateurism even further since, to the extent that the paid administrators bring rationality and efficiency to the performance of their task, the game's expansion is facilitated and the trend towards bureaucracy and professionalism, of which their own existence is an expression, is reinforced.

It is imperative to point out at this point to allay any misunderstanding, the degree of bureaucratisation, however advanced in scale since the early 1900s, remains small relative to the scale of work undertaken on a voluntary basis across all levels of the GAA. Rather, what we have sought to illustrate is the relative change over the decades and the shift in balance between amateurism and professionalism.

Gate-taking continued to be the dominant source of income. But since the 1970s commercialisation and other monetisation processes also advanced as commercial advertising and sponsorship were permitted and gradually expanded in the following decades. The value and scale of media contracts also increased. For instance in 1962, the GAA received a 'nominal' fee of £10 from RTÉ for the broadcast rights (Corry, 2009, p. 111); by 1976 this had increased to £15,000 (*Irish Times*, 29 March 1976, p. 3). In the decades that followed the number of media organisations involved expanded as did the GAA's income. By 2015 media rights were worth €11.2 m to the GAA (*Irish Independent*, 16 October 2016). The injection of funding from commercial advertisers, sponsors and media broadcast organisations connected with this has increased the dependency of the GAA on these organisations. And while commercialisation and monetisation processes were incremental processes, each increment has moved the association further along the continuum between amateurism and professionalism in the direction of the latter. It is perhaps important to explain why such developments are indicative of this movement. As we explained earlier in this chapter in the case of gate-taking, commercialisation processes are a result of spectator interest connected to on-field player performance—the economic exchange is based on players performing. The GAA's financial dependency on commercial activities, in particular media rights are in many ways an extension of gate-taking spectator dependence. Furthermore, it is from this income that 'elite players' (see Chap. 6) and administrators are compensated in varying ways and degrees and through which units of the GAA throughout Ireland receive funding. We have mentioned gate-taking throughout this chapter and its significance. Indeed, notwithstanding the expansion in other sources of income, gate-taking has remained the principal source of revenue within the GAA—right up to the present—and despite the fact that attendances fluctuated over the decades (declining in the 1980s), the overall trajectory has been increasing attendances. While this reflects the dependence on spectators, several other developments also illustrate it. These include the scheduling and timing of fixtures which is largely determined to enhance the size of the broadcast audience rather than in the interests of players. This process, combined with the other developments described in this chapter, serve to illustrate the gradual erosion of amateur aspects of Gaelic games and their replacement with characteristics associated with professional sport. In the next section we will explain why this has occurred.

EXPLAINING THE EROSION OF AMATEUR STRUCTURES IN THE GAA

As we have sought to illustrate thus far in this chapter, the process of professionalisation has incrementally increased since the foundation of the association. In saying this, we are not claiming the association has become professional, but rather the balance has tilted further in the direction of professionalism. The GAA is still characterised by aspects of amateurism but also by more and more elements of professionalism at both playing and administrative levels. The causes of this are multiple and connected to social processes at different tiers of social integration, as we now outline.

As we explained in Chap. 2, over the course of the late nineteenth and twentieth centuries the social interdependences bonding people in Ireland lengthened and changed. The more extensive reciprocal pressures and controls constrained people to exercise greater degrees of emotional restraint in their everyday activities. As Elias explains, as societies become more functionally differentiated in conjunction with expanding chains of social interdependences, there occurs a greater social constraint to exert greater and more stable degrees of emotional control. One consequence of this more emotionally restrained social environment is a need for activities which allow for the socially permitted arousal of emotions and pleasurable excitement, such as sport and other forms of leisure (Elias & Dunning, 2008). This emotional excitement is partly generated by the structure of sporting contests which has an oppositional character—it involves a struggle or contest between rival individuals and groups. The oppositional character of sport is also one of the reasons that sport has emerged as one of the principal realms in which collective identification can be experienced for it serves to reinforce 'in-group identification'; in-group or we-group identity and feelings are enhanced and strengthened by the presence of a rival they-group (Dunning, 2008). The significance of these processes in accounting for the shift in the balance between amateurism and professionalism in the GAA is that they tend to militate against the playing of sport for short-term fun and enjoyment. Instead, those involved at a playing level at club and county levels of the GAA are compelled to dedicate more time and commitment, physically and psychologically, towards longer-term sporting goals and ambitions. Similarly, those involved at an organisational level are also constrained to facilitate and contribute to this through greater functional differentiation and specialisation (involving full-time professionals).

The compulsions and pressures generated by these processes are experienced and find expression in different ways for players, administrators and spectators. For players the playing of Gaelic games does itself generate pleasurable excitement for them personally. They are also a source of meaning and collective identification for them. And while this generates a compulsion to participate in more serious ways, it is the fact that they are representatives of wider social units which further propels greater seriousness of involvement and an achievement orientation. Administrators experience similar compulsions and pressures to those of players, and while they do not play their involvement at an organisational can be a further source of meaning. For spectators too, sport (Gaelic games) has become a central source for meaning, for collective identification and for the arousal of the emotions. In this regard, both players (and administrators) and spectators remain highly interdependent. However, the socio-spatial structure of the GAA is also significant in shaping the interdependences between players and spectators. As players must live or be born in the geographical unit they represent, the we-identification between players and spectators is closely aligned—there is little scope for players to play for a different unit. Furthermore, GAA units largely align with many existing social units—parishes, towns and counties. This adds to both the level of social identification between those comprising a GAA unit and their difference from those in other areas. Consequently, as players are both members and representatives of these sporting units, they are also aware of how others comprising their we-group are dependent upon them for social needs—social meaning, identification and excitement is generated and aroused by players through sporting encounters. Awareness of this by players and administrators alike generates a pressure for seriousness of involvement and an achievement-striving orientation. This as we have illustrated had a compelling and escalating element over the decades.

Other processes, as we now explain, also reinforced the shift in the balance between amateurism and professionalism towards the latter. Although no significant direct threat came—in terms of GAA players switching codes to earn a wage[3]—from professional sports[4] in Ireland, other professionalising pressures did emerge from the figuration of sporting organisations. From the 1960s, in particular, there was expansion in the mediatisation of sport as English and Scottish professional soccer, as well as national and international sports, were increasingly amplified across different mediums in Ireland. This, allied with changes in the social habitus of people in Ireland (see Chaps. 2 and 7), intensified the competitive pressures and anxieties experienced by GAA administrators. One manifestation of this was that they became more sensitive about how to retain and attract membership and audience (see also Chaps. 6 and 7). Consequently, they felt under increased pressure to counter these threats through greater functional specialisation, and many of these new functions needed to be filled on a full-time (professional) basis (Connolly & Dolan, 2012). For example, by 2019 County Dublin GAA employed 54 games promotion officers (*Irish Independent*, 25 June 2019, p. 52).

THE PERSISTENCE OF AMATEUR STRUCTURES

Although, as we illustrated, the tension balance between amateurism and professionalism has tilted more in the direction of the latter, significant elements of amateurism persist in the playing and organising of Gaelic games. As we argued, both concepts are processual and need to be considered relationally on a continuum. In that sense, while the GAA has become 'more' professional or in other words 'less amateur' there is still further it could go along that continuum (in the direction of professionalism). In addition, while we explained in the previous section the processes that tend to erode amateur structures other processes have served in an unplanned and unintended way to push against professionalising pressures.

The initial form of amateurism instituted and the lack of a strong ideological motivation for amateurism amongst those at administrative levels at the time, in no small part due to their social class, served to permit the accommodation of professional characteristics through the decades. This more practical and malleable form that developed permitted the integration of elements of professionalism without generating open conflict between its members. This in a way acted as a valve through which tensions and pressures brought to bear on particular groups, such as players, by pristine amateur structures could be released without generating internecine conflict or schisms of a scale that could have fractured the organisation. Intertwined with this dynamic was the relatively decentralised (and multipolar power) structure of the GAA (see Chap. 4) which facilitated the distribution of financial resources to various social units and for different purposes—not just to sustain 'elite' player training and preparations. This was also connected with the fact that although 'elite' players as a social group have become more functionally important (see Chap. 6), their power chances are constrained by the structure of the figuration which also includes several other social groups with different interests and demands. Furthermore, though we stated that rugby and soccer in Ireland are professional sports, the threat they pose as professional sports has remained limited. Soccer has a club structure unable to consistently support a comprehensive and secure professional financial structure. Similarly, the professional structure of rugby remains limited to a relatively small number of players connected to four provinces (or clubs). There is limited attraction to switch codes for financial reasons for the vast majority of GAA players. A further constraint emanating from the structure of the GAA figuration, which we explain below, is the multiple we-identifications of 'elite' players, which means the county (elite) we-identification exists in tandem with other we-identifications where the culture and benefits of amateurism and volunteerism is stronger because it is more functionally important. For instance, 'elite' players (inter-country players) continue to play and identify with their clubs, which are organised through, and highly dependent upon, volunteerism.

This constellation of processes and the related structure of interdependence has had a relatively persistent aspect over the generations. And it is this structure and power balance which has sustained a culture in which 'amateurism' is perceived as beneficial. This value and attachment to the culture of amateurism/volunteerism has found expression through the decades in varying ways. For instance, at a discussion on the professionalisation of the function of county secretary in 1974, one group of voluntary county secretaries stated:

> On the question of having a full-time paid secretary we felt that in the ideal situation it would be an excellent idea for all counties to have full-time paid secretaries…We were afraid too I think that the voluntary nature of the Association might suffer. (GAA, 1974)

Similarly, in 1977 the then GAA president speaking at the annual congress in 1977 noted:

> I must refer to administration at county level... and the ever increasing work load is of constant concern ... [We must] relieve the pressures and ensure a tolerable situation both for the sake of the Association and the individuals concerned bearing in mind the need to retain the voluntary commitment which is one of the greatest assets of the association. (GAA, 1977)

Concerns and similar views were also expressed at the 1983 annual congress and in a GAA manual for administrators (GAA, 1985). This ambivalence towards professionalism is not confined to administrators. Over the decades many elite players have been opposed to outright professionalism (See *Sunday Independent*, 10 December 1989). Commenting (in 2018) on a proposal to pay a direct allowance to elite players, one elite player suggested:

> I don't think at all it should happen
>   The reason everyone loves hurling is it's amateurs playing an amateur sport ... It would take away from the love of the game. If you're getting paid, you could go training and wander around because 'it doesn't matter, I'm getting paid anyway'. I don't think it should come in. Every team gets their expenses. (cited in https://www.the42.ie/austin-gleeson-allowance-inter-county-3937325-Apr2018/)

We argue that this attachment to a culture of 'moderated' amateurism within the habitus of many contemporary players and officials, in parallel with other processes, has acted as a counter tension pulling against professionalising pressures.

CONCLUSION

The unintended and unplanned erosion (though gradual) of amateur structures and values and their replacement by professional ones has evolved over several generations. It has not been caused by any single individual or group comprising the GAA, and it is a process no single individual or group planned or intended. More importantly, this movement in the direction of professionalism is a relative movement; Gaelic games and the organisation governing them, the GAA, continue to exhibit significant elements of amateurism and volunteerism. What has occurred is a movement in the balance between amateurism and professionalism in the direction of the latter. One of the processes we alluded to in this chapter has been the increasing stress on the seriousness of involvement and in the next chapter we also illustrate aspects of this. In particular, we explain how it was connected with a shift in the balance of power between players and administrators. This change also facilitated professionalisation processes, although the erosion of amateur principles does not simply refer to the remuneration of players. Indeed, in the next chapter we relate how the concept of amateurism came to be increasingly amplified in tandem with the rise in the power chances of 'elite' players from the 1970s onward.

Notes

1. Some of the rising commercial middle classes were aligned with them and collectively they were coming to form a reconstituted social elite along.
2. Cusack's reports of matches often refer to men playing in Freize coats. Such clothing was associated with lower-class peasantry.
3. A very small number of players over the decades (often high profile) did leave to play professionally for soccer clubs in Ireland, England and Scotland, and more recently to Australian Rules clubs.
4. Soccer officially went professional in 1894, but in the decades that followed the number of fully professional clubs remained limited. Many struggled with financial difficulties, while others went semi-professional. The vast bulk of clubs were largely amateur. rugby only went professional in 1995.

References

Conboy, T. (2002). The forties. In T. Moran (Ed.), *Stair CLG Chonnacht 1902–2002* (pp. 53–72). Carrick-on-Shannon, Co. Leitrim: Carrick Print.

Connolly, J., & Dolan, P. (2012). Sport, media and the Gaelic Athletic Association: The quest for the 'youth' of Ireland. *Media, Culture & Society, 34*(4), 407–423.

Corry, E. (2009). The mass media and the popularisation of Gaelic games, 1884–1934. In D. McAnallen, D. Hassan, & R. Hegarty (Eds.), *The evolution of the GAA: Ulaidh, Éire agus eile* (pp. 100–111). Belfast: Stair Uladh.

Curran, C. (2015). *The development of sport in Donegal, 1880–1935.* Cork: Cork University Press.

Dolan, P. (2005). *The development of consumer culture, subjectivity and national identity in Ireland, 1900–1980.* PhD thesis, Goldsmiths College, University of London, London.

Dunning, E. (2008). The dynamics of modern sport: Notes on achievement-striving and the social significance of sport. In N. Elias & E. Dunning (Eds.), *Quest for excitement: Sport and Leisure in the civilising process* (Rev. ed., pp. 203–221). Dublin: University College Dublin Press.

Dunning, E., & Sheard, K. (1979). *Barbarians, gentlemen & players: A sociological study of the development of rugby football.* Canberra: Australian National University Press.

Elias, N., & Dunning, E. (2008). *Quest for excitement: Sport and leisure in the civilising process* (Rev. ed.). Dublin: University College Dublin Press.

GAA. (1911). *Minutes of annual congress.* Dublin: GAA.

GAA. (1914). *Gaelic Athletic Association. Official guide. 1914–1915.* Wexford: GAA.

GAA. (1920, March 17). *Minutes of annual convention of Ulster council.* GAA.

GAA. (1925). *Motions for annual congress.* Dublin: GAA.

GAA. (1929). *Minutes of special annual congress.* Dublin: GAA.

GAA. (1930). *Minutes of annual congress.* Dublin: GAA.

GAA. (1934a). *Minutes of annual congress.* Dublin: GAA.

GAA. (1934b, July 6). *Minutes of Armagh county committee.* GAA.

GAA. (1936). *Minutes of annual congress.* Dublin: GAA.

GAA. (1946). *Minutes of annual congress.* Dublin: GAA.

GAA. (1947). *An comhdháil bhliantúil.* Dublin: GAA.

GAA. (1954). *An comhdháil bliantúil.* Dublin: GAA.

GAA. (1971). *Report of the commission on the GAA.* Dublin: Gaelic Athletic Association.

GAA. (1974). *Report of the development conference for officers of county committees and provincial councils.* Dublin: Irish Management Institute.

GAA. (1977). *Minutes of annual congress.* Dublin: GAA.

GAA. (1978). *Minutes of annual congress.* Dublin: GAA.

GAA. (1985). *Manual for county committees and provincial councils.* Dublin: GAA.

GAA. (1997a). *Minutes of annual congress.* Dublin: GAA.

GAA. (1997b). *Report of the committee established to review the GAA's amateur status.* Dublin: GAA.

GAA. (2002). *G.A.A. strategic review—Enhancing community identity.* Dublin: Gaelic Athletic Association.

Garnham, N. (2004a). Accounting for the early success of the Gaelic Athletic Association. *Irish Historical Studies, 34*(133), 65–78.

Garnham, N. (2004b). *Association football and society in pre-partition Ireland.* Belfast: Ulster Historical Foundation.

Higgins, J. J. (1914–1917). John J. Higgins collection, Leix and Ossory GAA, 1914–1917. *GAA archive.* Croke Park, Dublin: GAA

Hunt, T. (2008). *Sport and society in Victorian Ireland: The case of Westmeath.* Cork: Cork University Press.

Hunt, T. (2009). The GAA: Social structure and associated clubs. In M. Cronin, W. Murphy, & P. Rouse (Eds.), *The Gaelic Athletic Association 1884–2009* (pp. 183–202). Dublin: Irish Academic Press.

Mandle, W. F. (1987). *The Gaelic Athletic Association and Irish nationalist politics, 1884–1924.* Dublin: Gill & Macmillan.

McAnallen, D. (2009). The greatest amateur association in the world? The GAA and amateurism. In M. Cronin, W. Murphy, & P. Rouse (Eds.), *The Gaelic Athletic Association 1884–2009* (pp. 157–182). Dublin: Irish Academic Press.

McElligott, R. (2013). *Forging a kingdom: The GAA in Kerry 1884–1934.* Wilton, Cork: Collins Press.

Mullan, M. (1995). Opposition, social closure, and sport: The Gaelic Athletic Association in the 19th century. *Sociology of Sport Journal, 12*(3), 268–289.

Ó Riain, S. (1994). *Maurice Davin (1842–1927): First president of the G.A.A.* Dublin: Geography Publications.

O'Callaghan, L. (2011). *Rugby in Munster: A social and cultural history.* Cork: Cork University Press.

Rouse, P. (2015). *Sport & Ireland.* Oxford: Oxford University Press.

CHAPTER 6

The Amplifying of Professionalism and Amateurism, and the Emergence of 'Player Power'

COMPETITIVE TENSIONS AND AMPLIFICATION PROCESSES

Following the establishment of the GAA, the main axis of tension was between those representing the GAA and those aligned with the sports bodies claiming to govern athletics and also cycling in Ireland. However, the efforts to promote the sports of Gaelic football and hurling by appealing to existing clubs of other football codes (rugby and association football or soccer) brought them into conflict with those constituting representative associations for those codes—the Irish Football Association (IFA) and the Irish Rugby Football Union (IRFU)—and their activists. In the mid to late 1880s, both these codes were organised along amateur lines too. As noted in the previous chapter, the competition between GAA activists and their rivals varied by region; in some parts rugby was the stronger, while soccer was dominant or the main rival in other parts. As we note later in this chapter, the relatively localised playing structure of all codes, the tendency to play multiple codes throughout the year, and the ease with which clubs could, and did, switch allegiance, whether due to emotional identification, internecine disputes or sporting preference, added to the tensions between the competing associations. Gaelic football, in particular, involved aspects of play which mirrored and/or were compatible with the competing codes and this further complicated matters (see also Chap. 2). Competition for the allegiance of young men and their respective clubs by the rival associations persisted over the course of the 1890s. In some cases, the lack of competition, owing to the absence

© The Author(s) 2020   117
J. Connolly, P. Dolan, *Gaelic Games in Society*, Palgrave Studies
on Norbert Elias, https://doi.org/10.1007/978-3-030-31699-0_6

or decline of a rival code, precipitated the strengthening of a code. For instance, the waning of the GAA in County Kerry in the 1890s ran in tandem with the growth of rugby in that county (McElligott, 2013, pp. 104–105).

Both rugby and soccer would remain an object of ridicule for GAA activists in the coming years (see also Chap. 7). Meanwhile, the IFA, under competitive pressures from professional Scottish and English soccer clubs, had decided, but not without internal strife, to legalise professionalism in 1894 (Garnham, 2004). Notwithstanding, few soccer clubs in Ireland had the financial resources to maintain a fully professional team (Garnham, 2004, p. 87). Despite the relative growth of the GAA, and perhaps too because of its decline in the 1890s, soccer remained popular in many parts of Ireland (Curran, 2015; Toms, 2015). The loyalty of clubs to one particular code or sport was often relatively weak. For instance, teams would disband and reform under a different code for a variety of reasons: where they were unable to compete owing to a lack of opposition in a similar code; to contravene a disciplinary penalty imposed by a governing body; and to partake in different and/or rival codes on a seasonal or even shorter basis (Hunt, 2009, p. 156; O'Donoghue, 1987, p. 78). The nature of these transient practices added to the existing tensions generated by the inter-organisational rivalry and fuelled attempts to develop more enduring affiliations.

This felt pressure on GAA activists was embodied in the increasing vitriolic denunciation of soccer and professionalism and the desire for a ban on the playing of rival sports by GAA activists in 1901 (see Chap. 7). By the early 1900s the IFA closely rivalled the GAA for affiliations in parts of the country, and soccer was clearly the most popular sport in some regions, both urban and rural (Curran, 2015; Toms, 2015). The continued strength of soccer—the numbers of clubs and related attendances in the early 1900s—led to the increased stigmatisation of professionalism, and by default soccer, often the real target, by GAA organisers and administrators. While professionalism was stigmatised in an effort to strengthen the GAA, and simultaneously weaken soccer, and indeed other sports, there was no concerted effort by GAA activists to strongly espouse the ethos of amateurism in this competitive struggle. Indeed, the discourse of amateurism was generally de-amplified. For instance, in an article in a GAA periodical in 1908 on the progress of the GAA in the province of Ulster the author claimed:

Belfast, like the large cities of England and Scotland, has in athletics become simply spectatorial; it pays to see a football or cricket match as it would pay to see a music hall performance, to watch a number of trained and paid performers take part in a game in which they themselves are too emasculated to participate. Add to this the spirit of professionalism which it breeds, the secret ambition which it sows in every boy's breast to become—not a clean athlete—but a paid performer and to receive the plaudits of the mob who have paid—not to indulge in a healthful game but to watch others do so. (GAA, 1908–1909, p. 19)

Certainly rugby remained amateur, and in some parts of the country it competed strongly against the GAA for people's affiliation, particularly amongst sections of the higher middle classes. It is reasonable to suppose that this may have been the reason for the general de-amplification of amateurism by GAA activists. However, we believe there were other reasons too for the general de-amplification of amateurism by GAA activists at this time. First, although professionalism in Irish soccer had been permitted for some time, the actual number of professional soccer clubs and players in Ireland were relatively limited, and primarily concentrated in the urban centres of the north east of Ireland (Garnham, 2004, p. 99). In addition, given the relatively weak level of centralisation of the IFA, some regional units of the soccer organisation continued to operate under amateur rules; in the north west, professionalism was only given official sanction by the ruling authorities there in 1902 (Garnham, 2004, p. 73). Many within the IFA umbrella remained hostile to professionalism and continued to espouse the benefits of amateurism, mirroring developments in Britain which sprung from wider social class tensions.

So, for most GAA units there was no significant competitive threat from professional soccer. Soccer, at the local level, where it vied competitively for the allegiance of players and spectators with GAA clubs, was essentially an amateur sport. The vilification of professionalism was merely a form of blame gossip (Elias & Scotson, 2008)—in reality the threat from professional soccer was negligible; amateur soccer was the real threat. The perceived threat from soccer was no mere illusion; by 1914 it was 'a major gate-money sport, with an administrative structure that spanned the entire country and thousands of regular players' (Garnham, 2004, p. 133).

The blame gossip of professionalism employed by GAA activists then was part of a wider narrative through which GAA activists sought to enhance the legitimacy of the GAA and thereby extend and broaden its membership. In contradistinction with other sports, Gaelic games were labelled 'truly Irish', conflated with both cultural and militant nationalism (see also Chap. 7). This vilifying of other sports was a reflection of the frustrations and insecurities many GAA activists felt owing to the continued popularity of these competing sports. The fact that many Irish people across the social classes continued to partake in other non-GAA sports merely reinforced these feelings.

Alongside this disparagement of other sports was the espousal of a GAA praise gossip (Elias & Scotson, 2008). Within this praise gossip the GAA was often aligned with the struggle for independence and Irish nationalism. Incorporated within this narrative was a conception of Gaelic games as the very embodiment of an authentic Gaelic culture. We emphasise the structure and content of both these narratives of blame gossip and praise gossip to illustrate a more fundamental point—the relative absence of any direct and explicit espousal of amateurism as the organising principle of Gaelic games. As we illustrated, in several GAA publications in which 'professionalism' and 'soccer' are targeted (GAA, 1908–1909, 1910–1911), the conflation of Gaelic games with amateurism is rarely deployed. Consequently, we contend the main reason for the de-amplification of amateurism within a GAA praise gossip, up to the 1920s, was because the competitive threat from rival professional sports never really surfaced. The threat was from amateur sports—rugby and soccer.

Although the membership of the GAA grew in the 1920s, soccer and rugby continued to be popular in different regions of Ireland post-partition and the formation of the Free State (Curran, 2015; Ó Maonaigh, 2017; Toms, 2015; Tynan, 2013). As increasing numbers of soccer fixtures were now played on a Sunday in the Free State it further intensified competition between those representing the different codes—in some cases physical altercations broke out over the use of public playing pitches (Tynan, 2013, p. 190).

As before, soccer was the primary target of various broadsides by GAA activists as it presented a significant threat in some parts. This invective generally fused soccer with Anglicisation in particular, but soccer was also excoriated for being a professional sport. At a meeting of GAA administrators in County Wexford in 1924, one official warned 'that the G.A.A. was, in a sense, on a firm footing, but they could lose their ground very easily. The "Soccer crowd" had, in his opinion, lowered sport by professionalism' (cited in *Irish Times*, 21 March 1924, p. 3).

The achievement of partial independence may have added to the insecurities and frustrations here too; the presence of the British could no longer be assumed as the cause of Irishmen playing 'non' Gaelic sports—it was now a choice taken by some[1] 'free' Irish people. By the latter half of the 1920s the stigmatisation and amplification of professionalism continued but it was now accompanied by increasing amplification of the amateur ethos by GAA administrators and activists. This was connected with the increasing seriousness of involvement and the achievement orientation within Gaelic games which we referred to in the previous chapter.

SERIOUSNESS OF INVOLVEMENT AND THE AMPLIFICATION OF PROFESSIONALISM AND AMATEURISM

As we noted in Chap. 4, the expansion of inter-club GAA competitions had initially been slow and sporadic in many counties while team and/or individual preparation was limited in those early decades following the establishment of GAA competitions. Gradually teams and their mentors did begin to see the benefits of greater on-field coordination. Pre-match preparation started to become a feature of GAA clubs (O'Donoghue, 1987, p. 172). Nonetheless the available evidence would suggest training was generally sporadic with skill and fitness levels less advanced than in later years. Such a conclusion can be deduced from the many match reports of the time (see also Chap. 2). For example, writing about the All-Ireland Hurling final of 1903, one journalist reported:

> [S]ome of the Cork team seem absolutely bewildered, and not infrequently failed to hit the ball when quite alone, and, towards the end of the second period they tired palpably, whether from the heavy going or disgust, we cannot tell. (*Sport*, 8 August 1903)

The trajectory was, however, towards more structured and scientifically informed training. Trainers were increasingly engaged and deployed by teams at the highest level of competition, including those who had obtained a reputation as trainers of soccer teams (Garnham, 2004, p. 30). These were relatively short-term appointments, often only engaged by teams in the latter stages of competition (Looney, 2008). The games themselves became less structured around strength and physicality. One feature of this was greater specialisation of players in relation to their on-field position and tactics. This advance in specialisation was facilitated by modifications in the rules—a reduction in the number of permitted on-field players and the greater demarcation of competitions based on age and ability (see also Chap. 2). Indicative of this overall trend was a book published in 1914 by the Kerry footballer Dick Fitzgerald—*How to play Gaelic football*. In it he discusses the various on-field positions of players and the type of preparation for skill enhancement associated with each role—'half-backs', 'midfielder', 'wing men'. Fitzgerald, a successful footballer and trainer, maintained that pre-match preparations could, and should, be distinguished from 'professionalism'. While Fitzgerald prescribed and encouraged more structured and skilful play he simultaneously warned of the dangers of specialised training, the emulation of methods associated with other sports, and professionalism. At the same time the intensification of competitive dependences between GAA teams, and the related advance in the stress on seriousness of involvement, manifested itself on several fronts in both on- and off-field activities. The practice of team training and preparation assumed greater importance with players required to dedicate increasing amounts of time to training and its associated logistics. As working men, they were also required to navigate the complexity of this in relation to their employment. As we noted in Chap. 5, the economic constraint this often imposed led GAA administrators to address this through what were called 'broken time' payments. This involved (as we outlined in the previous chapter) paying men to replace those who had to leave their workplace to train for Gaelic teams.

The increasing stress on seriousness of involvement and achievement orientation by teams and related functionaries was interconnected with a process in which the importance of sport as a medium through which social meaning, emotional arousal and satisfaction through specific we-feelings and identification was increasingly generated and maintained (Dunning, 2008). As we explained in the previous chapter, the functions of both players and administrators comprising GAA units became more tightly bound to the maintenance and enhancement of the emotional satisfaction and social meaning of the wider groups they represented. It was this overall structure of compulsions and constraints which generated advances and innovations in the organisation and frequency of training.

The competitive tensions channelled into greater preparation by GAA teams was mirrored by often bitter off-field relations between the representatives of GAA units, as we illustrated in Chap. 4. These disputes and related tensions would soon interweave with developments in pre-match preparations. In 1927 the issue of broken-time payments by the Kilkenny

County committee was raised at the Annual Congress of the Leinster Council by a representative of the Dublin County committee. The minutes of the meeting recorded the following:

> Mr. Walsh (Kilkenny) said there was no question of paying men who had taken part in the game, but they did pay men, whom they had got to replace the men whom they had taken from their work to train. The chairman said he was convinced that Mr. Walsh's explanation would quash talk of professionalism, that was going around. He reminded Mr. Tarrant [Laois delegate] that in 1913 Leix [County Laois] players were taken from their work and paid, when training for the All Ireland final. He was opposed to grants some years ago but the time had come when players should be trained as the public expected it of them. (GAA, 1927)

The pressure for financial supports to offset the costs of training county teams continued to increase in the 1920s, as did the practice of seeking public subscriptions for 'Training Funds' (Devine, 2002). Equally, representatives of county committees continued to request greater financial supports to be allocated by the central governing units of the GAA so as to cover costs associated with training and playing matches (GAA, 1929). This is evident from the motions at the GAA's annual congresses (see previous chapter). It was in this context that a discourse of professionalism now came to be increasingly amplified. Certainly, the perceived threat from soccer was still experienced and efforts to stigmatise soccer on the grounds of professionalism still persisted. However, indicative of the increasing anxiety over the stress on seriousness of involvement and the achievement orientation in Gaelic games was the widening of the vituperative discourse on professionalism in soccer to incorporate this dimension. As part of this, the amateur ethos, either explicitly or implicitly, was given greater expression. For instance in his 1934 book *Our Native Games*, PJ Devlin, a former GAA administrator and by then journalist, declared:

> This Gaelic Athletic Association has no room for gladiatorial shows or subsidised competitors. Either would be well calculated to defeat its main objective—the physical welfare of the race by high-spirited rivalry on a fair field. If victory and trophies become the predominant pursuit, the chivalry that it is part of its purpose to foster, and the popular benefits it exists to provide, must disappear. If we want to develop our games upon the lines of the great commercial winter pastime across the channel, then let us import the methods and the men who have brought that business to such a pitch of

efficiency. Let us be thorough even in our treason to native ideals, or else eliminate agencies and practices that discredit our own games by ineptness and disloyalty. A Gaelic team that would put a price upon participation in a championship final is unfitted for the privilege of such a competition. Yet this has been attempted. (p. 68)

The provision of financial resources associated with training camps or other forms of preparation was largely the function of county committees and specific functionaries within this unit. The primary means through which county committees sought to offset this was through the income generated through gate-taking within the county, seeking voluntary contributions to organised training funds from the general public, and from grants awarded by higher-tier central units of the GAA. Such was the escalating burden of costs that county committees continued to petition the central units of the GAA to allocate further resources. For instance, one delegate at the GAA annual congress of 1946 declared: 'Counties are being very badly treated. It costs a lot of money to put a County into the All-Ireland finals. You must put out a trained team. It cost us nearly £420 last September. The grants should be increased' (GAA, 1946).

The increasing seriousness of involvement and achievement orientation associated with the men's senior inter-county competitions also percolated downwards—those involved in others tiers of competition now became subject to pressure for the need for greater preparation. The diffusion of more intensive training practices to more grades, to younger age-graded competitions in particular, generated anxieties for those in functions vested with overall coordination and development of the GAA, perhaps fearful of the financial resources now being directed at these activities or that it may foster an orientation towards professional sport (GAA, 1942, 1950). So by the 1940s a discourse conflating the scale and structure of training with professionalism becomes more noticeable. Training, it was claimed by one administrator, 'was destroying the amateur status' (GAA, 1947).

The stress on winning and the training connected with this was viewed by some GAA administrators and journalists as creating an obsession with winning at all costs. This, they argued, was detrimental to the GAA and its ethos—amateurism (*Irish Times*, 14 October 1943, p. 2). Other journalists, perhaps less sympathetic to the GAA, had some years earlier claimed that '"broken time" payments was essentially professionalism' (*Irish Times*, 19 January 1939, p. 3). The conflation of professionalism with training began to tighten and the concepts of amateurism and professionalism became increasingly amplified in debates and discussions and at different tiers of the association:

> If men are taken away out of their jobs and paid for one or two or three weeks, and fed and groomed in hotels, it was professionalism. (Delegate at the County Offaly Annual convention, 1939 cited in *Irish Press*, 10 January 1939, p. 13)
> This is tending towards professionalism ... I do not agree that this special training is improving the game. (A delegate at GAA Annual Congress, 1946)

The concerns over training were underpinned by different social inter-dependences including GAA intra-organisational tensions. One reflection of this was the divisions that surfaced over the status and meaning of 'wholetime collective training'. This sensitivity towards the type and scale of pre-match preparation reflected a fear by some GAA administrators that this system of training was, or could in the future be, a disadvantage to the sporting chances of the GAA unit they represented in the GAA's national sporting competitions and from which much emotional satisfaction and social meaning was derived. Consequently, some began to question the practice and intensification of training regimes more generally. In so doing they appropriated and amplified the discourse of amateurism and profes-sionalism to embellish and legitimise their critique. Others took a conflict-ing standpoint, based though on the very same fears:

> It is the duty of Co. Boards to field out their county teams for the inter-county championships. It is their obligation to patrons to equip their sides so that their play will be efficient as possible. To do this, players far removed from each other must come together to evolve the standard of play that is expected in these important tests. (GAA, 1953a)

Tensions around training climaxed to such an extent that a review com-mittee was established in 1953 to consider:

1. Is such training consistent with the amateur status of the members of this Association?
2. Is it otherwise objectionable?
3. Should it be allowed to continue or should it be prohibited or lim-ited? (GAA, 1953b)

The outcome of the review which was later passed by annual congress was to instigate a ban on collective wholetime training. So, by the 1940s and 1950s the meaning and function of the concepts of amateurism and professionalism had shifted. The connection between amateurism and the type, structure and extent of training tightened, and the ethos of amateurism as a defining feature of Gaelic games had been greatly amplified. It is important to reiterate, as we explained in the previous chapter, that it was with the growing seriousness of involvement and achievement orientation within Gaelic games rather than from 'outside' threats from professional sports that a discourse of amateurism and professionalism was now articulated, and so strongly and so tightly connected with team preparation.

The Figuration of Players and Administrators and the Amplification of Professionalism

The advance in the functional importance of training—the growing seriousness of involvement and achievement orientation which it reflected more generally—certainly generated new pressures on players, particularly those representing their county. Simultaneously though, and in an unplanned way, it increased the functional importance of the inter-county player and led to a shift in the power balance between players and administrators. This shift in the power balance would find its clearest expression from the late 1960s onwards.

As we noted previously, the GAA's inter-county competition had evolved from one where a county was represented by one club to one in which a county team now comprised representatives of several clubs. This development too was a result of the increasing achievement orientation and the spiral of competiveness connected with it as the club team representing a county began supplementing their team with better players from other clubs within the county. As representative county teams emerged, county committees (administrators), which were comprised by representatives of clubs within a county, obtained the function of selecting such teams. This process often generated considerable enmity between representatives of clubs within a county. The we-identity of the club for many administrators remained stronger than county identity and there was often a strong element of local determination in team selection. For instance, the Armagh county team of the 1930s was selected by a committee comprising representatives from seven different clubs in the county (GAA, 1935). And as we outlined in Chap. 4, county committees also retained the functions of: administering and governing Gaelic games within a county's boundaries; appointing delegates to the GAA's national congress at which the GAA's rules for playing and governance could be changed; and appointing a delegate to the central council of the GAA, the unit charged with governing the organisation between annual congresses. It was these functions that gave the county committee and those comprising it the source of their power. Indeed, as illustrated in Chap. 4, struggles over the functions retained by county committees were a persistent feature of annual congresses.

Of course administrators were dependent on players; without players no games existed. Aside from needing players for the completion of sporting events—to sustain the very existence of Gaelic games—it was these events which had also come to generate the main source of income for GAA units—gate-taking (see previous chapter). Furthermore, it was players in playing which generated the excitement and choreography surrounding sporting events, both before and after. This was an essential ingredient in the increasing promotion of Gaelic games in the media. In that sense, while the overall balance of power favoured administrators in those early decades (both before and after the turn of the twentieth century) administrators were still dependent on players. What had occurred gradually over the following decades was a shift in this power balance between administrators and what were known as county players in the direction of the latter. There also occurred a related shift in the balance between county and non-county players, again in favour of county players. This was linked to a large degree to the rise in status of the men's senior inter-county competitions and the wider processes we referred to in the previous chapter concerning social meaning and identification. Indeed, awareness of the status of senior inter-county players was increasingly recognised by administrators. For instance, in 1931 the General Secretary of the GAA stated during a debate on the allocation of expenses to different categories of players: 'Senior teams deserved the preferential treatment they received as it was they that made the money' (GAA, 1930).

Despite this shift in the power balance between administrators and inter-county players, the balance still lay in favour of administrators. Indicative of this, and a source of their power, was the fact they continued to exercise considerable control over the selection of county teams and in the resources made available to players. This on occasion led to tensions between players and administrators. The gradual erosion in the power symmetry between players and administrators would become more apparent in the 1960s. It was underpinned by several interwoven social processes at different tiers of social integration. From the 1940s through to the 1960s inter-county competitive dependences, combined with an increasing achievement orientation and heightened levels of seriousness of involvement, propelled greater functional specialisation in team preparation. Coaches and trainers began to be deployed on a longer term basis than they had in the past (McKeever, 2009, p. 33). The rise in the functional importance of coaching was driven not only by competitive sport interdependences and functional specialisation but also by wider inter-organisational competition between the GAA and other sports organisations (see Chap. 7).

The rise in the perceived importance of coaching and those deemed to be specialist in that domain had the unplanned and unintended effect of weakening the power resources of administrators. The function of selecting and managing county teams had remained the preserve of the county committee right through to the 1960s in most counties. As the former GAA administrator in County Down, Maurice Hayes, recalled:

> Like most other counties, the county board took seriously its responsibility for county teams by insisting on selecting the teams themselves. The whole board (all twenty-five or thirty of them) picked the teams, voting on each position in turn, fighting for 'their' man, one by one, with no great idea what the finished article would look like. (Hayes, 2009, p. 25)

This rise in the status of coaching was reflected in the focus directed at that activity within GAA administrative manuals and in the formation of educational development courses on coaching. By the late 1970s the year-long appointment of coaches had become a standard characteristic of inter-county training structures, and they were increasingly perceived as essential to 'success' (Conboy, 2002, p. 124). Coaches now gradually took over the function of preparation and their perceived expertise and importance increased their power chances. Many administrators, benignly in some cases and more reluctantly in others, were forced to accede to the demands of coaches. For instance, one former inter-county player recalling his experience of training in 1970 stated:

> I remember him [new coach] going into the Gaelic Grounds one night and demanding two sliotars for every hurler [player]. Now there are buckets of sliotars. Prior to that, the trainer might have a couple of sliotars in his pocket.

He wanted all sorts of equipment. I remember looking at the faces of the county board officials [administrators] and it was like a death sentence to them. (Martin, 2009)

Tensions also emerged over the function of team selection as managers and players with the support of some administrators sought the transfer of this function away from county committees (Martin, 2009). Contests for control of this function occurred at different intensities within individual counties, but gradually coaches obtained this function, albeit the process differed temporally and in structure from county to county. Indeed, as the function of coaching grew in importance, county committees began to compete for the services of 'successful' coaches—this process also filtered down to clubs. Combined with the advance in the stress on achievement orientation and seriousness of involvement, and in a spiralling process of competition and emulation, some clubs began to offer enhanced expenses and reportedly 'under the counter payments' (*Irish Times,* 4 August 1988, p. 3). By the 1990s the power balance between county committees and coaches had shifted in the direction of coaches to such an extent that some coaches were capable of influencing the timing of club championships within a county and in demanding more resources for training and pre-match preparation (O'Connor, 2010). One unintended outcome of the increased functional importance attached to coaches/managers and their related conflation with sporting success was a renewed focus around 'payments' to managers. By the 1990s questions and concerns at club and inter-county level about the paying of managers had become more amplified in parallel with concerns about contraventions of the amateur ethos of the GAA.

These developments occurred at the same time as the professional bureaucracy of the GAA was expanding (see previous chapter). The units governing the GAA experienced pressure for more differentiated and specialised professional administrative and organisational functions as one of the responses to real and felt competitive threats (see also Chap. 7). A feature of this was the emergence of a discourse of professionalism pertaining to organisational and communication tasks in which professionalism was construed as essential and imbued with positive connotations. For instance, in a GAA report in 1971 a section on reorganisation and strategy deemed the professionalisation of some administrative functions essential:

No worthwhile organisation can hope to succeed without a framework of full-time staff to put plans into action. In an organisation of the size of the GAA it is imperative that there be a full-time staff of professional people—professional in the sense of first-class ability for a particular job; specific qualifications to undertake particular work; concern with the pursuit of excellence. A major defect in the past has been the Association's failure to exploit opportunities. For the future there must be more full-time effort to ensure that this defect is eliminated; to ensure that plans and projects of the Association's voluntary leaders, many of whom are aware of required improvements, are brought to fruition. (GAA, 1971)

This compulsion to develop models of organising based on commercial business organisations also reflected increasing commercialisation and industrialisation in Ireland as a whole, the functional importance of these processes, and the wider global expansion of companies, capital exchanges and international trade. GAA administrators at the highest tiers sought to elevate 'planning', 'development' and 'promotion' functions as essential, while a discourse of professionalism was amplified and repeatedly connected with social expectations around administrative and organisational activities. For instance, notes distributed at a seminar for club secretaries (one of the lower administrative tiers of the GAA) in 1980 stated:

We live in a highly critical age and the general public have come to demand professional standards in most things. It is important therefore that we in the G.A.A. have that professional look about us. Slipshod and hit or miss methods are not good enough. (*GAA seminar for club secretaries*, 28 April 1980)

In parallel with this amplification of professionalism in administration, the discourse concerning professionalism in on-field activities also underwent a change. The concept of a 'professional' approach to pre-match preparations took on more positive connotations and came to be associated with the preparations of 'successful teams' (see *Gaelic World*, May 1980). Certainly, the processes that underpinned the shift in the balance between amateurism and professionalism contributed to this. But it was also connected with the changing power balance between inter-county players and administrators and other groups constituting the GAA. Indeed, it was also this constellation of processes that led to the increasing amplification of amateurism from the mid-1980s by various individuals and groups comprising the GAA.

The Amplification of Amateurism and 'Player Power'

As we noted earlier in this chapter, the power balance between inter-county players and administrators had been gradually shifting in a more equal direction prior to the 1960s. This was largely impelled by the wider social processes connected with the increased meaning of GAA inter-county sport and the advances in seriousness of involvement and achievement orientation connected with it. The increasing importance attached to coaching that had emerged from this dynamic, in an unplanned way, led to a loss of function for county committees. Specialised trainers had gradually subsumed some of the functions previously undertaken or controlled by county committees. This in turn weakened inter-county player dependence on county committees (administrators). Several other processes now served to impel this dynamic further, including the more equal relations between younger and older generations (Dolan, 2005). Consequently, previous levels of deference and subordination to the interests and values of older generations diminished somewhat (see Chap. 7 for a more detailed account). This was reflected also in relations between players (which tended to come from younger generations) and administrators (which tended to be drawn from older generations).

By the 1970s the decline in the power imbalance was becoming more perceptible and players began to make more demands, and in a more organised way. Indicative of this were the efforts by some players for greater material rewards for their playing sacrifices. This also served to heighten tensions between players and administrators. For example in 1972 the then reigning All-Ireland football champions, Offaly, sought additional expenses from their county committee for a trip to America as part of a formally sanctioned and organised GAA tour. The GAA's executive committee at central level intervened to prohibit the Offaly County committee from doing so, on the grounds that it did not 'accord with the amateur status of the Association'. And they went further, condemning 'the attitude of the Offaly players' and regarded 'it as a grievous breach of discipline, and one that will not be condoned' (GAA, 1972). These contests of strength between players and administrators continued through the 1970s across the country. The Cork senior football team was suspended in 1977 over a row with administrators over the wearing of playing gear which was not supplied through the county committee but which was given to the players by a different commercial apparel company as a form of promotion (*Irish Times,* 28 July 1977, pp. 1, 3; *Irish Times,* 25

November 1978, p. 3). By the late 1970s the power ratio between players and administrators had become even more equal and was felt to be so in comparison with times past. For instance, in 1979 one writer in the GAA themed magazine *Gaelic Word* (November 1979, p. 11) noted:

> In years gone by it was the norm for players to "to feel-the-pinch"—loss of wages because of absence from work was not uncommon. Many a player suffered in silence because of his love for the game.
> The climate abroad such times dictated that players, like children, should be seen, not heard. To speak out on such issues was to rock the boat and one ran the risk of sinking without a trace from the scene.
> Happily, a more informed light shines down on the G.A.A. today. It is recognised that players have a not inconsiderable influence on the Association … no longer are they regarded as a lower order.
> That the players have a powerful voice is a fact of life. Their silent vigil is part of history.

Though this was an exaggeration somewhat—players had relatively limited influence in comparison to later years—it does indicate that there was an increasing recognition that players had a right to 'influence'. The power symmetry which still lay in favour of administrators continued to move in a more symmetrical direction. The winning of the senior men's inter-county competition remained the pinnacle of achievement for players and for those they represented—their wider 'county' communities. Indeed, as before, the inter-county competition and the we-feelings connected with this impelled a pressure on players to prepare more intensely (see also previous chapter). More broadly, it led to a spiral of increasing competitiveness which was pervasive across all levels. This exerted a considerable pressure on administrators, particularly for the preparation of inter-county teams, to increase the financial resources to facilitate this. County level administrators also constituted an element of the GAA intra-unit competitive figuration that exerted a strong social pressure for sporting success. The social desire for success from within the wider communities of which administrators were representative, had increased administrator dependence on those functionaries who could attain this (through winning)—players and coaches. A further dynamic advancing administrator dependence on inter-county players was the long-term processes of expanding mediatisation and globalisation of sport in Ireland, and concerns about integrating youth into the GAA within the context of increasing competitive interdependences (see Chap. 7). GAA administrators became more aware that Gaelic games were competing with other sports for a share of an expanding and more differentiated media space. On the one hand these processes provided the momentum for the further expansion and speciali-sation of media and communications functions within the GAA. On the other, it also led GAA administrators to encourage and facilitate greater publicity around individual inter-county players. This in turn gave inter-county players another function on which administrators depended. Of course, the interdependences between players and administrators were complex and they were bonded through both conflictual and cooperative interdependences. For instance, they could and did experience the same we- and they-feelings around county identification.

By the 1970s the demands on inter-county players' time and commit-ment to training and playing had grown yet again. These pressures were often amplified through sympathetic journalists (see *Irish Times*, 13 December 1979, p. 2). The common issues facing inter-county players across Ireland and the widening scope of identification between them led to the formation of a national players union in 1980 with the expressed desire of obtaining better training and playing facilities and conditions (Gaelic Players Association, 1980). The new organisation was open to all senior GAA players, not just inter-county players, and it sug-gests that the we-identification and we-feelings of 'inter-county' players as a distinct group had not materialised to the extent it would in later years. The nascent player's association was short lived but the demands on players continued to escalate. Trials of strength between inter-county players and administrators continued. The issues involved widened from player welfare and material recompense to control over the selection process for the function of manager/coach (See *Sunday Independent*, 20 January 1980, p. 28). Through the 1980s the pressures on players increased further. Many, exasperated by the situation, spoke out indi-vidually arguing for more concessions in recompense for the commit-ments now expected of them (*Irish Times*, 4 August 1988, p. 3). Reports of players accepting payments for off-field sporting-related events such as attending functions and the presentations of medals began to circulate (*Irish Times*, 24 May 1988, p. 3; *Irish Times*, 22 March 1989, p. 2), as did reports of a small number of players going to the USA to play Gaelic games during the summer months where they received cash payments or some form of benefit-in-kind. There were also rumours of payments to coaches (managers) (*Irish Times*, 17 May 1983, p. 3). It was in this con-text that amateurism and professionalism began to be re-amplified. At the GAA's annual congress in 1985 the president warned of creeping professionalism and the need to guard 'one of our most precious resources'—amateurism (*Irish Times,* 1 April 1985, p. 4). An internal review on the amateur status of the GAA was instigated by administrators in 1986. Indeed, between 1983 and 1997 the issue of amateurism was examined on seven occasions (GAA, 1997). This latter report noted that amateurism was still to be valued and aspired to, while the spectre of professionalism was deemed to threaten 'the "very roots" of the Association' (GAA, 1997, p. 2). Interestingly, the 1997 report also noted that there was 'very little evidence of abuse' of the amateur status rules by players but 'there were allegations about payments to a very small number of coaches of county teams and to a much larger number of coaches of club teams' (p. 2).

The identification between inter-county players from different counties had also advanced since the 1980s. They met more frequently through both sporting and non-sporting events—national awards ceremonies, inter-provincial championships, and through education as greater numbers of younger people accessed third-level education. The issues of common interest to inter-county players, their greater integration as a group and an advance in the moulding of a common identification, all facilitated the development of a players union in 1999—the Gaelic Players Association (GPA) (Cusack, 2009). Unlike its predecessor of the early 1980s, membership was restricted to inter-county players. This group now sought to establish its legitimacy as the voice of 'elite' Gaelic players and push their interests. A struggle ensued with central administrators of the GAA and the term 'player power' was now increasingly deployed and amplified. The GPA's attempt to act as the legitimate voice for inter-county players was strongly resisted by some administrators. For instance, shortly after the formation of the GPA the then president of the GAA, Joe McDonagh, himself a former inter-county player in the 1970s and 1980s, stated: 'We take serious issue with any group which would negotiate a sponsorship at national level outside of our organization on behalf of our members as long as they remain members of our association' (cited in *Sunday Independent,* 19 March 2000, p. 30). Despite this declaration, and indicative of the strength of the players' position relative to the central administrators of the GAA, within a few years the GPA negotiated several sponsorship deals, while their efforts to obtain other concessions and benefits for inter-county players were also successful to varying degrees. These included individual financial grants,[2] a financial payment if attending third-level education, the provision of free clothing and sportswear, and sponsored cars. They also benefited from enhanced team holidays financed by the GAA, better training and playing facilities and social and material supports connected with this, including physiotherapy, food, biomedical advice and monitoring.

As we noted previously, the increasing social significance of sport and the process of inter-organisational rivalry between sports organisations had added further to central GAA administrator dependence on players. They needed the players for their on-field performances for the completion of inter-county competitions, which attracted spectators and generated directly and indirectly the vast bulk of the GAA's revenues. Players too were becoming more aware of this and of the physical, temporal and social commitments they gave which sustained this. For instance, in their quest for acceptance as a players union they threatened to organise for strike action (*Irish Times*, 29 April 2002, p. A1).

Tensions and trials of strength between both the GPA and administrators, and between other groups of players and administrators, at different levels continued in the proceeding years. For example, inter-county player groups became more militant over the selection process for the inter-county management function as administrators sought to retain control over it. For instance, in 2009 a senior administrator in County Clare in a dispute with the senior hurling players over the selection of the management team declared: '... in all truth, player power cannot dictate. Certainly, they can have a voice but their input cannot be the final dictate as regards policy and decision making' (cited in *Irish Times*, 29 December 2009, p. A11). In that sense, the use and amplifying of the phrase 'player power' was often deployed in a pejorative way by administrators as they sought to preserve their declining power position.

Again, and indicative of the shift in the balance of power, there have been further concessions to players including the transfer of functions from administrators to inter-county players. In many cases they have attained significant input over the selection process for inter-county managers/coaches. When considered in the long-term then, one can see how this function has largely been lost by administrators and gained by inter-county players. This too is part of the context in which professionalism, amateurism and indeed the concept of player power came to be increasingly amplified from the 1980s onwards.

Since its formation, the we-identity of those comprising the GPA has solidified. Furthermore, the greater confidence, status and power sources of inter-county players has expressed itself on many fronts. The GPA has become more greatly integrated into the existing institutional structures of the GAA, legitimated and accepted. They have obtained a position on the central council, previously the preserve of administrators, and they receive direct funding transfers from the central funds of the GAA to finance both the administration of the GPA and services for inter-county players. More of their interests have been catered for and elite players have secured greater financial and non-financial rewards. As the power differential between inter-county players and central administrators became more even, and despite the initial enmity, greater mutual trust and identification has emerged. The longstanding strength and scale of mutual dependences and the emotional connections between elite players and central administrators certainly contributed to this.

CONCLUSION

In this chapter we described and explained the processes through which narratives, though at times different and contradictory, of amateurism and professionalism have been amplified by various groups and individuals comprising the GAA. In more recent times the ethos of amateurism has come to be expressed primarily in relation to inter-county player practices and demands. One manifestation of this was the emergence and amplification of the term 'player power' itself. Since the GAA's foundation the power balance between administrators and players has largely favoured administrators (though it has become more symmetrical between inter-county players and administrators over the decades). This structure in conjunction with other processes (see previous chapter) has shaped how the concepts of amateurism and professionalism have been treated by various groups comprising the GAA. The issue of payments to coaches/managers too have been increasingly alluded to in various official GAA reports and media coverage since the early 1990s in particular. This has also contributed to the amplification of professionalism and amateurism since the 1990s. And while it is connected with the processes of increasing seriousness of involvement and achievement orientation as discussed in Chap. 5, it was also underpinned by a shift in the power ratio between managers and administrators in the direction of the former.

NOTES

1. The partition of Ireland meant a large group of people who identified with an independent Ireland were in a territory that remained under British control.
2. These grants were paid by the Republic of Ireland state as a part of an agreement with the Irish Sports Council rather than the GAA.

REFERENCES

Conboy, T. (2002). The seventies. In T. Moran (Ed.), *Stair CLG Chonnacht 1902–2002*. Carrick-on-Shannon, Co. Leitrim: Carrick Print.

Curran, C. (2015). *The development of sport in Donegal, 1880–1935*. Cork: Cork University Press.

Cusack, D. Ó. (2009). *Come what may: The autobiography*. Dublin: Penguin.

Devine, L. (2002). The twenties. In T. Moran (Ed.), *Stair CLG Chonnacht 1902–2002* (pp. 23–36). Carrick-on-Shannon, Co. Leitrim: Carrick Print.

Devlin, P. J. (1934). *Our native games*. Dublin: M. H. Gill & Sons.

Dolan, P. (2005). *The development of consumer culture, subjectivity and national identity in Ireland*, 1900–1980. PhD thesis, Goldsmiths College, University of London, London.

Dunning, E. (2008). The dynamics of modern sport: Notes on achievement-striving and the social significance of sport. In N. Elias & E. Dunning (Eds.), *Quest for excitement: Sport and leisure in the civilising process* (Rev. ed., pp. 203–221). Dublin: University College Dublin Press.

Elias, N., & Scotson, J. L. (2008). *The established and the outsiders* (Rev. ed.). Dublin: University College Dublin Press.

Fitzgerald, D. (1914). *How to play Gaelic football*. Cork: Guy & Co.

GAA. (1908–1909). *The Gaelic athletic annual*. Dublin: GAA.

GAA. (1910–1911). *The Gaelic athletic annual*. Dublin: GAA.

GAA. (1927). *Minutes of annual convention of Leinster council*. Dublin: GAA.

GAA. (1929). *Minutes of annual congress*. Dublin: GAA.

GAA. (1930). *Minutes of annual congress*. Dublin: GAA.

GAA. (1935, February 8). *Minutes of Armagh county committee*. Dublin: GAA.

GAA. (1942). *Minutes of annual congress*. Dublin: GAA.

GAA. (1946). *Minutes of annual congress*. Dublin: GAA.

GAA. (1947). *Minutes of annual congress*. Dublin: GAA.

GAA. (1950). *An comhdháil bhliantúil*. Dublin: GAA.

GAA. (1953a). *Minutes of annual convention of Leinster council*. Dublin: GAA.

GAA. (1953b, February 28). *Minutes of central council*. Dublin: GAA.

GAA. (1971). *Report of the commission on the GAA*. Dublin: GAA.

GAA. (1972, March 11). *Minutes of executive committee of GAA*. Dublin: GAA.

GAA. (1997). *Report of the committee established to review the GAA's amateur status*. Dublin: GAA.

Gaelic Players Association. (1980). *Constitution and rules*.

Garnham, N. (2004). *Association football and society in pre-partition Ireland*. Belfast: Ulster Historical Foundation.

Hayes, M. (2009). Down through the years. In D. McAnallen, D. Hassan, & R. Hegarty (Eds.), *The evolution of the GAA: Ulaidh, Éire agus eile* (pp. 20–29). Belfast: Stair Uladh.

Hunt, T. (2009). The GAA: Social structure and associated clubs. In M. Cronin, W. Murphy, & P. Rouse (Eds.), *The Gaelic Athletic Association 1884–2009* (pp. 183–202). Dublin: Irish academic Press.

Looney, T. (2008). *Dick Fitzgerald: King in a kingdom of kings*. Dublin: Currach Press.

Martin, H. (2009). *Unlimited heartbreak: The inside story of Limerick hurling*. Cork: Collins Press.

McElligott, R. (2013). *Forging a kingdom: The GAA in Kerry 1884–1934*. Wilton, Cork: Collins Press.

McKeever, J. (2009). The coming of age of Gaelic games in Ulster, 1950–1970. In D. McAnallen, D. Hassan, & R. Hegarty (Eds.), *The evolution of the GAA: Ulaidh, Éire agus eile* (pp. 30–41). Belfast: Stair Uladh.

Ó Maonaigh, A. (2017). 'Who were the shoneens?': Irish militant nationalists and association football, 1913–1923. *Soccer & Society, 18*(5–6), 631–647.

O'Connor, C. (2010). *The club*. Dublin: Penguin.

O'Donoghue, N. (1987). *Proud and upright men*. Indreabhán, Galway: Clódóirí Lurgan Teo.

Toms, D. (2015). *Soccer in Munster: A social history 1877–1937*. Cork: Cork University Press.

Tynan, M. P. (2013). *Association football and Irish society during the inter-war period, 1918–1939*. PhD thesis, University of Ireland, Maynooth, Maynooth.

CHAPTER 7

Integrating Irish Youth, National Identification and Diminishing Displays of Superiority

Towards Social Controls

In the social context from which the GAA came to be established (Chap. 4), its founders had, in the course of attempting to form such an organisation, deployed both a nationalist blame and praise gossip (Elias & Scotson, 2008). Within this narrative many existing (competing) sports and their representative organisations were characterised as English, effeminate, unnatural (to Irish people) and essentially inferior (McDevitt, 1997). This discourse was generated by the coloniser–colonised figuration. It was this figuration which also simultaneously shaped the praise gossip deployed in the efforts to establish the GAA (and later in attempts to strengthen it following its foundation). GAA activists increasingly sought to equate true Irishness with Gaelic games and simultaneously with membership or affiliation with the GAA. The competitive tensions between those representing the GAA and their opponents in both the newly established IAAA and the Irish Cyclists Association soon intensified. Caught in a double-bind dynamic, GAA activists increasingly sought to stigmatise other sports as British. Another tactic (in 1885), in exerting greater social control over what sport Irish people would partake in, was to prevent athletes from competing at GAA-organised athletics meetings if they had competed in events organised under the rules of other sports organisations (Rouse, 1993). The ban was rescinded a year later as the conflict over athletics affiliation subsided (Rouse, 1993).

© The Author(s) 2020
J. Connolly, P. Dolan, *Gaelic Games in Society*, Palgrave Studies on Norbert Elias, https://doi.org/10.1007/978-3-030-31699-0_7

Aside from the divide over control of athletics, no competing organisation controlled or sought control of 'Gaelic' games (football and hurling). GAA activists were soon in conflict with those representing other sports organisations as they sought to 'convert' sports clubs associated with other sports (such as rugby and soccer) to play Gaelic games, and affiliate to the GAA. Many Irish men, across the social class divide, patronised other competing sports organisations and the games and leisure activities they coordinated. Indeed, these games were still the most popular sports in certain pockets of the country. Furthermore, as we alluded to in Chap. 3, many more 'clubs' or gatherings remained unaffiliated to any sports organisation, instead playing ball games by locally derived rules in ad hoc arrangements. Consequently, by 1886 some GAA activists now sought to attain greater affiliation by preventing existing GAA clubs from competing against non-affiliated GAA clubs (Rouse, 1993). Its remit was soon widened so as to prevent members of other sporting organisations from being members of the GAA. Yet again these constraints were soon broadened further to prohibit the police—the Royal Irish Constabulary (RIC) and Dublin Metropolitan Police (DMP)—from membership of the GAA, as the IRB's influence in the GAA increased (Mandle, 1987). Such rules illustrate the extent to which social constraints were brought to bear in playing Gaelic games.

While the ban on RIC members was removed in 1893 (Rouse, 1993), the stigmatisation of other sports continued. They continued to be conflated with Englishness and were thereby considered less Irish. Indeed, with the rise of nationalist sentiment more generally across Ireland by the turn of the twentieth century, the nature of the invective solidified. It was driven by competitive interdependences between those representing the various sports organisations. The insecurities and pressures felt by some GAA activists stemmed from the continued participation of many Irish men in other sports codes. For instance, between 1905 and 1910 the number of soccer clubs affiliated to the IFA increased from 278 to 430 (Garnham, 2004b, p. 7); the GAA comprised 311 affiliated clubs by 1900 (Mandle, 1987, p. 116). In several parts of the country both cricket and soccer remained the most popular sports (Curran, 2015; Hunt, 2008; Toms, 2015) as did rugby in other parts (McElligott, 2013; O'Callaghan, 2011). Combined, these processes impelled the desire for the imposition of greater social constraints as a means to integrate people into the GAA. At the 1901 GAA annual congress, the Kerry GAA official, Thomas O'Sullivan, proposed:

That we the representatives of the Gaels of Ireland in convention assembled hereby pledge ourselves to resist by every means in our power the extension of English pastimes to this country, as a means of preventing the Anglicisation of our people: that County Committees be empowered to disqualify and suspend members of the Association who countenance sports which are calculated to interfere with the preservation and cultivation of our national pastimes: that we call on the young men of Ireland not to identify themselves with rugby or association football or any other form of imported sport which is likely to injuriously affect the national pastimes which the G.A.A. provides for self-respected Irishmen who have no desire to ape foreign manners and customs. (cited in Mac Lua, 1967, pp. 40–41)

By 1905 the rule and related sanctions were more precise: 'That any persons who play rugby, soccer, hockey, cricket or any imported games shall be suspended for two years' (Rouse, 1993, p. 348). These constraints would widen further over the next 5 years while vigilance committees were established to enforce the rules. Of course not all GAA administrators or activists were in favour of imposing such constraints. And the fact that vigilance committees were required, and that many Irish people opted to partake in other sports, indicates how weakly the association between Gaelic games and Irishness had been internalised by them.

In the following decades, the invective directed at competing sports—soccer and rugby in particular—and those deemed sympathetic to them, such as particular media outlets, intensified. Not only were such sports labelled British, they were increasingly stigmatised through the metaphor of the 'garrison games', meaning the games of the 'British military':

There are papers in Dublin which on Saturday's print a special football issue, giving the latest soccer news. The Dalymount [soccer stadium] and Lansdowne [rugby stadium] get lauded to the skies, column after column is filled with details of play and players, photographs are given of prominent (sometimes "very" prominent) exponents of the garrison games. But we seldom if ever get a photo or word of praise for any of the prominent Gaelic players. (*Gaelic Annual*, 1908–1909, p. 30)

The open hostility to some media outlets by some GAA activists was mirrored in similar public pronouncements about competing sports in which the desired destruction of these sports was openly declared:

Few people will deny we have knocked a good shake out of the Rugby and Soccer...but how do we stand in regard to athletics and cycling? ... It may be said: why does not the G.A.A. promote international contests? The answer is: our exclusive rules block the way so long as our enemies exist... But is there no remedy? There is; it is at hand, and should be availed of. The remedy is to smash the rival organizations root and branch. Can we do it? We can if the business be approached in a determined manner. We have been sparring now for some years, and it is nearly time we came to hard blows.... There can be no compromise, and there certainly cannot be any peace, until some Association or Associations go under, and that Association cannot be the G.A.A. (*Gaelic Athletic Annual*, 1910–1911, pp. 60–61)

Certainly not all GAA activists held such views. Indeed, Mandle (1987) suggests that those writing within the realm of the *Gaelic Annual* represented the views of the more extreme nationalists. Nevertheless, what it illustrates is how comfortable some GAA activists were at the time in openly desiring the destruction of other Irish sports organisations.

So while the actual extent of the association between the GAA and the militant uprisings which eventually led to partial independence in 1921 is contested, the allusion to that association was increasingly amplified by GAA activists in the years that followed. GAA activists, and others, post the Civil War began to increasingly insinuate and amplify the GAA's—its leadership and wider membership—role and commitment to the militant nationalist cause (Ó Maonaigh, 2017). This praise gossip formed part of a wider frame in which GAA activists as well as national and local politicians sought to conflate true national identity with membership of the GAA (Cronin, 1999; Garnham, 2004a; Mandle, 1987; McDevitt, 1997; O'Callaghan, 2013; Ó hAnnrachain, 2008; Rouse, 1993; Tynan, 2013). Yet many Irish people did not submit to these social controls—stigmatisation through blame-gossip and the bans. Although the GAA expanded rapidly in terms of general membership, club affiliation and spectatorship in the 1920s, so too did soccer, the primary competition to Gaelic games (Tynan, 2013), which also grew in popularity (McCabe, 2011; Ó Maonaigh, 2017). In other cases, some did submit to the pressure of these social constraints. For instance, Ó Maonaigh (2017, pp. 636–637) notes how one former soccer and rugby player became 'a zealous GAA convert' citing the attack on 'foreign games' in Nationalist periodicals as the motivation (see also Curran, 2015, pp. 210–211).

The increasing social significance of sport more generally in Ireland was indicative of a wider sportisation process in which sport attained greater functional importance in generating we-feelings and excitement for people. This process was reflected also in the increased mediatisation of sport. Newspaper editors and related functionaries continued to expand sports coverage. One of the most popular newspapers of time, the *Irish Independent*, devoted two columns weekly to soccer, while a weekly sports magazine primarily dedicated to soccer was also launched (McCabe, 2011). The popularity of soccer and rugby in many parts of Ireland and the capacity of their respective sporting organisations to field 'national' teams and participate in international competitions contributed to insecurities and hostility felt amongst some GAA activists. A further source of antagonism for many GAA administrators was the continued patronage of rugby in particular by some schools and the sporting emphasis on non-Gaelic games. The response by various GAA administrators at different organisational levels was again to resort to social controls through stigmatisation. The allusion to the playing of non-Gaelic games was labelled a form of national betrayal. For instance, in 1936 the president of the GAA verbally castigated those schools involved in non-Gaelic games, declaring: 'I hope that those responsible in these colleges will reconsider their attitude and that before any action can be taken the call of the Motherland will bring them back to their fidelity to the national games' (cited in *Irish Times*, 13 April 1936, p. 8). The willingness to openly censure those deemed supportive of other sports was no mere verbal threat. In 1934 Douglas Hyde, president of the Irish Free State and patron of the GAA, was expelled from the association for attending an International soccer match in his function as president (Moore, 2012).

Stigmatisation was directed at many organisations deemed in anyway supportive of non-Gaelic games. The national radio broadcaster in the Irish Free State, 2RN, came under considerable attack in the 1930s for the failure to institutionalise the primacy of the GAA and Gaelic games over other sports in their coverage. In 1936, soon after 2RN began the practice of broadcasting the results for different sports, the general secretary of the GAA declared at the GAA's annual congress of that year:

The most objectionable of these was the linking up of Gaelic results with the reports of foreign games. The Council considered this an insidious method of introducing non-Gaelic pastimes to the attention of the Irish public at large. It is a debatable question whether the advantages of Wireless publicity are not entirely neutralised by the manner in which it is provided at present. (GAA, 1936)

The web of interdependences within which GAA functionaries and media functionaries were bound to one another were, however, diverse. Since its introduction in Ireland, the technology of radio had changed the spatial dimensions and temporal boundaries in which sport, and the 'quest for excitement' (Elias & Dunning, 2008), could be experienced by those who could not attend many sporting events. Consequently, condemnation of the radio authorities (and other media), for the level and type of coverage, ran in parallel with other more cooperative interdependences. For example, representatives of regional GAA units in the 1940s sought greater coverage of provincial fixtures (GAA, 1945). Indeed, the structure of interdependence meant GAA functionaries increasingly sought to accommodate the media. The general secretary of the GAA—the same individual who had castigated the radio authorities above—sought to empower the central organisational units of the GAA with the authority to arrange match fixtures in advance 'because of the widespread demand for the broadcasting of our important games' (GAA, 1946, p. 15). It was in many ways this dependence on media functions which fuelled their disappointment and anger when those they depended upon adopted approaches and positions they disliked. Furthermore, their we-feelings for the GAA were strong and greatly shaped their reactions to those they were interdependent with.

The openness of the verbal attacks on various individuals and organisations reflected not only the structure of the blame gossip but also the open expression of superiority. In 1943 when the Minister for Defence in the Irish Free State, Oscar Traynor, who was also then president of the Football Association of Ireland (FAI) (soccer), sought to give official status to the playing of all sports within the Army (and not just Gaelic games as had been the case) he was accused of 'national betrayal' by the president of the GAA for 'putting foreign games on the same status with the national games [Gaelic games]'(Mac Lua, 1967, p. 85). This vituperative reaction was made at the GAA's annual congress. It illustrates how open displays of hostility towards, and superiority over, other sports were considered acceptable. There was no sense of embarrassment around such condemnations. These displays of superiority and the blame and praise gossip connected with them were invoked by status competition. Despite the popularity of Gaelic games, the competing sports of soccer and rugby still thrived and remained popular; they had an international structure with representative national teams. Feelings of superiority and insecurity went hand in hand.

Wrapped up with this insecurity was the belief that people needed to be protected from the temptations of 'foreign games', protected from themselves. This was partly the function of the ban and the vigilance committees associated with it. Of course other GAA activists and administrators opposed the ban, not to mention players and spectators, and attempts were made to rescind it in 1947 (see *Irish Press*, 28 January 1947, p. 8). This was illustrative of the weak inculcation of the association between nationality and the playing of Gaelic games within many GAA members. Nonetheless, the tactic of praise-blame gossip and the broader emphasis on social controls this reflected persisted through the 1950s. Leading GAA administrators continued to conflate GAA membership with 'true' Irishness as a form of praise gossip. It was a form of social control to be exercised over others, its function being to shame people into joining the GAA. Indicative of this praise gossip was a declaration in 1951 by the Secretary of Ulster Council of the GAA:

> The games sponsored by our Association are the many native ones of our country, and they are second to none where athletic skill and prowess are concerned. Furthermore, they are entwined with true nationality, and this very fact entitles them to general support. (GAA, 1951)

The deference to social controls was a reflection of the Irish personality structure more generally of the time where the balance between external social controls and internal self-restraints lay more towards the former (Dolan, 2009). Social controls were still considered essential by many and the ban continued to be enforced. For instance, in 1953 three players of the Combined Universities Gaelic football team were suspended for attending the Ireland versus England rugby international match played in Dublin (*Irish Press*, 2 March 1953, p. 7). The exercise of other social constraints also found expression. In 1954 the GAA authorities refused to allow the broadcast of a national final due to the fact that Radio Éireann (the new name for the national radio broadcaster in what was now the Republic of Ireland) intended to include coverage of an International soccer match between the Republic of Ireland[1] and Scotland during half-time in the GAA fixture (Boyle, 1992, p. 629).

Anxieties that young people might take up other sports if they were not protected or prevented from doing so underpinned such policies. Young people, their impulses and emotions, could not be trusted unless specific social controls were in place to safeguard and direct them. Otherwise they could or would be easily converted by the seductive and powerful forces of competing sports and the media. Social controls and blame gossip were seamlessly moulded as means to protect youth from themselves. Indicative of this was the warning in 1958 by the president of the GAA that youth clubs were contributing to the de-nationalising of youth through the fostering of various leisure and sporting activities—non-Gaelic games (*Irish Press*, 7 April 1958, p. 5).

Movements in the Balance of Social Controls and Self-Controls

The focus, and perceived importance, on the integration of young people into the GAA intensified for GAA administrators in the 1960s. Several intertwined processes served to increase the felt anxieties of administrators around the issue, including the expansion of the medium of television and the related increase in the mediatisation of sport (Connolly & Dolan, 2012). Linked with this is a noticeable change in how young people were considered and viewed by administrators. The latter point as we will explain was connected to expanding social interdependences and changing power balances between different social groups in Ireland, including intergenerational relations.

As we outlined in Chap. 2, expanding social interdependences and the less unequal power relations this invoked between different social cohorts in Ireland had become a feature of Irish society during the first half of the twentieth century, and earlier (Dolan, 2005). In the 1960s the scale of this process was more advanced and the pace more rapid. Relations between younger and older generations were becoming less unequal; the expansion of free state education and more industrial employment opportunities from the mid-1960s would propel this dynamic even further in the 1970s. Hints of this change in the power balance are noticeable from the early 1960s. For instance, during a debate on the removal of the 'ban on foreign games' at the GAA's annual convention of 1962 one delegate, M. O Ruairc, claimed:

> ... that it had often been stated that the voice of the players was not heard, but he saw no reason why it should be. In schools, colleges and universities the students had no say in the curriculum, because they were too immature to make decisions of major importance. (cited in *Irish Independent*, 23 April 1962, p. 17)

O Ruairc's comment reflects a habitus and a way of life in which younger people were considered fairly subordinate to older generations (Dolan, 2005). But, by the 1960s, the decreasing gap in the power differential between older and younger generations, which had been receding for some decades, now emboldened youth, and they began to be more vocal in their demands. Indeed, this dynamic can be observed in a response to O Ruairc which appeared in a GAA magazine of the time:

> At home we listen even to the voices of children and, indeed, parents who don't soon see the children go. Players are not children; yet Miceal O Ruairc, I suspect, regards them as such by drawing a parallel with college students. (*Gaelic Sport*, June–August 1962, p. 33)

The rejoinder also illustrates the younger generation's awareness of their power resources—they were less dependent on their parents—as the phrase 'parents who don't soon see the children go' indicates. The balance would tilt more comprehensively by the latter stages of the decade and again in the 1970s.

This shift in the inter-generational power relation also partly underpinned the change that occurred in relation to the narrative of true national identity and Gaelic games—then perceived by many as a means in attempting to integrate youth into the GAA. Certainly, through the 1960s, the narrative fusing Gaelic games and 'true' national identity was still invoked. For instance, in 1966 the then GAA president lamented: 'You may serve another nation's language, or games, or way of life for motives of your own, but you cannot claim that such service is for Ireland's sake' (*Our Games*, 1966, p. 43). There is a slightly nostalgic aspect to this—a realisation of newly emerging mores and expectations. There was now though an increasing, though perhaps reluctant, acceptance amongst some administrators that as a means to encourage youth to partake in Gaelic games the association with national identity, in their eyes, had lost, or was losing, some of its potency. The belief that existed amongst many GAA administrators that the conflation of Gaelic games with 'true' national identity was, or should be, a reason for membership was being questioned. It was part of a wider reflective process about how people more generally, and in particular 'youth', ought to be treated. For instance in 1969 the president of the Ulster Council of the GAA argued: 'We must provide more appeal ... [and get involved in] any other type of social activity that will attract the youth in our clubs so that they will become imbued with a pride in our traditions handed down to us by our predecessors' (GAA, 1969, p. 5). There is melding here between the older approach and the newer regime of considering the choice and needs of youth. Three years later the president of the Ulster council again declared in his annual address that 'youth is influenced to a decreasing degree by the tenets of traditions'. And he went on to add,

> In the years ahead I believe the G.A.A. cannot rely solely on the traditional appeal it had for our youth. It must, as an Association, show itself to be actively interested in the youngsters if it is to have any hope of winning their allegiance. (GAA, 1972, p. 4)

Similarly, Sean O'Neill, a 30-year-old former player, and then GAA administrator, suggested in 1972 in an interview for the GAA magazine *Our Games* that:

> the G.A.A. has only tolerated youth, not encouraged and fostered their needs and claims... Modern youth were more discerning than their fathers were at a similar age; they knew what they wanted and had certain standards which they demanded when it came to the organisation and playing of games. (1972, p. 61)

Echoing this in a similar article, Dan McAreavy claimed:

> It is no longer sufficient to say that you must play Gaelic games because they are Irish. Today's youth seeks better reasons than that. They have alternative games to turn to and if they find in these things missing in the G.A.A., the haemorrhage will continue.

There was a greater recognition that younger generations had the right to choose (and indeed the right to play other sports).

The former regime of seeking to integrate youth was also one which involved a greater recourse to issuing commands, by older generations directed at younger generations, who were expected to listen rather than be heard. Previously youth were talked about and referred to but there was limited recognition of, and mechanisms for hearing, their voice. Such a regime reflected a greater emphasis on social controls and a belief in their necessity. By the 1960s a shift in direction of self-restraint was occurring. The removal of 'the ban', itself, in 1971 was a further manifestation of this trend, as were other changes. It was now increasingly accepted by many GAA administrators that the demands, interests and values of youth must receive greater consideration. Indicative of the changes referred to is the following extract from the 1971 report on the status of the GAA, which had been authorised by the central council some years earlier. In a section headed 'Youth', it stated:

> Youth is being exposed to a much wider range of ideas than formerly and standards of performance are often set by what is seen on the television screen. Educational opportunities are greater. There is more money to spend, and more ways and more leisure time in which to spend it. Young people too are more articulate and demand to be involved in any decision making that affects them. (GAA, 1971, p. 88)

The newer regime, more sensitive towards the needs and desires of youth, also involved greater trust. This too is a reflection of the shift towards greater self-restraint. Administrators came to accept that people could make the 'correct' choice, in their eyes, of joining the GAA and could be trusted to do so, without the need for social constraints such as the ban. They also took a more 'detached' view in relation to why young people would participate in Gaelic games. For example, one administrator in 1980 argued that 'that the national aspect of Gaelic games does not now attract young members—they play for whatever enjoyment they can get' (*Gaelic World*, 1980, January, p. 37). Nor is there any sense of embarrassment or a feeling of shame in making the observation that the link to nationality was no a longer a significant reason for playing. The comment (and the wider article from which it was drawn) reflects the change in habitus of both younger people and also administrators—a change in the social habitus of people in Ireland more generally had occurred. As the social interdependences in which people in Ireland were enmeshed increased, the scope of identification people experienced also changed. Elias (2010) developed the concept of the we–I identity balance to explain the process. As people become less bound to their traditional protective we-groups such as family and community, the accent on the I-identity can become stronger, especially where the state expands and subsumes some of the functions provided by familial and other local networks. Certainly, in the case of the Republic of Ireland, from the 1960s the emotional charge connected with the national we-group remained but its strength relative to the I aspect of people's identity weakened somewhat (Dolan,

2009). By the 1980s the accent on the I-identity which people experienced was also becoming more tangible and visible to many. A 1985 manual for GAA administrators acknowledged that:

> [t]he Association must accept the increasing emergence of independent-minded people with sharply critical power of selection and rejection of a sports body, its games and its services. The G.A.A. must also accept the unpleasant implication that if it fails to identify with the motivation of its members, players, and supporters; fails to seek out and solve their problems; fails to find out what they need and how to give it to them, the organisation will quickly lose its pre-eminent position in Irish sport. (GAA, 1985)

The examples provided reflect both the receding preference for social controls and the actual shift in the balance between social and self-controls in the regimes for integrating people into the GAA. In Chaps. 2 and 3 we outlined how this tilting of the balance between social and self-restraints reflecting a wider social transformation in the social habitus of people in Ireland—though the extent varied across classes and generations—shaped both player and spectator behaviour and feelings. The expansion and lengthening of social interdependences facilitated a reduction in the power inequality between many formerly outsider social groups, such as women and those drawn from younger generations, and more established groups—men, and older generations. This decline in the power inequality between the generations brought with it a greater level of identification with those from the rising social group—the younger generations (Wouters, 2007). Consequently, the needs and values of these formerly outsider groups framed more of how all people were permitted and expected to behave and think. There was now greater social acceptance of wider and more different ways of living and behaving.

These changing social interdependences, in an unintended and unplanned way, led to a change in how GAA administrators envisaged youth and younger generations generally. As we have illustrated, GAA administrators now felt a greater compulsion to recognise and identify with the needs of younger generations. In the wider social climate of less unequal power relations, the more authoritarian approach to dealing with young people was increasingly tabooed. This, we argue, found expression also in how GAA administrators were coming to deal with youth. The previous approach to youth (and Irish people generally) was one where greater social controls—the ban and vigilance committees, shaming mechanisms—were deemed essential to ensure people joined the GAA. Without such external controls a person's own self-restraints might give in to the temptations of 'foreign' sports. The commanding of people to participate in Gaelic games on the grounds that a failure to do so was a betrayal of true national identity reflected this more authoritarian regime.

The trajectory of the process also shaped in an unplanned way a greater stress on media and communications by GAA administrators occupying higher-tier functions. In a social context where individual motivations, needs and desires are believed to be, and become, a significant driver of behaviour, the demand for greater social and self-knowledge increases (Wouters, 2007). People must, and are expected to, navigate a greater number of more varied options in a wider set of social contexts on their 'own'. And, where there is greater sensitivity towards the exercise of more authoritarian social restraints and/or where they are deemed more socially unacceptable, the necessity for other social steers and functions in helping people to 'choose' increases. So as the more command and authoritarian style approach loses functional importance, other approaches that facilitate and accommodate choice, and which can play upon individual needs and motivations, take up the baton of functional import. Communications, promotion and media, as functions which permit such approaches, take on greater importance and thus prominence. Combined with processes of inter-organisational sports competition they propelled a social pressure on senior GAA administrators for more extensive media and communications. The dependence of GAA functionaries on various media and communications functions increased as did awareness of this dependency. For instance, at the GAA's annual congress of 1977 the president of the GAA stated:

> A liaison group has been formed by the journalists in the press and R.T.E. which will operate on an ongoing basis with the Association on matters of mutual interest... The Association and the Media need one another and we must endeavour to use the media to the Association's best advantage. We must treat their representatives with respect. (GAA, 1977)

The increased dependency on media and communications functionaries is reflected in a whole series of developments. By the 1970s new and more differentiated organisational functions concerning media and communications were advocated by senior administrators of the GAA (and in turn created)—a process that continued in later decades.[2] More GAA units and different tiers were expected to develop specialist communications functions while relations between GAA functionaries and media functionaries became more cooperative. As we explained, this was not driven solely by competitive tensions and the expansion of media such as television, but the intertwining of these processes with the changing social habitus of people.

Interestingly, many of the wider social changes we alluded to—urbanisation, more individualised behaviour and thinking, the rise of youth and women—did not go unnoticed amongst GAA administrators at the time. Leading GAA administrators at different tiers of the organisation commissioned sociologists and other specialist researchers to examine these developments (see GAA, 1971; O'Connor & Whelan, 1971). The beliefs behind such action are themselves based on a figurational shift that produced feelings of individuality and uniqueness, an indication of the wider trend towards greater individualisation in Ireland in the 1970s (Dolan, 2009, p. 137).

The movement in the direction of greater social control toward greater self-control was accompanied by a more tolerant approach to other sports. This too was connected with more even social relations emerging across Irish society where expressions of superiority were becoming more taboo and increasingly avoided. We argue that a process in which displays of superiority diminished also came to frame how GAA administrators and activists considered competing sporting bodies from the 1960s onwards.

DIMINISHING DISPLAYS OF SUPERIORITY

As we illustrated earlier, from the early years of the GAA's foundation right through to the 1950s, GAA administrators and activists often adopted an openly hostile attitude towards competing sports. In particular, GAA activists adopted an air of superiority in respect of 'true' national identity. A further feature of this process was the fact that expressions of this nature were openly displayed—even to the extent of challenging senior state functionaries (as we noted earlier in respect of the Minister for Defence). Such displays of superiority did not disappear by the 1960s, as the next example below illustrates, but they did gradually diminish in the decades that followed. In 1960 the GAA's annual congress included a discussion of a programme developed and broadcast by the state radio service, Radio Éireann. The broadcaster had introduced a roundtable structure to a radio programme in which various sports, including Gaelic games, were discussed. Many GAA delegates were dismayed and angered at this development:

> ...we would be better off if we were excluded from these programmes from Radio Éireann ... particularly since it introduced these round table treatments of the various sporting events of the week in which one game is made to look as good as another. We cannot accept that position at all.
>
> Uachtarán [president of the GAA]: If that is the opinion of congress we will get in touch with the Radio Éireann authorities with the view to having that wish granted. Is this the opinion of Congress?
>
> Cries of "Yes". (GAA, 1960)

Certainly not all administrators comprising congress held such views but it is indicative of the feelings of some GAA administrators of the time. As in previous decades Gaelic games were deemed superior and this sense of superiority was openly expressed. Gaelic games were conflated with 'national' games and it was claimed this entitled them to more, and separate (from others sports), media coverage. At meetings of the policy committee of the GAA in 1966 the committee unanimously rejected the idea of 'mixed sports programmes'; expressed their dissatisfaction that some GAA games 'had been previewed from a broadcasting unit based in Lansdowne Road' (the stadium in which Irish international rugby matches were played);[3] and disapproved of a non-sports TV programme 'The Late Late Show' hosting a panel of guests to discuss the upcoming rugby international between Wales and Ireland (*Minutes of Policy Committee*, GAA, 19 March, and 2 April 1966).

Yet, as we explained earlier, by the early 1960s changes to this type of thinking and feeling were becoming more evident and it is reflected in relations with other sports also. A more circumspect attitude to criticising other sports begins to appear. For instance, following the development of broadcast television in Ireland in the early 1960s, one columnist in a GAA magazine commenting on the sports programmes broadcast by the new state service, Teilifís Éireann, expressed the view:

> Having watched all three over the early weeks of Teilifís Éireann's short existence, one thing is clear to me at least. Hurling and Gaelic football have been treated as just two of the many sports to be dealt with.
>
> Whether this is right or wrong is something on which opinions differ, and I'm sure that the Radio Éireann authorities, depending as they are on direct income from licence holders and advertisers, are mindful of the fact that all tastes must be catered for. (*Gaelic Sport*, March–May, 1962, p. 49)

It also illustrates how some GAA supporters were adopting a more restrained and moderate approach to displays of superiority towards other sports. By the 1970s it was even more perceptible. In 1970 the secretary general of the GAA attended a formal banquet hosted by a group of rugby school 'Old boys' (*Irish Times*, 16 November 1970, p. 11). His attendance and the extensive media attention directed at his participation illustrate both the increasing mutual accommodation between the sports and the embryonic nature of this phase of reciprocity. The removal of the ban itself was in effect another example of the softening of the censure previously directed towards other sports. It reflected a greater tolerance and a diminishing sense of superiority in respect of other sports too. The wider media debate that ensued around the removal of ban at the time is also demonstrative of this trend. One columnist with *Gaelic Sport* writing after the ban noted:

> The temptation to try soccer or rugby or any other game in the gaps of waiting for the next fixture on the G.A.A. club calendar needs no longer to be glorified with the name "temptation". It is now an honourable tendency, and will be followed without stigma—even with encouragement. (March 1971, p. 11)

Similarly, in 1971, the editorial in *Gaelic Sport*, and also after the decision to repeal Rule 27, suggested:

> Positive encouragement of the national ideal, in an unrestricted environment, will now be the mode of operation. We believe that G.A.A. members and supporters, and perhaps, many others, will respond gladly to the new challenge. Gaelic games are **the national games** [original emphasis] and not only must their traditional motivation not be lost, it must not be diluted. (*Gaelic Sport*, April 1971, p. 3)

As this example illustrates, the 'national' association with Gaelic games could still be invoked but a more restrained approach to criticising other sports is taken. A feature of this is that the stigmatising of other sports as less national fades. Certainly some GAA activists continued to hold such views and they did give expression to them but overall it is less amplified. The we-identification and related we-feelings towards the GAA remained strong and in a charged emotional setting verbal attacks on competing sports could still occur. In some cases, the habitus of GAA administrators lagged behind the newly emerging social standards, precipitating critical outbursts with overt declarations of superiority. For example, one delegate at annual congress in 1974 claimed:

[I]t is apparent that R.T.É. are carrying out a deliberate policy of downgrading Gaelic games due to the inadequate coverage and unfair treatment meted out in the past few years, so blatant it is beyond belief, and yet soccer, rugby, racing, snooker and other sports command extensive coverage to the detriment of the national games of Ireland. (GAA, 1974, p. 24)

The process of diminishing expressions of superiority was far from linear and occasional counter movements took place. Notwithstanding, the tendency to decry other sports as less national or even foreign subsided somewhat and came to be replaced by a less hostile view of these other sports. And while some activists and administrators would continue to hold such views they became more restrained in making their views known.

Appraisals of other sports remained, and of the media coverage they received, but the critique, where it did occur, was more nuanced. Critical comparisons were directed at other perceived 'differences' such as the skill levels required and in perceived public popularity. It could still involve the air of superiority but in a more moderated form, subtler and more nuanced. For instance, in an article in *Gaelic World* in 1979 Gaelic football was compared with other codes—soccer, Rugby Union, Rugby League, Australian Rules and American football. In the case of rugby, the author notes: 'The "Ollie Campbells" and "Tony Wards" [Irish international rugby players at the time] may get the points but too often it is "the forwards" that swung the game—and weight, height and strength hardly make up three of the most necessary components of skill' (9 May 1980, p. 7). Soccer was treated in a more sympathetic fashion, with Gaelic football and soccer described as 'out in front' in terms of skill. There is no overt reference to soccer or the other sports being less national as might have been the case in the past. The author then wrote:

However, in this country where the public have a choice whether to attend either game, more people opt for Gaelic football.
    No doubt the Gridiron (a more apt name indeed!) experts in the U.S., the Aussie Rules people and supporters of both Rugby codes see the argument in an entirely different light, but then who was it said that the world revolves on a healthy difference of opinion? (9 May 1980, p. 7)

The expression of superiority is moderated somewhat—less explicit than it might have been in the past. Even then, the allusion to superiority is countered by suggesting that one's opinion is no more superior than those of advocates for other sports. This is indicative of how expressions of feelings of superiority over other sports were coming to be deemed somewhat distasteful. Wouters (2007) argues that in social contexts of more even social relations expressions of superiority come to be increasingly avoided.

This process would advance further in following decades. By the 1990s, alongside diminishing displays of superiority and greater tolerance of other sports, was a movement towards greater inclusiveness and greater mutual accommodation. For instance, in 1991 the chairman of the Kerry County board, Seán Kelly, stated:

> Ecumenism is as desirable in sport as it is in the churches, and I think an organisation so strong, so self-relying as the GAA, has within its scope the power to make at least occasional ecumenical gestures at national level towards other organisations without compromising our principles or creating all-embracing knock-on precedents. Friendly rivalry should be our motto, not open hostility. A calm business-like approach and mature reflection must be brought to bear on these major questions of the day. (cited in Kelly, 2007, p. 181)

The process was far from linear involving both reversals and advances. Indeed, in the same year of Kelly's contention a fundraising effort by a Dublin-based GAA club, Clanna Gael Fontenoy, involving the playing of a 'friendly' inter-county GAA match between the counties of Dublin and then All-Ireland champions Down, on the same bill as a local League of Ireland soccer match at a non-GAA vested ground, was stopped by the central council. Despite the decision, the reaction actually indicates the overall social dynamic we are referring to. Various GAA administrators openly disagreed with the decision while using terms such as 'ashamed' and 'embarrassed' (see *Irish Times*, 16 December 1991, p. 18). The overall trajectory in the following decades was one of increasing mutual accommodation and more cordial relations. In 2005, when the IRFU (in conjunction with the FAI) sought to redevelop their main ground, Lansdowne Road, for international matches, the GAA changed its rules (Rule 42) to permit the playing of international soccer and rugby matches in Croke Park during the redevelopment (Fulton & Bairner, 2007). This was followed a few years later by the central council of the GAA' decision to support the IRFU's bid (ultimately unsuccessful) to host the 2023 Rugby World Cup by permitting the use of GAA stadia for use in the competition.

Since the 1960s references to the superiority of Gaelic games over other sports has faded and where it does occur it has become subtler or perhaps hidden. It has become increasingly taboo to proffer the type of displays of superiority that appeared in earlier times. Yes, the cultural alignment with Irishness and Gaelic games continued, and continues, to be made but it is freed, or detached to a great extent, from any explicit inference that the other sports played by Irish people are 'less' Irish. But displays of superiority over other sports do still find expression, though in changed ways from the past. More contemporary exhortations are largely in the context of a specific Gaelic games match itself. The function here is more towards expressively choreographing the event and occasion. Nonetheless, even commentary of this nature is open to condemnation. For instance, a journalist writing in August 2018 following the weekend of two All-Ireland hurling semi-finals suggested:

> Rather than simply enjoy the matches for their own magnificence, there was yet another rush to anoint hurling as the greatest of all games and decry others while doing so. For what it's worth, hurling is this column's favoured code but the impulse to acclaim it over all others isn't as prevalent here as it seems elsewhere.
>
> How often do you hear pundits, commentators and former players from other sports hail their game as the greatest in the world? Occasionally, maybe. By and large they're satisfied just to judge a particular match on its own merits and outline why it might have been particularly good rather than rushing to declare their code the greatest of all which, given their association with it, is likely what they happen to believe... Just celebrate hurling for what it is, not what other sports aren't. (*Irish Mirror*, 2 August 2018)

Such injunctions are but a further illustration of the wider social pattern towards diminishing displays of superiority.

CONCLUSION

The allusion to national identity and Gaelic games did not disappear between the 1960s and the present. Certainly the we-identification of the GAA and of the 'Nation'[4] remained strong for many people throughout Ireland but, as we illustrated, significant changes did occur. Other forms of identification grew in strength; they took on a greater emotional charge— the I-identity of people in particular. As we explained (and in Chap. 2) this individualisation process was connected to lengthening social interdependences, greater social competition, differentiation and functional specialisation which impel feelings of distinction amongst people. More and more people see themselves as distinct from others in more and more ways. This individualisation process over many generations encourages a *homo clausus* (closed person) habitus (Elias, 2010). It is also an example of a shift in the balance between social and self-restraints in the direction of the latter. It was partly this dynamic which contributed to the change in the scale and nature of the narrative used by many GAA administrators and activists. Social restraints, as a means to integrate young people into the GAA, were increasingly superseded by a focus on individual needs and motivations. As we explained, this occurred in tandem with the emergence of a more tolerant approach to other sporting organisations. Overt expressions of superiority became more unacceptable and embarrassing.

Overall these changes reflect a shift in the balance between social and self-restraints. We argue that these changes, in the attitudes, beliefs and thinking of GAA administrators, were connected with changes in the psychic make-up of people more generally and in changing social structures in Ireland interrelated with this (Dolan, 2009). The changes in emotion regulation, and the corresponding need to supress overt feelings of superiority, became more dominant aspects of Irish people's habitus partly because these new regimes and codes of living were connected to broader social acceptability. To contravene these standards risked social embarrassment and shame. One manifestation of this was a less authoritarian regime to the integration of youth in the GAA. Another was appealing more strongly on the grounds of 'individual' values and needs of younger people. It is also important to reiterate that this was not a linear process. It was marked with reversals and ambivalence at times. Nonetheless, the overall trajectory when viewed in the long term is one of change in the balance between social and self-restraint in the direction of the latter and diminishing displays of superiority.

NOTES

1. The Irish Free State became officially recognised as the Republic of Ireland in 1949.
2. By 2010 the central administrative unit of the GAA comprised the following communications and media functions: 'brand manager'; 'director of communications'; 'communications manager'; and 'director of commercial and marketing' (GAA, 2010).

3. Interestingly RTÉ promised this would not be repeated. Any future previewing of GAA games would be from the RTÉ studios.
4. The Nation can refer to both the Republic of Ireland and the whole of Ireland. Indeed, people can experience positive we-feelings towards both.

REFERENCES

Boyle, R. (1992). From our Gaelic fields: Radio, sport and nation in post-partition Ireland. *Media, Culture and Society, 14*(4), 623–636.

Connolly, J., & Dolan, P. (2012). Sport, media and the Gaelic Athletic Association: The quest for the 'youth' of Ireland. *Media, Culture & Society, 34*(4), 407–423.

Cronin, M. (1999). *Sport and nationalism in Ireland: Gaelic games, soccer and Irish identity since 1884.* Dublin: Four Courts Press.

Curran, C. (2015). *The development of sport in Donegal, 1880–1935.* Cork: Cork University Press.

Dolan, P. (2005). *The development of consumer culture, subjectivity and national identity in Ireland, 1900–1980.* PhD thesis, Goldsmiths College, University of London, London.

Dolan, P. (2009). Developing consumer subjectivity in Ireland: 1900–1980. *Journal of Consumer Culture, 9*(1), 117–141.

Elias, N. (2010). *The society of individuals* (Rev. ed.). Dublin: University College Dublin Press.

Elias, N., & Dunning, E. (2008). *Quest for excitement: Sport and leisure in the civilising process* (Rev. ed.). Dublin: University College Dublin Press.

Elias, N., & Scotson, J. L. (2008). *The established and the outsiders* (Rev. ed.). Dublin: University College Dublin Press.

Fulton, G., & Bairner, A. (2007). Sport, space and national identity in Ireland: The GAA, Croke Park and rule 42. *Space and Polity, 11*(1), 55–74.

GAA. (1936). *Minutes of annual congress.* Dublin: GAA.

GAA. (1945). *Minutes of annual congress.* Dublin: GAA.

GAA. (1946). *Minutes of annual congress.* Dublin: GAA.

GAA. (1951). *An comhdháil bhliantúil.* Dublin: GAA.

GAA. (1960). *Minutes of annual congress.* Dublin: GAA.

GAA. (1969). *Minutes of annual convention of Ulster council.* Dublin: GAA.

GAA. (1971). *Report of the commission on the GAA.* Dublin: GAA.

GAA. (1972). *Minutes of annual convention of Ulster council.* Dublin: GAA.

GAA. (1974). *Minutes of annual congress.* Dublin: GAA.

GAA. (1977). *Minutes of annual congress.* Dublin: GAA.

GAA. (1985). *Manual for county committees and provincial councils.* Dublin: GAA.

GAA. (2010). *An comhdháil bhliantúil.* Dublin: GAA.

Garnham, N. (2004a). Accounting for the early success of the Gaelic Athletic Association. *Irish Historical Studies, 34*(133), 65–78.

Garnham, N. (2004b). *Association football and society in pre-partition Ireland.* Belfast: Ulster Historical Foundation.

Hunt, T. (2008). *Sport and society in Victorian Ireland: The case of Westmeath.* Cork: Cork University Press.

Kelly, S. (2007). *Rule 42 and all that.* Dublin: Gill & Macmillan.

Mac Lua, B. (1967). *The steadfast rule.* Dublin: Cuchulainn Press Ltd.

Mandle, W. F. (1987). *The Gaelic Athletic Association and Irish nationalist politics, 1884–1924.* Dublin: Gill & Macmillan.

McCabe, C. (2011). *Football Sports Weekly* and Irish soccer, 1925–1928. *Media History, 17*(2), 147–158.

McDevitt, P. F. (1997). Muscular Catholicism: Nationalism, masculinity and Gaelic team sports, 1884–1916. *Gender & History, 9*(2), 262–284.

McElligott, R. (2013). *Forging a kingdom: The GAA in Kerry 1884–1934.* Wilton, Cork: Collins Press.

Moore, C. (2012). *The GAA v Douglas Hyde: The removal of Ireland's first president as GAA patron.* Cork: Collins Press.

Ó hAnnrachain, T. (2008). The heroic importance of sport: The GAA in the 1930s. *International Journal of the History of Sport, 25*(10), 1326–1337.

Ó Maonaigh, A. (2017). 'Who were the shoneens?': Irish militant nationalists and association football, 1913–1923. *Soccer & Society, 18*(5–6), 631–647.

O'Callaghan, L. (2011). *Rugby in Munster: A social and cultural history.* Cork: Cork University Press.

O'Callaghan, L. (2013). Rugby football and identity politics in Free State Ireland. *Éire-Ireland, 48*(1–2), 148–167.

O'Connor, R., & Whelan, B. (1971). *Attitudes of young people to games and pastimes.* Dublin: Economic and Social Research Institute.

Rouse, P. (1993). The politics of culture and sport in Ireland: A history of the GAA ban on foreign games 1884–1971. *International Journal of the History of Sport, 10*(3), 333–360.

Toms, D. (2015). *Soccer in Munster: A social history, 1877–1937.* Cork: Cork University Press.

Tynan, M. P. (2013). *Association football and Irish society during the inter-war period, 1918–1939.* PhD thesis, University of Ireland, Maynooth, Maynooth.

Wouters, C. (2007). *Informalization.* London: Sage.

CHAPTER 8

Cultural Hybridisation as an Essentialising Strategy: The Development of a New Sport—International Rules Football

HYBRID SPORTS AND REPRESENTATION

In this chapter we examine the attempts of GAA administrators and players to build hybrid versions of football as a means of creating the honour of international representation through national sport. There is an irony here of course in that Gaelic games have historically been promoted as symbols of the 'true' Gael (see also Chap. 7) through their very uniqueness in the world of sport. Though Gaelic football itself can be considered a form of hybrid activity, in that its rules were influenced, either through emulation or deliberate distinction, by other sports and leisure pursuits already in existence. As we illustrate in Chap. 2, all sports are in fact processes, changing over time to accommodate rising moral principles or to meet shifting expectations of excitement. Despite the perceived distinctiveness of Gaelic football, various people connected with the sport sought or embraced the opportunity to emulate other sports regularly played as international contests in terms of their capacity to represent the nation. They did this through the identification of another 'indigenous' code of football—Australian Rules football (this name is more recent, as the game was first played in Melbourne, then in other areas of Victoria, which remains a stronghold for the sport (McConville & Hess, 2012, p. 2361))— itself seen as unique to its country of 'birth', Australia. The fact that these codes somewhat resembled each other allowed for the construction of a composite hybrid code. But the uniqueness of both codes, less in the substance of the play and rules, and more in the geographical limits of

J. Connolly, P. Dolan, *Gaelic Games in Society*, Palgrave Studies on Norbert Elias, https://doi.org/10.1007/978-3-030-31699-0_8

where they were played, meant that both organisations controlling their codes in their respective territories entered a kind of double bind. The hybrid sport could not expand because no other countries played a similar kind of football. Representation could only be achieved through playing a new sport, not Gaelic football, against one other nation, Australia.

Cultural Hybridisation

Nederveen Pieterse (2009) writes of globalisation as global mélange, a mixing of pre-existing cultural forms into new hybrids based on interaction and interdependence. Such hybridisation can entail new organisational frameworks to govern new practices and sets of social relations (p. 73), though we argue here that essentialising tendencies prohibit the emergence of such forms where the hybrid cultural form is intentionally created to further the interests and cultural policies of the constituent organisations. This acts as a cultural barrier, or 'drag effect' (Elias, 2010, pp. 188–190), preventing the advance towards a higher level of organisational integration. Hybridity assumes both difference and similarity in that the distinction between the pre-existing constituent elements are recognisable, thereby facilitating mixture by definition, but also similar enough to invite comparison (Nederveen Pieterse, 2009, p. 83). Nederveen Pieterse also notes that the elements becoming part of a new hybrid are themselves likely to be historical hybrids, though their very hybridity could be forgotten. The normalisation of the new compound creates a kind of cultural amnesia permitting the cultural practice or form to flourish. But we argue that the prospects of such amnesia and the creation of an established hybrid as a relatively autonomous social practice depend on the initial intentions of the participants involved in such hybridisation processes. Ironically the intention of creating and maintaining an explicit cultural hybrid diminishes its long-term appeal; this is an unintended consequence of such efforts.

The failure to recognise the provenance of different elements that constitute cultural practices is often central to the indigenisation process (Holton, 2000, p. 151). Hybrid practices are created as part of a broader nationalising or unifying process, either to symbolically represent a new plane of social integration at a higher level, such as a federation, or one at a lower level, such as an ethnic or national group seceding from such a broader federation. Prior hybridity is removed from collective memory, or never acknowledged in the first instance, in order to preserve the myth of purity (Gilroy, 2000). Also, new cultural hybrids are no guarantee of cosmopolitan openness and the decline of essentialism, as Morris (2010) shows in relation to music that hybrids can assume an essentialising form over time, such as country music and its signification of whiteness. Rather, essentialism and hybridity can exist in tension.

As Nederveen Pieterse (2001, p. 220) notes, hybridity only merits attention to the extent that prior boundaries have been essentialised, and therefore draw attention upon their trespass or transgression. So hybridisation is based on prior conditions of indigenisation, and this relates specifically in our case to the development of 'native' sports in Ireland and Australia during the nineteenth century—Gaelic football and Australian Rules football. Though the games were based on regional and national boundaries, thereby facilitating subsequent hybridisation, both sports have entailed some limited degree of diffusion. However, this has largely been based on emigrant groups continuing cultural practices in host countries, with some attempts at promoting the games within the local population.

Elias (2018b, p. 131) does use the word hybridisation to refer to the mixture of models and standards from different social ranks which produces new sports. The potential and degree of hybridisation between class-specific models and standards was also related to the social distance and ease of relations between classes, which is why sportisation advanced more in Britain than in France (see also Dolan, 2018; Elias, 2018a). Such groups were already in the same state territory and enmeshed in multiple forms of interdependence. Though changing, the balance of mutual dependencies, and therefore of power, still favoured the upper classes at the time most folk games were transformed into more regulated and standardised sports. These conditions did not pertain in the hybridisation process involving two established sporting organisations from distinct geographic and political territories. They needed each other to produce a hybrid game both could play to represent their countries and codes, but the function of national representation was also partly served by the belief in the cultural uniqueness of their national codes in the first instance. So the international relationship could be considered fragile, as well as exclusive in that no other sporting organisation could join the social network, or at least this has not been envisaged so far. Efforts to present the hybrid game with some degree of authenticity to some extent rested on the search for common origins of the two footballing codes, but as ever with such myths these efforts reveal more about the present than the past.

ORIGIN MYTHS

Australian Rules football (like other forms of football) is also likely to be a hybrid of different games brought to Australia during the nineteenth century from Ireland and Britain. Tom Wills, a former pupil at Rugby, is generally considered as the main founder of the sport, as he led a small group in devising rules in 1859 (McConville & Hess, 2012). McConville and Hess claim that the main influence in the establishment of the Victorian game were immigrants from Ireland rather than England, though Hibbins (1992) asserts an English origin. The contested origin of the sport in historical accounts lends credence to its very hybridity—new immigrants from different parts of Britain and Ireland had to construct a common game that all could play with some degree of established familiarity. Hay (2014) points out that early historians of the sport attributed its genesis to Irish folk football (known as 'caid'), and indeed reproduces 1840 newspaper accounts of a game played by Irishmen resembling this early form of what would become Gaelic football. Hay (2010) supports Blainey's contention that there is no clear lineage between Gaelic football and Australian Rules football, as many variants were combined, and that the focus on origin myths obscures the fact that the game developed as a process. For example, one of the characteristic features of modern Australian Rules football is the high mark, though this only became a common feature from the 1870s, while scrummaging was more common in earlier decades (Collins, 2011). The myth of aboriginal origins accompanied the transformation from the Victorian Football League to the Australian Football League in 1990 (p. 12), indicating that traditions are often invented to suit current social and cultural imperatives rather than transparent reflections of historical facts. Collins also claims that the myth of Gaelic descent spread due to Australian resentment at British restrictions on Commonwealth immigration following the decision to seek membership of the European Economic Community (EEC) (p. 14).

Syson (2013, p. 461) compares this sporting origin myth to a circular logic, whereby a game is identified through archival research of newspapers and other sources and the resemblance to some modern code of football ensures a clear lineage is drawn. Thus descriptive similarities usher in historical narratives. As Syson shows, several current Australian Rules football clubs played a game similar to soccer when they were first established. As Elias (2006, p. 249) notes: 'Nothing is more fruitless, when dealing with long-term social processes, than to attempt to locate an abso-lute beginning.' Of course origin myths can still be meaningful to social actors involved in cultural practices, particularly if such practices have been endowed with symbolic significance or shared rituals concerning various forms of identification like the nation. Indeed the development of 'International Rules' football (also known as 'Compromise Rules') was driven in large part as a vehicle of national prestige and representation for players of football codes hitherto excluded from such national representa-tion (Cronin, 1998).

Sportisation of International Rules Football

While the first official international matches between Ireland and Australia, following a set of rules combining both codes and agreed by the respective governing organisations, did not begin until 1984, there were challenge matches in the late 1960s between an Australian selection and prominent Gaelic county teams. From 1984, on an intermittent rather than necessar-ily annual basis, the games consisted of a series of two or three matches taking place over several weeks between an Australian selection and an Irish selection and played in one country, alternating for the next series. In the late 1960s, there was also a strong entrepreneurial element to these initial cultural encounters, as the project was largely promoted by the Australian broadcaster and former football umpire Harry Beitzel (Cronin, 1998). He had seen a touring Gaelic football team play the sport in Australia, and became convinced that an Australian selection of players could play Gaelic football due to some similarities in the codes—both codes permit ball handling as well as kicking, there is no offside, and both have a reputation for strong physicality (though unlike the Gaelic code, Australian Rules football allows a form of tackling with some similarities to tackling in rugby). Challenge matches between the then All-Ireland foot-ball championship winners, Meath, and an Australian selection occurred in 1967 in Ireland and again in 1968 in Australia. The game played was a slightly modified version of Gaelic football. This 'discovery' of similarity by Beitzel is another example of originating mythology at work, though in this case from the mind of a single individual. There is, however, evidence of the GAA president suggesting the development of cultural links with the Australian game from 1964, where the governing body agreed to invite an Australian Rules team (at that time a Victorian Rules team, of course) to Ireland (*Irish Times*, 25 May 1983).

The idea of playing international matches on a more official footing re-emerged in the 1980s. Similar to the sportisation process of other football codes, the two organisations had to agree upon a standardised rule and game structure in order for any matches to proceed. However, the problem of establishing composite rules is that one side or the other can subsequently claim the game is really 'not our game' and therefore the sense of national prestige or shame at the outcome of matches can be diminished (Cronin, 1998, p. 182). Furthermore, the attempt at hybridity (and it was often described as a 'hybrid game' in media reports) was undermined by the very labelling of the new sport as 'international' or 'composite'. Clearly it was devised as an instrument of international competition rather than as a new cultural practice in its own right. The sport could not obtain relative cultural autonomy from the constituting cultural elements. Despite these in-built limitations, players and organisers alike from both codes were drawn in part by the felt desire to transcend the national enclaves and boundaries of their pursuits. Eriksen (2007) notes that the development of 'indigenous' sports like Gaelic football enable a form of cultural nationalism and local pride, and ecologically such sports make sense in the context of cultural globalisation; they are survival strategies. But from a figurational perspective, such sporting organisations and participants act within a fluid social network involving other sports, some played on international stages, thereby attracting greater financial reward or stronger emotional we-identification assuming the integration plane of the nation is imbued with stronger feelings than that of the subnational county, town or region (of course, this may not always be the case). All sports exist in a figuration together, competing, and collaborating occasionally, for the attentions of new recruits and existing participants who may become attracted to other sports. This creates a status emulation between sporting codes, and participants seek the kind of cultural and economic rewards visible in other practices. This figurational dynamic propelled the governance bodies in Ireland and Australia to seek a hybrid practice together—international cooperation borne of intra-national competition.

This sportisation of International Rules football shows some parallels with accounts by Elias, Dunning and others (Dunning & Sheard, 2005; Elias & Dunning, 2008) in relation to rugby and soccer, particularly concerning the process of rule refinement and standardisation, as well as efforts to make the sport less violent over time. But International Rules did not develop from earlier folk versions which had quite loose, flexible and limited rules. Here, rule standardisation, or one could refer to the process as norm stabilisation in the cultural sense, involved the effective suppression of early forms of football through superior organisation and social control. The hybridisation process in this instance involved the selective combination of rules from two well-established and already sportised cultural practices within their respective territories. Rules for playing both Gaelic football and Australian Rules football were already more or less standardised and known by all participants. The national codes had acquired a high level of emotional significance as marks of national distinction, and so could not be simply replaced by a new standardised code. This was not the intention of the organisers, as the hybrid game was invented to provide an opportunity for international competition and thus emulate other global sports. So the hybrid code not only provided a platform for competition between two nations, but also between two pre-existing cultural codes of sporting practice, both also inflected with collective feelings of pride precisely based on the indigenous nature of the practice. Whereas most sports are played on the basis of common norms and standards of conduct on the field, this hybrid code involved a conflict of codes and norms. It was not simply a conflict between practitioners dedicated to the same cultural pursuit, but conflict based on divergent codes.

Both organisations—GAA and Australian Football League (AFL) — comprise a double-bind figuration due to the lack of substitutes. Their games are similar enough to permit hybridisation, and other sporting organisations within a broader field of similarity already operate at the international level of competition. There are other dependences within the figuration, reflecting broader international dependences. The development of the hybrid game has encouraged Australian Rules scouts to observe Gaelic footballers with a view to recruitment to the Australian game. Thus the collaboration between the two bodies also encompasses tensions and contradictions. In order to illustrate these processes, we present evidence from newspapers in both Ireland and Australia that traces the development of the code, and the varying responses to its implementation.

Hybridity as National We-Feeling

While in Ireland the hybrid game tends to be viewed from an Irish perspective, and particularly in terms of its impact on Gaelic football and footballers, it has also been warmly received in Australia as a vehicle for the expression of their national game. Both journalists and players expressed enthusiasm at the prospect of national representation:

It gives our players the chance to represent their country and, if you think the test series is small beer compared to other team sports, try telling that to the Australians who have played in previous tests in Ireland. (*Herald Sun*, 1 November 1990)

Andrew McLeod, a first-time All-Australian,[1] 'expressed equal delight in "having the opportunity to represent my country in my sport"' (*The Advertiser*, 16 September 1998). Here we see an example of the contradiction of playing international sport through a recently and deliberately invented hybrid code on the basis of displaying athletic prowess in another national code of football. Representing one's country at one's sport meant the hybrid code became a means towards this end, and suffered from a lack of relative cultural autonomy, and perhaps ultimately a deficit of respect as a code in itself. If we think of a code as an expected or desirable way of conducting oneself, in this case on the field of play, then the pursuit of that could become largely instrumental and secondary when viewed through the primary lens of another code. Prospective coaches of the national sides also interpreted representation in terms of both country and code: 'I've always had this burning desire to represent my country and when it comes to our game, this is it' (Leigh Matthews, Australian team coach, quoted in *The Age*, 6 October 1998).

The function of the hybrid game to represent distinct national football codes also facilitated displays of national superiority based on the competing national codes. The nation, at a relatively high level of social integration invested with strong feelings of belonging, pride and mutual destiny, was of greater significance than allegiance to a new hybrid game. The limited respect for the game, relative to the more established codes, also meant that transgression of rules was subject to less shameful experiences, compared to the potential feelings of pride evoked by victory for one's country and code. The fact that the rules were new and shifting, and from the perspective of players not necessarily 'our' rules anyway, exacerbated this tendency towards transgression and limited the prospect of 'advancing thresholds of shame' (Elias, 2012) about displays of aggression during matches. However, for some commentators outside the game, such national displays of aggression at least brought reflection:

The dangers of belligerent Australian nationalism have never been demonstrated better than in Perth last Saturday. Rather than interpret the contest as an opportunity to develop an exciting new game and foster international goodwill, we choose to demonstrate to the Irish, and more particularly our-selves, that we possess all the masculine virtues. But haven't we let ourselves down? (Brent Crosswell quoted in *Irish Times*, 16 October 1986)

Indeed it is revealing that an Irish journalist, Paddy Downey, sought out the reactions of Australian commentators in Australian newspapers, in this case Brent Crosswell, a former Australian Rules footballer. As the new game was following newly established norms, those commentating on games were keen to assess their own evaluations in a comparative context with others, trying to see the spectacle from the perspective of those some-what connected with the other side. For those closer to the action and more directly involved as players, managers or administrators, reactions tended to be more defensive of their own group and belittling of the other group, particularly in the face of perceived moral condemnation from members of that national group. After an Australian victory in the 1986 matches, the Australian manager referred to the Irish players as

a bloody crowd of wimps ... They'd make great soccer players ... but wouldn't have a hope of making the grade in Australian Rules. They're not tough enough to handle a real game. (Todd quoted in *Irish Times*, 20 October 1986)

Though this occurred in the social context of Irish journalists question-ing the conduct of the Australian players, Todd went on to refer to an attempted kick by an Irish player at an Australian as 'the lowest form of any foul act in Australian Rules' (*Irish Times*, 20 October 1986). This indicates the tendency to view the hybrid game through the lens of the more established national code of one side only. The characterisation of soccer players as more effeminate was perhaps a familiar insult to the Irish, as Gaelic football was often presented as more manly than soccer.

Where opposing players were deemed to have played with honour and dignity, despite occasional displays of violence, then it was possible to con-fer status upon the victors. But even then the prestige was given in the context of one's own national code. Eugene McGee (the Irish coach) said to the Australian players after their test victory:

You have enhanced the game of Gaelic football and entranced the Irish people with your whole attitude. The overall impression is that a great deal of good has been done for both codes of football and you can be proud. (McGee quoted in *Irish Times*, 2 November 1987)

Journalists too noted the tendency to view the new sport as an opportunity to display the virtues of the constituent codes: 'Neither country is
fond of the "compromise" tag that undermines the claims made for the
authenticity of the sport. But it remains, at heart, a showcase for two
domestic sports rich in pride and history' (Duggan, *Irish Times*, 14
October 2000).

The respect for the game was limited by this tendency to view it as not
'our' game. Loss could be attributed to the imagined bias in the rules
towards the other code. This was particularly the case from the Australian
perspective, and perhaps diminished the indignity of potentially losing to
amateur players:

> Irish team manager Kevin Heffernan blamed much of the friction on a con-
> fusion among players about the composite code, which owes more to Gaelic
> than Australian rules except for allowing a limited form of tackling which
> produced some bewildering umpiring. (*The Advertiser*, 13 October 1986)
>
> The Irish are always negative, never positive, about this new game. You
> want to play the game all your way. We go on and make the best of it. If we
> could sort out our problems between us, we'd have a great game of football,
> and we've got to compromise. With the round ball the Irish have 75 per
> cent of the advantage. Put our oval ball in and see if you can adapt to it, as
> we do to yours. (Todd [Australian team coach] quoted in *Irish Times*, 20
> October 1986)

When the International Rules series resumed in 1998, after a break
since 1990, the Australian coach Leigh Matthews also referred to the sport
as 'their' game:

> We know which game it's like and it's not ours … We hope our blokes are
> bigger and stronger but, when it comes to ball skills, our blokes have han-
> dled that ball about eight times in their life … Thank heavens we can tackle
> them because otherwise it's not our game. (quoted in *The Age*, 6
> October 1998)

Again in 2002, the Australian coach Garry Lyon affirmed his pride in
the Australian players as 'they are playing a game that is so foreign to
them' (quoted in *Irish Times*, 14 October 2002).

There were also dissenting voices in Ireland, among them Mickey
Harte, the highly successful manager of the County Tyrone Gaelic
football team:

We are engaging in a so-called international series, and yet it's not Gaelic games. Why should we pursue that when we have a wonderful product of our own that we could just as easily be pursuing worldwide? For me that's the criminal thing. ... these players are not representing Ireland in Gaelic games. We seem to forget that. (quoted in *Irish Times*, 26 October 2006)

For Harte, the focus by GAA administrators on the hybrid game necessarily detracted attention away from the global promotion of the national game of Gaelic football. Through sustained emigration over generations, many GAA clubs had emerged throughout much of the world (Darby, 2009; Darby & Hassan, 2008). Harte also did not see Gaelic footballers as representing the national code of Gaelic football simply because they were playing a new hybrid sport. Whether from an Irish or Australian perspective, and irrespective of the reasons, the act of increasing the cultural distance to the hybrid code inhibited the development of an emotional attachment to the new code as a potential object and ritual of collective effervescence (see Durkheim, 2001) and we-group representation.

The very hybridity of the sport, and the fact that this could not be forgotten in the context of its function to serve the representation of two constituent codes, contributed to ongoing tensions between those comprising the GAA and AFL—the various administrators, players and coaches.

Tensions and Cultural Perspectives

From the beginning of the hybrid code there was consistent confusion over the rules of the sport, particularly in relation to tackling and releasing the ball. While the rules were framed by representatives of both sporting organisations, no new governance structure emerged beyond occasional disciplinary committees to deal with severe breaches of the rules in the form of violent conduct on the field. The new sport became a cultural code without a supporting social organisation to sustain it. Though the hybrid was ostensibly under the control of both the GAA and AFL, the primary function of both organisations was to regulate and promote their own national codes, and as we have seen these divergent perspectives shaped the ongoing interpretation of the hybrid sport. What was acceptable in one code could be deemed unacceptable in another, or the codes could differ in their latitude of acceptable conduct and indeed the latitude of acceptable reactions to perceived breaches of expected conduct.

This led to outcomes that were unusual in either code, such as five players being dismissed by referees in a single match due to 'a series of flare-ups that marred an at times confusing code of Gaelic and Australian rules' (*The Advertiser*, 13 October 1986). The international matches have both an Australian and Irish referee on the pitch at the same time, again indicating the impossibility of nominating a neutral referee for a sport that nobody else plays. All sporting rules are open to interpretation, but confusion is likely to increase with more than one source of discipline and authority on the field. The definition of fair play or fair physical encounters between players also floundered on divergent interpretations of conduct deemed normal in one code but not in another: 'Although Australia won by a point, a difference of opinion on what constitutes a tackle resulted in the all-in brawl' (*The Australian*, 13 October 1998). Following the same match, the Irish coach Colm O'Rourke lamented the lack of clarity over the degree of physical interaction permitted between players: 'I know the Australians would say that's tough luck, but we need a fairly clearly defined line in the rough-house stakes—if the series is to continue (the rules) will have to be a bit more clear-cut' (quoted in *The Australian*, 13 October 1998). O'Rourke himself had played in an earlier series of the hybrid game, and yet was unclear of the permissible degree of aggression on the field. This was partly due to the changing nature of the rules precisely because of the continued violence on the field, and also to maintain a degree of unpredictability and excitement in the sport for spectators. If little physical contact was permitted the stronger Australians were unlikely to win, yet if too much was allowed they would nearly always win, while the Irish players would suffer defeat as well as injury.

Journalists, such as Keith Duggan, were critical of the game because of its imagined artificiality:

> But it is still hard to see it as anything other than a game that is annually forced into being rather than a sport that has evolved naturally. If International Rules (which sounds likes [sic] a United Nations term) is a game at all, then it is a game without soul. (*Irish Times*, 28 October 2006)

The question of authenticity in sport is sometimes invoked in contrast to hybridity. Historically many sports contained elements from other sports, and so the search for purity in sport is largely misguided. In the case of the International Rules hybrid sport, the problem is that players, spectators and commentators are unlikely ever to forget its hybridity.

Supporters and players of more established sports forget the hybrid history of such sports, or they are simply passed from one generation to the next without any word of their mixed heritage. As this mingling and refining process occurs over many generations, the 'authenticity' of particular sports is an aspect of the sport's longevity and its relative autonomy from other sports. Such relative autonomy developed many years ago, and since then its games are played by children over many countries and regions. International Rules has not achieved, and more than likely will never achieve a sufficient degree of autonomy from its constituent codes to enable its promotion on a widespread scale to children in schools and clubs. This too sustains the collective confusion regarding its rules, as people never internalise the rules so that playing feels 'natural'.

So an element of 'authenticity' in sport is the deeply internalised memory of particular sports so that they seem second nature to players and spectators alike. The infrequency of matches played under International Rules meant that the rules themselves had to be communicated through the media prior to each series of matches between Ireland and Australia. Changes to rules brought about by attempts to diminish violence or heighten the unpredictability of the likely winners also required repeated communication of rules for the benefit of spectators, both those attending matches and those watching on television. In more established sports, journalists do not state the rules of the game; this would be entirely superfluous given spectators' familiarity with the sport through repeated viewing and indeed playing from early childhood.

Habitus Formation and Athletic We-Feelings

When children learn to play a sport from childhood, this learning becomes embodied as second nature. This habitus formation ensures that people know how to conduct themselves by and large through habit, and each player normally behaves in terms of 'mutually expected self-restraint' (Goudsblom cited in Wouters, 1987, p. 422). Of course transgressions occur, as people generate greater emotional intensity through competition and conflict (Elias & Dunning, 2008), but these become rarer as players internalise the rules and customs of particular sports. The difficulty with the playing of International Rules is its very infrequency and its more or less complete monopolisation by elite adult players. The sport is not governed by a relatively autonomous organisation, and so there is no social or sporting infrastructure to nurture and develop the game from one generation to the next. Gaelic football players acquire a sporting habitus attuned to Gaelic football primarily through immersion in training and playing from an early age. Likewise, Australian Rules players acquire their distinct sporting habitus, with the added factor that theirs is highly specialised and central to their identity as professional sportsmen. While people can learn to play different sports, the ease of conduct shaped by the habitus formed in childhood is likely to emerge in situations requiring quick reactions. The two footballing codes of Gaelic football and Australian Rules entail different uses of the body and therefore different physical skills concerning kicking, catching, marking, handling, tackling, and even fouling. While fouling is obviously against the rules, in most sports players learn to circumvent rules to some extent for the sake of advancing the winning chances of the team.

Journalists noted the tendency of Irish players not to release the ball after tackles, which led to frustration on the part of the Australian players as well as 'angry clashes' (*Irish Times*, 7 October 1987):

> After all their practice the Irish players are still unable to tackle in the manner of the Australians. The tactics they used were too often those of Gaelic football while the Australians used every ploy and stratagem allowed in the hybrid code. (*Irish Times*, 2 November 1987)

Even by 2004 players expressed a lack of knowledge regarding the use of the tackle:

> The physical aspect has lessened in recent years. But you know if they hit you right in a one-on-one, it will hurt because we don't really know how to deal with those tackles yet and the fact is they are just in better shape than us by virtue of being professional. (Padraic Joyce [an Irish player] quoted in *Irish Times*, 16 October 2004)

As well as different skill requirements due to its hybrid nature, the new sport also entailed a different game flow and rhythm, which necessitated an adaptation of playing conduct. It proved difficult to attune to this conduct given the prevailing and deeply ingrained sporting habitus developed through playing the constituent codes. The Australian players engaged in a

> succession of fouls under the composite rules agreed for this series, but it is only fair to assume many of their infringements were instinctive rather than deliberate. It must also be said the Irish players invited crunching tackles

many times because of their tendency to dally in possession of the ball, espe-cially when they chose to play on after taking a "mark". (*Irish Times*, 22 October 1984)

Taking a mark is an option in Australian Rules whereby a player who catches the ball cleanly before interference from another player can claim a 'free' kick. This option did not exist in Gaelic football at the time,[2] so Irish players reverted to their 'natural' playing style. This style was carried into the hybrid game in other respects, such as the preferred mode of keeping possession of the ball: 'While the Australians again moved the ball quickly from man to man, either by hand or foot, the Irish players were often bogged down in the holding, carrying tactics of Gaelic' (*Irish Times*, 5 November 1984).

From the relatively detached (see Elias, 2007) perspective of journal-ists, it was clear to see an appropriate strategy and course of action to maximise the chances of success in the sport. During preparations for the 1998 series in Ireland, the ball was identified as 'the Gaelic variety' by an Australian journalist and for this reason difficult for the Australian players to control:

> The further out from goal they were, the more errant their kicking.
> Which is the biggest adjustment the Australians face. Modern football demands that players retain possession with short disposal by hand and foot, but their primal instinct remains to kick the ball long when in the clear. But in the composite game, that is a low-percentage play that invariably results in turnovers. Short kicks will be the order of the day at Croke Park, no mat-ter what the situation. (*The Age*, 6 October 1998)

Because of the function of the hybrid sport to represent the uniqueness of the constituent codes, as well as the infrequency of matches and the amateur and professional status of the Irish and Australian players respec-tively, little sense of mutual identification of the players as practitioners of the same pursuit emerged. This common we-feeling, despite the central aspect of competition, is often present in more established sports, so that players and observers alike can claim, for example, that 'rugby was the real winner'. The international dependences between the Irish and Australians facilitated the development of the hybrid sport, but only as an instrument of national distinction and representation. Each side used the other side to express the 'we'—using a they-group (see Elias, 2010, p. 186) to glorify the we-group. This lack of emotional identification to each other and to the hybrid sport diminished the prospect of developing a more integrated sporting habitus and also of adhering closely to the rules of the sport for fear of experiencing shame at transgressing codes of conduct or even at publicly displaying lack of knowledge about the hybrid sport. The athletic pride of the players revolved around their competence at their game:

> Our strength will be kicking the round ball, and that's where the Aussies would be at a serious disadvantage. They are used to kicking straight but we can kick around the corner, put a bit of spin on it and bend it. (Colm O'Rourke quoted in *The Weekend Australian*, 10 October 1998)

CONCLUSION

The development of International Rules football remains an interesting case of cultural innovation based on a top-down process of hybridisation from the administrators of two distinct codes of football. Many sports are hybrids in the sense that they have developed over time accommodating various elements from existing folk games and even other relatively standardised sports. But here the two distinct codes were already highly standardised and also served as symbols of national distinction and emotional identification. In that context the hybrid sport remained secondary to the primary constituent codes, for which the innovators were responsible for growing through club infrastructures in their respective territories. Within Ireland there were already two distinct national sports within Gaelic games—football and hurling—and local clubs continue to play both sports. Children can learn and play both but social pressure towards specialisation often emerges in the case of talented players coveted for representation in the favoured code within the club and county structure. Within Australia the singular code of Australian Rules is also played at local clubs, and nurtured during childhood, but talented players are channelled towards professionalism. Within these national contexts, the hybrid sport has little opportunity to occupy space and time within local club structures. Therefore the game remains primarily an adult-only elite sport played at international level very infrequently.

The conscious and intentional hybridity of the sport exacerbates difference, in the context of irregular performance (each instance is as likely to be compared to different national codes as to previous encounters involving the compromise code), and generally adult-only play, thereby undermining the level of sporting we-identification around the compromise code, as well as the potential of the new code to represent national we-identification as neither side is playing 'our' game.

The distinct national codes serve as frameworks for players, spectators, administrators and journalists for the interpretation of International Rules, so that the hybrid game cannot escape its hybridity—it cannot be forgotten where the sport comes from, and so it becomes less likely to function as an object of mutual attention and focus to generate emotional rituals of social solidarity in the sporting sense. The lack of frequency of games emphasises hybridity, and diminishes the prospect of narrative to build emotional tension. The need to maintain or generate spectator excitement means games should become even and unpredictable, but this requires frequent rule changes, potentially identified as favouring one side or the other thereby reducing the chances of collective ownership of the sport. The sport can be disavowed as 'their' game, so it never really becomes 'our' game, a sport beyond rivalry and competition that can be followed for its own sake.

Notes

1. At the end of every season a panel selects a team of players deemed best in their position in Australian Rules football; in the history of international rules it has been mainly All-Australian players who were considered for selection.
2. A version of the mark was introduced into Gaelic football in 2016.

References

Collins, T. (2011). The invention of sporting tradition: National myths, imperial pasts and the origins of Australian Rules football. In S. Wagg (Ed.), *Myths and milestones in the history of sport* (pp. 8–31). Basingstoke: Palgrave Macmillan.

Cronin, M. (1998). 'When the world soccer cup is played on roller skates': The attempt to make Gaelic games international: The Meath–Australia matches of 1967–1968. *Immigrants & Minorities, 17*(1), 170–188.

Darby, P. (2009). *Gaelic games, nationalism and the Irish diaspora in the United States.* Dublin: University College Dublin Press.

Darby, P., & Hassan, D. (Eds.). (2008). *Emigrant players: Sport and the Irish diaspora.* Abingdon: Routledge.

Dolan, P. (2018). Class relations and the development of boxing: Norbert Elias on sportisation processes in England and France. In J. Haut, P. Dolan, D. Reicher,

& R. Sánchez García (Eds.), *Excitement processes: Norbert Elias's unpublished works on sports, leisure, body, culture* (pp. 235–254). Wiesbaden: Springer.

Dunning, E., & Sheard, K. (2005). *Barbarians, gentlemen and players: A sociological study of the development of rugby football* (2nd ed.). London: Routledge.

Durkheim, É. (2001). *The elementary forms of religious life* (C. Cosman, Trans.). Oxford and New York: Oxford University Press.

Elias, N. (2006). *The court society* (Rev. ed.). Dublin: University College Dublin Press.

Elias, N. (2007). *Involvement and detachment* (Rev. ed.). Dublin: University College Dublin Press.

Elias, N. (2010). *The society of individuals* (Rev. ed.). Dublin: University College Dublin Press.

Elias, N. (2012). *On the process of civilisation* (Rev. ed.). Dublin: University College Dublin Press.

Elias, N. (2018a). Boxing and duelling. In J. Haut, P. Dolan, D. Reicher, & R. S. García (Eds.), *Excitement processes: Norbert Elias's unpublished works on sports, leisure, body, culture* (pp. 173–215). Wiesbaden: Springer.

Elias, N. (2018b). Fragments on sportisation. In J. Haut, P. Dolan, D. Reicher, & R. S. García (Eds.), *Excitement processes: Norbert Elias's unpublished works on sports, leisure, body, culture* (pp. 121–136). Wiesbaden: Springer.

Elias, N., & Dunning, E. (2008). *Quest for excitement: Sport and leisure in the civilising process* (Rev. ed.). Dublin: University College Dublin Press.

Eriksen, T. H. (2007). Steps to an ecology of transnational sports. *Global Networks, 7*(2), 154–165.

Gilroy, P. (2000). *Between camps*. London: Penguin.

Hay, R. (2010). A tale of two footballs: The origins of Australian football and association football revisited. *Sport in Society, 13*(6), 952–969.

Hay, R. (2014). Football in Australia before codification, 1820–1860. *International Journal of the History of Sport, 31*(9), 1047–1061.

Hibbins, G. M. (1992). The Cambridge connection: The English origins of Australian Rules football. In J. A. Mangan (Ed.), *The cultural bond: Sport, empire, society* (pp. 108–128). London: Frank Cass.

Holton, R. (2000). Globalization's cultural consequences. *ANNALS of the American Academy of Political and Social Science, 570*(1), 140–152.

McConville, C., & Hess, R. (2012). Forging imperial and Australasian identities: Australian Rules football in New Zealand during the nineteenth century. *International Journal of the History of Sport, 29*(17), 2360–2371.

Morris, D. (2010). Hick-hop hooray? "Honky tonk badonkadonk," musical genre, and the misrecognitions of hybridity. *Critical Studies in Media Communication, 28*(5), 466–488.

Nederveen Pieterse, J. (2001). Hybridity, so what?: The anti-hybridity backlash and the riddles of recognition. *Theory, Culture & Society, 18*(2–3), 219–245.

Nederveen Pieterse, J. (2009). *Globalization and culture: Global mélange.* Lanham, MD: Rowman & Littlefield Publishers.

Syson, I. (2013). The 'chimera' of origins: Association football in Australia before 1880. *International Journal of the History of Sport, 30*(5), 453–468.

Wouters, C. (1987). Developments in the behavioural codes between the sexes: The formalization of informalization in the Netherlands, 1930–1985. *Theory, Culture & Society, 4*(2/3), 405–207.

CHAPTER 9

Conclusion: Some Thoughts on Contemporary Developments

Contemporary Developments

In a 1987 article, Elias coined the phrase 'retreat into the present'. It was meant to connote a particular trend—and one which has largely continued since Elias's observation—whereby sociologists no longer sought to use evidence from the past to understand and explain contemporary sociological problems. We allude to this here because of the focus of this concluding chapter which is largely framed around a discussion of several contemporary issues and developments concerning Gaelic games and the GAA. However, as we will illustrate, a concentration on present issues does not negate the past. Contemporary developments are shaped and informed by previous, and ongoing, social interdependences, many of which we document in this book.

Gender, Gaelic Games and a Developmental Approach

The inclusion of a section with the title gender in it, in the last chapter of this book, might be seen by some as yet again an example of the proverbial 'token gesture'. That is certainly not the case! The issue of gender is interwoven throughout the syntheses of several of the chapters of this book (Chaps. 2, 3, 5, 6 and 7). For example, a central aspect of our analysis and synthesis involved documenting and explaining changes in the structure of Irish society and changes in the habitus of Irish people (both men and

© The Author(s) 2020
J. Connolly, P. Dolan, *Gaelic Games in Society*, Palgrave Studies on Norbert Elias, https://doi.org/10.1007/978-3-030-31699-0_9

women). In some chapters it may appear that we deal more specifically with changes in the male habitus—as in Chap. 2 with male GAA players. But, following a figurational approach, attempting to explain changes in the male habitus simultaneously involves a concern with gender relations (Dunning & Maguire, 1996). Indeed, one of the changes in the structure of interdependence and power we allude to in that chapter is the structure of gender relations itself—although like all 'causal' processes this dynamic was itself interconnected and interwoven with other social processes. Indeed, we expand on this below in illustrating the interconnection between the emergence of less unequal gender relations in Ireland, the increasing stress on achievement striving and seriousness of involvement and the changing age profile of male inter-county GAA players. In suggesting that aspects of gender relations are interwoven within parts of the synthesis of this book, we are not claiming to have fully addressed all or perhaps many of the issues of gender in the study of Gaelic games and the GAA.[1] Quite clearly there is scope for further investigations on that front. The same too can be said about other developments which we have not addressed in this book such as the increasing participation of people of other nations across the world in Gaelic games.

Examining the extent of feminisation processes is more complex too. Although women's Gaelic games are governed by separate associations, women also make up a significant part of the spectator base for male Gaelic games and are involved in the administration of GAA units—though this, particularly, at the higher-tier units and functions remains male dominated. In that sense, there are different social indices for considering changes in women's involvement in Gaelic games. Clearly some of these suggest that the trajectory is towards greater levels of involvement and a rise in the functional importance of women's Gaelic games. They include increasing participation, such as in Ladies Gaelic football—from 80,000 members in 2005 (Liston, 2005) to 188,000 in 2017 (LGFA, 2017); increases in spectator attendance; and an increased media profile. The latter includes the relatively recent integration of female analysts on media programmes or segments addressing coverage of men's Gaelic games competitions. Of course in suggesting more even power relations we are not claiming that established–outsider dynamics do not still exist; indeed, the tilting in the power balance towards less unequal relations could also exacerbate tensions.

In several chapters in this book we noted the trend towards less unequal power relations which have developed between various social groups in Ireland over the course of the twentieth century and beyond, including that between the genders. And while this has reshaped the habitus of female GAA players (see also Liston, 2005), it has also led to changes in aspects of the male habitus. One reflection of the changing power balance and the greater feminisation of society has been the increasing role men have come to play in relation to family child care and the household more generally. The extent of this change can also be seen from the level of internalisation of social standards and expectations around these social spheres involving members of both sexes. This process of course, as noted above, is not isolated from other processes but part of a deeply interwoven tapestry of social processes. One consequence of this is the development of 'new' social pressures, constraints and emancipations that emerge around a diverse range of social practices. For instance, in Chaps. 5 and 6 we refer to how the stress on achievement striving and seriousness of involvement, amongst other processes, have increased the sporting demands on elite inter-county male Gaelic players. But this process too forms part of a wider social landscape that is interwoven with the dynamic of gender power relations. Combined, these processes have increased or generated new pressures on some elite male Gaelic players, as a recent article by a sports journalist on player retirement illustrates:

> Injury isn't the only reason players get out early. Andriú MacLochlainn finished with Kildare in 2012 at 29. He retired with a heavy heart because he knew he had several good intercounty seasons left in him… 'I just knew I had too much going on at the time,' he says now. That didn't hinder him but when MacLochlainn married young and became a father, he soon discovered the difficulties of trying to juggle parenthood with an intercounty career. (*Irish Times*, 23 January 2016)

This issue of the time commitment required at the inter-county level and a decreasing age-profile of elite Gaelic players has been raised by representatives of the Gaelic Players Association (GPA) in recent years. Much of this has been informed by anecdotal evidence rather than a wider social scientific study—indeed, others have questioned the idea that a significant change in the age profile of elite players has or is occurring. Yet, the latter argument, if it is correct, does not in itself mean that players are not experiencing increased stress and demands due in part to less unequal gender power relations and changed social expectations and norms that emerge from this. For instance, the age profile could remain relatively consistent over the generations but the reasons for retiring may change.

That in a way brings us full circle, so to speak. To explore issues of this nature requires a developmental approach, as Elias so succinctly argued on numerous occasions. We believe it is important to re-emphasise Elias's position here given that this book forms part of the Norbert Elias series (by Palgrave) but also, ironically, given the expansion of the very trend that Elias himself so strongly railed against—the retreat into the present— even within figurational sociology. While many figurational studies follow Elias's position, others have digressed and adopted a more present-orientated approach (see Elliott & Maguire, 2008; Engh, Agergaard, & Maguire, 2013; Liston, 2005).

Inter-organisational Sporting Competition

Since the late 1980s the competition the GAA has faced from its main rivals—soccer and rugby—has intensified. This has partly been under-pinned by an advance in the mediatisation of sport and the further inter-locking of sports and media organisations connected with this. Yet despite this escalation in competitive pressures, relations between those represent-ing the various sporting organisations have become more cordial and har-monious over the last 40 years, as we illustrate in Chap. 7. Unlike in earlier decades, GAA administrators generally refrain from overt, and public, pro-nouncements of superiority while there is now a greater culture of ecu-menism between the sporting organisations representing Gaelic games, soccer and rugby. Not only have we documented this change, we have sought to explain it. Without a longer term view we can lose sight of such changes and, consequently, fail to explain contemporary developments in a more reality-congruent way. During the summer of 2018, GAA admin-istrators, and the GAA more generally, received considerable public criti-cism—including from some of its own members—over their initial[2] rejection of a proposal to play a charity soccer match on a GAA ground (in Cork city). The GAA's constitution and rules does not permit the playing of 'non-Gaelic' games in GAA owned property.[3] The proposed match between a Republic of Ireland/Celtic select team and a Manchester United select team was arranged to raise funds for the family of the former Republic of Ireland, Celtic and Manchester United player Liam Miller who died of cancer at the age of 36 earlier that year. Miller had also played Gaelic games in his childhood and teenage years as a member of the Éire Óg GAA club. The proposal to play the fixture at a GAA grounds was initiated because the ground in question could accommodate a crowd of

45,000 and it was believed more money could be raised as a result—the nearest soccer ground had a capacity of 7500.

The GAA's initial refusal provoked public condemnation—including veiled threats from some politicians over the public funding the GAA receives and what one journalist labelled 'a barrage of recrimination and name-calling on social media' (*Irish Times*, 25 July 2018), much of the latter framed by phrases such as 'bigots'. It is somewhat ironic then that this issue arose in the first place, and that the GAA received such febrile criticism, partly as a consequence of the change in the social habitus of Irish people generally, and which reshaped the values and attitudes of GAA administrators (Chap. 7). Such disputes would be less likely to have arisen without these changes: greater emotional flexibility and capacity for empathy, greater tolerance, and changed social expectations around the playing of multiple competing sports, and in respect of relations between competing sports organisations. This is not to pass judgement on the various positions, or to label specific sides of the debate as right or wrong, but rather to illustrate the relationship between long-term social processes and ongoing changing social standards and expectations which find expression in contemporary issues and developments. This book we hope will contribute to a more reality-congruent way of considering and explaining issues of this nature that may emerge in the future.

The changes in habitus and related change in how GAA activists sought to integrate young people into the association which we set out in Chap. 7 also allows us to consider a recurring concern for GAA administrators—advances in urbanisation or individualisation (GAA, 1971; *Irish Examiner*, 12 January 2019; Leinster GAA, 2017). Since the 1970s various internal GAA reports have identified urbanisation as a central challenge. Administrators sometimes perceive urbanisation as leading to the decline of community. As one GAA administrator in 2017 suggested, 'The more urbanised you get, the less community spirit that exists and the GAA is built on community and spirit'. Indeed, to some extent, there is a basis for such a contention. As we explain in this book, there is a relationship between wider social processes, such as urbanisation, and how people think, feel and act. Urbanisation expresses itself not just as a specific form of geo-social organisation but, following Elias, as a process which in conjunction with other social processes precipitates modes of living, thinking and feeling which are more individualised. So in that sense urbanisation processes are a specific example of increasing social independences that partly contribute to advances in individualisation as we explain in Chap. 2.

The contention by the GAA administrator referred to above is, however, indicative of a type of non-processual thinking. The implication of this is that individualisation is the antipode to community with individualism and community perceived as absolute unconnected substances. Elias's concept of we–I balances is a far more accurate or reality-congruent way for comprehending the actual structure of this process. For Elias (2010) both the I-identity and the we-identity are always present; what changes is the degree, layers, and pattern of the I–we relation. That is not to suggest that specific forms of we-identification do not weaken or dissolve but rather that individuals always have we-identifications and related we-feelings. What GAA reports such as the one mentioned above appear to be identifying is not the replacement of community by individualism but a growing accent on the I-identity as we discussed in Chap. 7, or perhaps in some parts of Ireland a weakening of specific forms of we-identification. If we think in terms of process we can then envisage how a person's social habitus is open to further individualisation.

In Chap. 7, we note how the habitus of Irish people became more individualised (see also Chaps. 2 and 3), and how this was connected to the marginalisation of the strategy of conflating the playing of Gaelic games with true national identity. In claiming this we are not suggesting that feelings of national identification have disappeared, but rather that changes in the strength and pattern of I–we feelings and identifications have occurred. Although individualisation processes have advanced, many young Irish people for instance wear 'county' GAA jerseys while living overseas as a means to publicly demonstrate a connection to their county and Ireland simultaneously (two layers of their we-identity). As we explain in Chap. 4, the strength of we-identifications and related we-feelings has also been interconnected with the structures and forms of organising in the GAA, a point we return to later in this chapter.

In many ways the GAA and Gaelic games could be described as hugely successful; it has a large membership, is a major spectator sport and financially strong. It is this very success as a sporting organisation that to some degree masks its significance. This is not a value judgment. The point we are making is that this 'success' occurred at a time when soccer, it is fair to say, has become the prominent sport in almost every other European country. Whether Gaelic games or soccer is the 'biggest' sport in Ireland depends to some extent on how one decides to measure this, but one would not be stepping too far to suggest that soccer and Gaelic games are the 'big' two[4] sports in Ireland. Despite this, GAA administrators and activists continue to compete with those representing other sports in attempting to integrate new, younger generations into their respective sports; those comprising organisations are compelled to compete with others to survive. The changes in the social habitus of people in Ireland certainly shaped how competitive relations were expressed but it did not diminish the intensity of competitive relations; for GAA administrators and activists at various levels, soccer and rugby provide a competitive function for them. The GAA's long established position—though this may have declined relative to other sports organisations over the decades—has meant its activists and administrators have a level of confidence and aspiration that comes with this. For instance, in a recent conversation with a GAA club coach in Dublin we mentioned that over half of a local primary school appeared to be involved in the club. The response from this coach was 'but what about the other half, why aren't they coming to us'. This short anecdote is matched by the emphasis placed by GAA administrators at a higher tier in their more strategic analysis of participation rates relative to the population—such analysis is a feature of GAA reports going back to the 1970s. Within these reports, either explicitly or implicitly, there is a focus on those not involved in Gaelic games—an ingrained belief that those not playing could be attracted to Gaelic games and integrated into the GAA. The sociogenesis of this way of thinking by individuals comprising the GAA stems from the figuration the GAA formed with other sports organisations and its position within this figuration. While this is perhaps changing, it may take longer for this form of thinking (and the aspiration expressed within it) by some GAA members to change; their habitus may lag the social conditions of a changed power balance between the sports.

Organising Dynamics

In 2017 a GAA Club Players Association (CPA) was established to represent the interests of GAA club players as opposed to GAA inter-county players who are represented by the GPA—of course all inter-county players are simultaneously club players. Indeed, several of the members of the CPA are former inter-county players. This organisation has yet to attain the same legitimacy and status as the GPA, while the we-feelings of many club players towards the CPA may yet be embryonic. Furthermore, at this point in time at least, they do not have the same power resources as the

GPA, which as we explained in Chap. 6 were enhanced by the meaning attached to the inter-county championships and financial income generated by inter-county competitions. Yet this new unit has added to the complexity of the overall GAA figuration.

Mennell (2001, p. 32) notes that, based on Elias's synthesis, 'we have learned to think in terms of centrifugal and centripetal forces contending against each other in state-formation processes'. In Chap. 4 we explained how this same dynamic of centrifugal and centripetal forces also shapes organising processes and the organisational structures instigated. While we document 'past' developments we are of course explaining processes—organisational units and structures are ongoing processes. For instance, in 2018 the then general secretary of the GAA, Padraic Duffy, stated that a reduction in the size of congress would be a preferred organising structure on the grounds of being more effective (GAA, 2018). This is but another example of an element of these contending forces—in this instance centralising desires (perhaps pressures too)—in a contemporary setting. We believe that this book makes comprehending this tension, the overall direction and the reasons for it, more accessible. Change in organisational structures and the processes of organising are not the outcome of rational thinking nor of any single individual or group. It is largely a blind process, the unintended outcome of the interweaving of the plans and actions of various individuals, which in turn shapes the plans and desires of later generations.

The tension balance between amateurism and professionalism discussed in Chap. 5 is another example of a blind process. As higher-tier GAA functionaries and units have instigated policies stemming from felt competitive pressures, their actions and resultant practices have in an unplanned and unintended way pushed the GAA further along the continuum between amateurism and professionalism in the direction of the latter. For instance, the changes to the inter-county hurling championship in 2018, in which inter-county players play more matches and which greatly amplified the media profile and coverage of hurling, could, though unintended and unplanned, increase the time commitments and related pressures on the players and coaches involved.

Concluding Remarks

In this concluding chapter we sought to discuss some contemporary issues and developments concerning Gaelic games and the GAA. Our selection of topics is neither comprehensive nor based on a ranked order of importance; there are many issues we do not discuss. Our motivation is to illustrate how a book based on historical data connects to and helps explain different contemporary issues. History is not merely a prelude to the present. Furthermore, the content of this book is, we believe, also an attempt to transcend the oft-repeated, and rather platitudinous, claims made within some academic scholarship, and non-academic commentary, that developments in the GAA or Gaelic games are a reflection of a change in Irish society. As we state in our introductory chapter, the 'how' is generally overlooked within such assertions. Instead, throughout this book we seek to explain through empirical-theoretical elaboration precisely the relationship between changing social structures (Irish society) and specific developments in both the GAA and Gaelic games, and the channels connecting them. It is apt we feel to conclude by paraphrasing from a quote by Eric Dunning (1999) (in this the year of Eric's passing), which we feel encapsulates our feelings in relation to this manuscript: we have tried to carry the torch a little further from where Elias, Eric and others have left off.

NOTES

1. It should also be borne in mind that although comprising part of the 'family of Gaelic games', women's Gaelic football and hurling (known as camogie) are governed by separate sporting organisations—the Camogie Association and the Ladies Gaelic Football Association. The on-field games while very similar in structure are different and there are distinct sets of rules for women's Gaelic games. In 2018 senior officials representing the GAA, the Camoige Association and the Ladies Gaelic Football Association signed a memorandum of understanding but they remain separate organisations with no overlap in administration.
2. The game was later permitted to go ahead.
3. Exceptions have been made (which we documented in Chap. 7) but are subject to a process involving central decision-making bodies of the GAA.
4. Rugby's status is amplified by the media coverage it attracts in Ireland partly due to the internationalisation of the sport and the position of Irish teams within this. This masks the level of player numbers relative to Gaelic games and soccer as well as spectator interest beyond the international setting. By international here we are also referring to the four provincial teams' participation in inter-country competitions.

REFERENCES

Dunning, E. (1999). *Sport matters: Sociological studies of sport, violence and civilization*. London: Routledge.

Dunning, E., & Maguire, J. (1996). Process-sociological notes on sport, gender relations and violence control. *International Review for Sociology of Sport, 31*(1), 295–318.

Elias, N. (1987). The retreat of sociologists into the present. *Theory, Culture & Society, 4*(2–3), 223–247.

Elias, N. (2010). *The society of individuals* (Rev. ed.). Dublin: University College Dublin Press.

Elliott, R., & Maguire, J. (2008). "Getting caught in the net": Examining the recruitment of Canadian players in British professional ice hockey. *Journal of Sport and Social Issues, 32*(2), 158–176.

Engh, M. H., Agergaard, S., & Maguire, J. (2013). Established–outsider relations in youth football tournaments: An exploration of transnational power figurations between Scandinavian organizers and African teams. *Soccer & Society, 14*(6), 781–798.

GAA. (1971). *Report of the commission on the GAA*. Dublin: GAA.

GAA. (2018). *Report of the ard stiúrthóir*. Dublin: GAA.

Leinster GAA. (2017). *Rural communities workgroup report*. Dublin: GAA.

LGFA. (2017). *Ladies Gaelic Football Association strategic roadmap 2017–2022*. Dublin: LGFA.

Liston, K. (2005). Established–outsider relations between males and females in male-associated sports in Ireland. *European Journal for Sport and Society, 2*(1), 25–33.

Mennell, S. (2001). The other side of the coin: Decivilizing processes. In T. Salumets (Ed.), *Norbert Elias and human interdependencies* (pp. 32–49). Montreal: McGill-Queen's University Press.

BIBLIOGRAPHY

NEWSPAPERS, MAGAZINES AND PERIODICALS

Anglo-Celt
Australian
Celtic Times
City Tribune
Connacht Tribune
Cork Examiner
Freeman's Journal
Gaelic Athlete
Gaelic Athletic Annual
Gaelic Sport
Gaelic World
Herald Sun
Irish Independent
Irish Mirror
Irish Press
Meath Chronicle
Nenagh Guardian
Our Games
Southern Star
Sport
Sunday Business Post
Sunday Independent
The Age

© The Author(s) 2020
J. Connolly, P. Dolan, *Gaelic Games in Society*, Palgrave Studies
on Norbert Elias, https://doi.org/10.1007/978-3-030-31699-0

The Advertiser
Weekend Australian
Westmeath Examiner

GAA ARCHIVE AND COLLECTIONS, CROKE PARK

Central Council Minutes, 1899–
Minutes of Annual congress, 1901–
Leinster council minutes, 1915–
John J. Higgins Collection

THE CARDINAL TOMÁS Ó FIAICH MEMORIAL LIBRARY AND ARCHIVE, ARMAGH

CÓFLA Gaelic games collection

LIMERICK CITY LIBRARY

Séamus Ó Ceallaigh GAA Collection

NATIONAL ARCHIVES OF IRELAND

Census of Ireland 1901/1911

BOOKS, BOOK CHAPTERS, AND JOURNAL ARTICLES

Bairner, A. (2002). The dog that didn't bark? Football hooliganism in Ireland. In E. Dunning, P. Murphy, I. Waddington, & A. Astrinakis (Eds.), *Fighting fans: Football hooliganism as a world phenomenon* (pp. 118–130). Dublin: University College Dublin Press.
Boyle, R. (1992). From our Gaelic fields: Radio, sport and nation in post-partition Ireland. *Media, Culture and Society, 14*, 623–636.
Carey, T. (2007). *Croke park: A history.* Cork: The Collins Press.
Clark, S. (1978). The importance of agrarian classes: Agrarian class structure and collective action in nineteenth-century Ireland. *British Journal of Sociology, 29*(1), 22–40.
Clark, S. (1979). *Social origins of the Irish Land War.* Princeton, NJ: Princeton University Press.
Collins, R. (2008). *Violence: A micro-sociological theory.* Princeton, NJ: Princeton University Press.

Collins, R. (2009). The micro sociology of violence. *British Journal of Sociology, 60*(3), 566–576.

Collins, T. (2011). The invention of sporting tradition: National myths, imperial pasts and the origins of Australian Rules football. In S. Wagg (Ed.), *Myths and milestones in the history of sport* (pp. 8–31). Basingstoke: Palgrave Macmillan.

Conboy, T. (2002a). The forties. In T. Moran (Ed.), *Stair CLG Chonnacht 1902–2002* (pp. 53–72). Carrick-on-Shannon, Co. Leitrim: Carrick Print.

Conboy, T. (2002b). The seventies. In T. Moran (Ed.), *Stair CLG Chonnacht 1902–2002*. Carrick-on-Shannon, Co. Leitrim: Carrick Print.

Connolly, J., & Dolan, P. (2010). The civilizing and sportization of Gaelic football in Ireland: 1884–2008. *Journal of Historical Sociology, 23*(4), 570–598.

Connolly, J., & Dolan, P. (2011). Organizational centralization as figurational dynamics: Movements and counter-movements in the Gaelic Athletic Association. *Management & Organization History, 6*(1), 37–58.

Connolly, J., & Dolan, P. (2012). Sport, media and the Gaelic Athletic Association: The quest for the 'youth' of Ireland. *Media, Culture & Society, 34*(4), 407–423.

Connolly, J., & Dolan, P. (2013a). The amplification and de-amplification of amateurism and professionalism in the Gaelic Athletic Association. *International Journal of the History of Sport, 30*(8), 853–870.

Connolly, J., & Dolan, P. (2013b). Re-theorizing the 'structure–agency' relationship: Figurational theory, organizational change and the Gaelic Athletic Association. *Organization, 20*, 491–511.

Cooney, M. (2003). The privatization of violence. *Criminology, 41*(4), 1377–1406.

Cooney, M. (2009). The scientific significance of Collins's *Violence*. *The British Journal of Sociology, 60*(3), 586–594.

Corry, E. (1989). *Catch and kick*. Swords, Co. Dublin: Poolbeg.

Corry, E. (2005). *An illustrated history of the GAA*. Dublin: Gill & Macmillan.

Corry, E. (2009). The mass media and the popularisation of Gaelic games, 1884–1934. In D. McAnallen, D. Hassan, & R. Hegarty (Eds.), *The evolution of the GAA: Ulaidh, Éire agus eile* (pp. 100–111). Belfast: Stair Uladh.

Courtney, P. (Ed.). (2005). *Classic All-Ireland finals*. Galway: Leinster Leader Ltd.

Cronin, M. (1998). 'When the world soccer cup is played on roller skates': The attempt to make Gaelic games international: The Meath–Australia matches of 1967–1968. *Immigrants & Minorities, 17*(1), 170–188.

Cronin, M. (1999). *Sport and nationalism in Ireland: Gaelic games, soccer and Irish identity since 1884*. Dublin: Four Courts Press.

Cronin, M., Duncan, M., & Rouse, P. (2009). *The GAA: A people's history*. Cork: The Collins Press.

Cronin, M., Murphy, W., & Rouse, P. (Eds.). (2009). *The Gaelic Athletic Association, 1884–2009*. Dublin: Irish Academic Press.

Curran, C. (2015). *The development of sport in Donegal, 1880–1935*. Cork: Cork University Press.

Curtis Jr., L. P. (1988). Moral and physical force: The language of violence in Irish nationalism. *Journal of British Studies, 27*(2), 150–189.

Cusack, D. Ó. (2009). *Come what may. The autobiography*. Dublin: Penguin.

Daly, M. E. (Ed.). (2001). *County and town: One hundred years of local government*. Dublin: Institute of Public Administration.

Darby, P. (2009). *Gaelic games, nationalism and the Irish diaspora in the United States*. Dublin: University College Dublin Press.

Darby, P., & Hassan, D. (Eds.). (2008). *Emigrant players: Sport and the Irish diaspora*. Abingdon: Routledge.

De Búrca, M. (1984). *Gaelic games in Leinster*. Mullingar: Comhairle Laighean, CLG.

De Búrca, M. (1989). *Michael Cusack and the GAA*. Dublin: Anvil Books.

De Búrca, M. (1999). *The GAA: A history* (2nd ed.). Dublin: Gill & Macmillan.

Devine, L. (2002). The twenties. In T. Moran (Ed.), *Stair CLG Chonnacht 1902–2002* (pp. 23–36). Carrick-on-Shannon, Co. Leitrim: Carrick Print.

Devlin, P. J. (1934). *Our native games*. Dublin: M. H. Gill & Sons.

Dolan, P. (2005). *The development of consumer culture, subjectivity and national identity in Ireland, 1900–1980*. PhD thesis, Goldsmiths College, University of London, London.

Dolan, P. (2009a). Developing consumer subjectivity in Ireland: 1900–1980. *Journal of Consumer Culture, 9*(1), 117–141.

Dolan, P. (2009b). Figurational dynamics and parliamentary discourses of living standards in Ireland. *British Journal of Sociology, 60*(4), 721–739.

Dolan, P. (2018). Class relations and the development of boxing: Norbert Elias on sportisation processes in England and France. In J. Haut, P. Dolan, D. Reicher, & R. Sánchez García (Eds.), *Excitement processes: Norbert Elias's unpublished works on sports, leisure, body, culture* (pp. 235–254). Wiesbaden: Springer.

Dolan, P., & Connolly, J. (2009). The civilizing of hurling in Ireland. *Sport in Society, 12*(2), 196–211.

Dolan, P., & Connolly, J. (2014a). Documents and detachment in the figurational sociology of sport. *Empiria, 30*, 33–52.

Dolan, P., & Connolly, J. (2014b). Emotions, violence and social belonging: An Eliasian analysis of sports spectatorship. *Sociology, 48*(2), 284–299.

Dunning, E. (1989). A response to R. J. Robinson's "The 'civilizing process': Some remarks on Elias's social history". *Sociology, 23*(2), 299–307.

Dunning, E. (1994a). The social roots of football hooliganism: A reply to the critics of the 'Leicester School'. In R. Giulianotti, N. Bonney, & M. Hepworth (Eds.), *Football violence and social identity* (pp. 128–157). London: Routledge.

Dunning, E. (1994b). Sport in space and time: "Civilizing processes", trajectories of state-formation and the development of modern sport. *International Review for the Sociology of Sport, 29*(4), 331–347.

Dunning, E. (1999). *Sport matters: Sociological studies of sport, violence and civilization*. London: Routledge.

Dunning, E. (2008a). The dynamics of modern sport: Notes on achievement-striving and the social significance of sport. In N. Elias & E. Dunning (Eds.), *Quest for excitement: Sport and leisure in the civilising process* (Rev. ed., pp. 203–221). Dublin: University College Dublin Press.

Dunning, E. (2008b). Social bonding and violence in sport. In N. Elias & E. Dunning (Eds.), *Quest for excitement: Sport and leisure in the civilising process* (Rev. ed., pp. 222–241). Dublin: University College Dublin Press.

Dunning, E., & Maguire, J. (1996). Process-sociological notes on sport, gender relations and violence control. *International Review for Sociology of Sport, 31*(1), 295–318.

Dunning, E., Murphy, P., & Waddington, I. (2002). Towards a global programme of research into fighting and disorder at football. In E. Dunning, P. Murphy, I. Waddington, & A. Astrinakis (Eds.), *Fighting fans: Football hooliganism as a world phenomenon* (pp. 218–224). Dublin: University College Dublin Press.

Dunning, E., Murphy, P., Waddington, I., & Astrinakis, A. (Eds.). (2002). *Fighting fans: Football hooliganism as a world phenomenon*. Dublin: University College Dublin Press.

Dunning, E., Murphy, P., & Williams, J. (1986). Spectator violence at football matches—Towards a sociological explanation. *British Journal of Sociology, 37*(2), 221–244.

Dunning, E., Murphy, P., & Williams, J. (1988). *The roots of football hooliganism: An historical and sociological study*. London: Routledge.

Dunning, E., & Sheard, K. (1979). *Barbarians, gentlemen & players: A sociological study of the development of rugby football*. Canberra: Australian National University Press.

Dunning, E., & Sheard, K. (2005). *Barbarians, gentlemen and players: A sociological study of the development of rugby football* (2nd ed.). London: Routledge.

Durkheim, É. (1984). *The division of labour in society* (W. D. Halls, Trans.). Hampshire: Macmillan.

Durkheim, É. (2001). *The elementary forms of religious life* (C. Cosman, Trans.). Oxford and New York: Oxford University Press.

Elias, N. (1987a). On human beings and their emotions: A process-sociological essay. *Theory, Culture & Society, 4*(2–3), 339–361.

Elias, N. (1987b). The retreat of sociologists into the present. *Theory, Culture & Society, 4*(2–3), 223–247.

Elias, N. (2006). *The court society* (Rev. ed.). Dublin: University College Dublin Press.

Elias, N. (2007a). *An essay on time* (Rev. ed.). Dublin: University College Dublin Press.

Elias, N. (2007b). *Involvement and detachment* (Rev. ed.). Dublin: University College Dublin Press.

Elias, N. (2008a). An essay on sport and violence. In N. Elias & E. Dunning (Eds.), *Quest for excitement: Sport and leisure in the civilising process* (Rev. ed., pp. 150–173). Dublin: University College Dublin Press.

Elias, N. (2008b). Introduction. In N. Elias & E. Dunning (Eds.), *Quest for excitement: Sport and leisure in the civilising process* (Rev. ed., pp. 3–43). Dublin: University College Dublin Press.

Elias, N. (2010). *The society of individuals* (Rev. ed.). Dublin: University College Dublin Press.

Elias, N. (2012a). *On the process of civilisation* (Rev. ed.). Dublin: University College Dublin Press.

Elias, N. (2012b). *What is sociology?* (Rev. ed.). Dublin: University College Dublin Press.

Elias, N. (2013). *Studies on the Germans* (Rev. ed.). Dublin: University College Dublin Press.

Elias, N. (2018a). Boxing and duelling. In J. Haut, P. Dolan, D. Reicher, & R. S. García (Eds.), *Excitement processes: Norbert Elias's unpublished works on sports, leisure, body, culture* (pp. 173–215). Wiesbaden: Springer.

Elias, N. (2018b). Fragments on sportisation. In J. Haut, P. Dolan, D. Reicher, & R. S. García (Eds.), *Excitement processes: Norbert Elias's unpublished works on sports, leisure, body, culture* (pp. 121–136). Wiesbaden: Springer.

Elias, N., & Dunning, E. (1986). *Quest for excitement: Sport and leisure in the civilising process*. Oxford: Basil Blackwell.

Elias, N., & Dunning, E. (2008). Dynamics of sports groups with special reference to football. In N. Elias & E. Dunning (Eds.) *Quest for excitement: Sport and leisure in the civilising process* (Rev. ed., pp. 189–202). Dublin: University College Dublin Press.

Elias, N., & Scotson, J. L. (2008). *The established and the outsiders* (Rev. ed.). Dublin: University College Dublin Press.

Elliott, R., & Maguire, J. (2008). "Getting caught in the net": Examining the recruitment of Canadian players in British professional ice hockey. *Journal of Sport and Social Issues, 32*(2), 158–176.

Engh, M. H., Agergaard, S., & Maguire, J. (2013). Established–outsider relations in youth football tournaments: An exploration of transnational power figurations between Scandinavian organizers and African teams. *Soccer & Society, 14*(6), 781–798.

Eriksen, T. H. (2007). Steps to an ecology of transnational sports. *Global Networks, 7*(2), 154–165.

Felson, R. B. (2009). Is violence natural, unnatural, or rational? *British Journal of Sociology, 60*(3), 577–585.

Finnane, M. (1997). A decline in violence in Ireland? Crime, policing and social relations, 1860–1914. *Crime, Histoire & Sociétés/Crime, History & Societies, 1*(1), 51–70.

Fitzgerald, D. (1914). *How to play Gaelic football*. Cork: Guy & Co.
Fullam, B. (1999). *Off the field and on*. Dublin: Wolfhound Press Ltd.
Fullam, B. (2004). *The throw-in: The GAA and the men who made it*. Dublin: Wolfhound Press.
Fulton, G., & Bairner, A. (2007). Sport, space and national identity in Ireland: The GAA, Croke Park and rule 42. *Space and Polity, 11*(1), 55–74.
GAA. (1907). *Gaelic Athletic Association. Official guide, 1907–8–9*. Wexford: GAA.
GAA. (1908–1909). *The Gaelic athletic annual*. Dublin: GAA.
GAA. (1910–1911). *The Gaelic athletic annual*. Dublin: GAA.
GAA. (1911). *Minutes of annual congress*. Dublin: GAA.
GAA. (1913). *Minutes of annual congress*. Dublin: GAA.
GAA. (1914). *Gaelic Athletic Association. Official guide. 1914–1915*. Wexford: GAA.
GAA. (1920). *Minutes of annual convention of Ulster Council*. Dublin: GAA.
GAA. (1925). *Motions for annual congress*. Dublin: GAA.
GAA. (1927). *Minutes of annual convention of Leinster Council*. Dublin: GAA.
GAA. (1929). *Minutes of special annual congress*. Dublin: GAA.
GAA. (1930). *Minutes of annual congress*. Dublin: GAA.
GAA. (1934a). *Minutes of annual congress*. Dublin: GAA.
GAA. (1934b). *Minutes of Armagh County Committee*. Dublin: GAA.
GAA. (1935a). *Minutes of annual congress*. Dublin: GAA.
GAA. (1935b). *Minutes of Armagh County Committee*. Dublin: GAA.
GAA. (1936). *Minutes of annual congress*. Dublin: GAA.
GAA. (1939). *Minutes of the annual congress*. Dublin: GAA.
GAA. (1940). *Minutes of the annual congress*. Dublin: GAA.
GAA. (1942). *Minutes of annual congress*. Dublin: GAA.
GAA. (1943). *Minutes of annual congress*. Dublin: GAA.
GAA. (1945). *Minutes of annual congress*. Dublin: GAA.
GAA. (1946). *Minutes of annual congress*. Dublin: GAA.
GAA. (1947a). *An comhdháil bhliantúil*. Dublin: GAA.
GAA. (1947b). *Minutes of annual congress*. Dublin: GAA.
GAA. (1950). *An comhdháil bhliantúil*. Dublin: GAA.
GAA. (1951a). *An comhdháil bhliantúil*. Dublin: GAA.
GAA. (1951b). *Minutes of the annual congress*. Dublin: GAA.
GAA. (1952). *Minutes of annual congress*. Dublin: GAA.
GAA. (1953a). *Minutes of annual congress*. Dublin: GAA.
GAA. (1953b). *Minutes of annual convention of Leinster Council*. Dublin: GAA.
GAA. (1953c). *Minutes of central council*. Dublin: GAA.
GAA. (1954). *An comhdháil bliantúil*. Dublin: GAA.
GAA. (1955). *Minutes of annual congress*. Dublin: GAA.
GAA. (1960). *Minutes of annual congress*. Dublin: GAA.

GAA. (1962). *An comhdháil bhliantúil.* Dublin: GAA.

GAA. (1963). *An comhdháil bhliantúil.* Dublin: GAA.

GAA. (1969). *Minutes of annual convention of Ulster Council.* Dublin: GAA.

GAA. (1971). *Report of the commission on the GAA.* Dublin: GAA.

GAA. (1972a). *Minutes of annual convention of Ulster Council.* Dublin: GAA.

GAA. (1972b). *Minutes of executive committee of GAA.* Dublin: GAA.

GAA. (1972c). *Minutes of special congress 1972.* Dublin: GAA.

GAA. (1974a). *Minutes of annual congress.* Dublin: GAA.

GAA. (1974b). *Report of the development conference for officers of county committees and provincial councils.* Dublin: Irish Management Institute.

GAA. (1977). *Minutes of annual congress.* Dublin: GAA.

GAA. (1978). *Minutes of annual congress.* Dublin: GAA.

GAA. (1985). *Manual for county committees and provincial councils.* Dublin: GAA.

GAA. (1991). *An comhdháil bhliantúil.* Dublin: GAA.

GAA. (1997a). *Minutes of annual congress.* Dublin: GAA.

GAA. (1997b). *Report of the committee established to review the GAA's amateur status.* Dublin: GAA.

GAA. (2002). *G.A.A. Strategic review—Enhancing community identity.* Dublin: Gaelic Athletic Association.

GAA. (2010). *An comhdháil bhliantúil.* Dublin: GAA.

GAA. (2018). *Report of the ard stiúrthóir.* Dublin.

GAA Ulster Council. (2008). Committees. Retrieved from http://ulster.gaa.ie/council/committees/

Gaelic Players Association. (1980). Constitution and rules.

Garnham, N. (1999). Origins and development of Irish football. In N. Garnham (Ed.), *The origins and development of football in Ireland: Being a reprint of R.M. Peter's Irish football annual of 1880* (pp. 1–29). Belfast: Ulster Historical Foundation.

Garnham, N. (2004a). Accounting for the early success of the Gaelic Athletic Association. *Irish Historical Studies, 34*(133), 65–78.

Garnham, N. (2004b). *Association football and society in pre-partition Ireland.* Belfast: Ulster Historical Foundation.

Garvin, T. (1986). Priests and patriots: Irish separatism and fear of the modern, 1890–1914. *Irish Historical Studies, 25*(97), 67–81.

Gilroy, P. (2000). *Between camps.* London: Penguin.

Grimes, P. (2009). *The Moortown story.* Moortown, Co. Tyrone: St. Malachy's GAA Club.

Guiney, D. (1976). *Gaelic football.* Dublin: Gaelic Press.

Hassan, D., & O'Kane, P. (2012). Terrorism and the abnormality of sport in Northern Ireland. *International Review for the Sociology of Sport, 47*(3), 397–413.

Hay, R. (2010). A tale of two footballs: The origins of Australian football and association football revisited. *Sport in Society, 13*(6), 952–969.

Hay, R. (2014). Football in Australia before codification, 1820–1860. *International Journal of the History of Sport, 31*(9), 1047–1061.

Hayes, M. (2009). Down through the years. In D. McAnallen, D. Hassan, & R. Hegarty (Eds.), *The evolution of the GAA: Ulaidh, Éire agus eile* (pp. 20–29). Belfast: Stair Uladh.

Hibbins, G. M. (1992). The Cambridge connection: The English origins of Australian Rules football. In J. A. Mangan (Ed.), *The cultural bond: Sport, empire, society* (pp. 108–128). London: Frank Cass.

Higgins, J. J. (1914–1917). John J. Higgins collection, Leix and Ossory GAA, 1914–1917. In GAA (Ed.), *GAA archive*. Dublin: Croke Park.

Holton, R. (2000). Globalization's cultural consequences. *ANNALS of the American Academy of Political and Social Science, 570*(1), 140–152.

Hunt, T. (2008). *Sport and society in Victorian Ireland: The case of Westmeath*. Cork: Cork University Press.

Hunt, T. (2009a). The GAA: Social structure and associated clubs. In M. Cronin, W. Murphy, & P. Rouse (Eds.), *The Gaelic Athletic Association, 1884–2009* (pp. 183–202). Dublin: Irish Academic Press.

Hunt, T. (2009b). Parish factions, parading bands and sumptuous repasts: The diverse origins and activities of early GAA clubs. In D. McAnallen, D. Hassan, & R. Hegarty (Eds.), *The evolution of the GAA: Ulaidh, Éire agus eile* (pp. 86–99). Belfast: Stair Uladh.

Kee, R. (2000). *The green flag: A history of Irish nationalism*. London: Penguin.

Kelly, S. (2007). *Rule 42 and all that*. Dublin: Gill & Macmillan.

Kilminster, R. (2007). *Norbert Elias: Post-philosophical sociology*. Oxon: Routledge.

Lee, J. (1989). *The modernisation of Irish society: 1848–1918*. Dublin: Gill & Macmillan.

Leinster GAA. (2017). *Rural communities workgroup report*. Dublin: GAA.

Lennon, J. (1997). *The playing rules of football and hurling, 1884–1995*. Gormanstown, Co. Meath: Northern Recreation Consultants.

Lennon, J. (1999). *A comparative analysis of the playing rules of football and hurling 1884–1999*. Gormanstown, Co. Meath: The Northern Recreation Consultants.

Lennon, J. (2000). *Towards a philosophy for legislation in Gaelic games*. Gormanstown, Co. Meath: The Northern Recreation Consultants.

Lennon, J. (2001). *The playing rules of hurling 1602–2010; Gaelic football 1884–2010; hurling–shinty internationals 1933–2000*. Gormanstown, Co. Meath: The Northern Recreation Consultants.

LGFA. (2017). *Ladies Gaelic Football Association strategic roadmap 2017–2022*. Dublin: LGFA.

Liston, K. (2005). Established–outsider relations between males and females in male-associated sports in Ireland. *European Journal for Sport and Society, 2*(1), 25–33.

Looney, T. (2008). *Dick Fitzgerald: King in a kingdom of kings*. Dublin: Currach Press.

Mac Lua, B. (1967). *The steadfast rule*. Dublin: Cuchulainn Press Ltd.

Maguire, C. (2011). *Peasants into patriots: Instruments of radical politicisation in Clare 1800–1907*. PhD thesis, Mary Immaculate College, Limerick.

Mahon, J. (2000). *A history of Gaelic football*. Dublin: Gill & Macmillan.

Mandle, W. F. (1987). *The Gaelic Athletic Association and Irish nationalist politics, 1884–1924*. Dublin: Gill & Macmillan.

Martin, H. (2009). *Unlimited heartbreak: The inside story of Limerick hurling*. Cork: Collins.

McAnallen, D. (2009). 'The greatest amateur association in the world? The GAA and amateurism. In M. Cronin, W. Murphy, & P. Rouse (Eds.), *The Gaelic Athletic Association 1884–2009* (pp. 157–182). Dublin: Irish Academic Press.

McAnallen, D., Hassan, D., & Hegarty, R. (Eds.). (2009). *The evolution of the GAA: Ulaidh, Éire agus eile*. Belfast: Stair Uladh.

McCabe, C. (2011). *Football sports weekly* and Irish soccer, 1925–1928. *Media History, 17*(2), 147–158.

McConville, C., & Hess, R. (2012). Forging imperial and Australasian identities: Australian Rules football in New Zealand during the nineteenth century. *International Journal of the History of Sport, 29*(17), 2360–2371.

McDevitt, P. F. (1997). Muscular Catholicism: Nationalism, masculinity and Gaelic team sports, 1884–1916. *Gender & History, 9*(2), 262–284.

McElligott, R. (2013). *Forging a kingdom: The GAA in Kerry 1884–1934*. Wilton, Cork: Collins Press.

McGee, O. (2005). *The IRB: The Irish Republican Brotherhood from the Land League to Sinn Fein*. Dublin: Four Courts Press.

McKeever, J. (2009). The coming of age of Gaelic games in Ulster, 1950–1970. In D. McAnallen, D. Hassan, & R. Hegarty (Eds.), *The evolution of the GAA: Ulaidh, Éire agus eile* (pp. 30–41). Belfast: Stair Uladh.

Mennell, S. (1998). *Norbert Elias: An introduction*. Dublin: University College Dublin Press.

Mennell, S. (2001). The other side of the coin: Decivilizing processes. In T. Salumets (Ed.), *Norbert Elias and human interdependencies* (pp. 32–49). Montreal: McGill-Queen's University Press.

Mennell, S. (2007). *The American civilizing process*. Cambridge: Polity.

Moore, C. (2012). *The GAA v Douglas Hyde: The removal of Ireland's first president as GAA patron*. Cork: Collins Press.

Morris, D. (2010). Hick-hop hooray? "Honky tonk badonkadonk," musical genre, and the misrecognitions of hybridity. *Critical Studies in Media Communication, 28*(5), 466–488.

Mullan, M. (1995). Opposition, social closure, and sport: The Gaelic Athletic Association in the 19th century. *Sociology of Sport Journal, 12*(3), 268–289.

Mulvey, J. (2002a). A new dawn. In T. Moran (Ed.), *Stair CLG Chonnacht 1902–2002* (pp. 11–22). Carrick-on-Shannon, Co. Leitrim: Carrick Print.

Mulvey, J. (2002b). Sowing the seed. In T. Moran (Ed.), *Stair CLG Chonnacht 1902–2002* (pp. 1–10). Carrick-on-Shannon, Co. Leitrim: Carrick Print.

Murphy, P., Dunning, E., & Williams, J. (1988). Soccer crowd disorder and the press: Processes of amplification and de-amplification in historical perspective. *Theory Culture & Society, 5*(3), 645–673.

Nederveen Pieterse, J. (2001). Hybridity, so what?: The anti-hybridity backlash and the riddles of recognition. *Theory, Culture & Society, 18*(2–3), 219–245.

Nederveen Pieterse, J. (2009). *Globalization and culture: Global mélange*. Lanham, MD: Rowman & Littlefield Publishers.

Nolan, W. (Ed.). (2005). *The Gaelic Athletic Association in Dublin 1884–2000* (Vol. 1). Dublin: Geography Publications.

Ó Gráda, C. (1994). *Ireland: A new economic history*. Oxford: Oxford University Press.

Ó hAnnrachain, T. (2008). The heroic importance of sport: The GAA in the 1930s. *International Journal of the History of Sport, 25*(10), 1326–1337.

Ó Maonaigh, A. (2017). 'Who were the shoneens?': Irish militant nationalists and association football, 1913–1923. *Soccer & Society, 18*(5–6), 631–647.

Ó Riain, S. (1994). *Maurice Davin (1842–1927): First president of the G.A.A.* Dublin: Geography Publications.

O'Callaghan, L. (2011). *Rugby in Munster: A social and cultural history*. Cork: Cork University Press.

O'Callaghan, L. (2013). Rugby football and identity politics in free state Ireland. *Éire-Ireland, 48*(1–2), 148–167.

O'Connor, C. (2010). *The club*. Dublin: Penguin.

O'Connor, M. (2014). Investment in edification: Reflections on Irish education policy since independence. *Irish Educational Studies, 33*(2), 193–212.

O'Connor, R., & Whelan, B. (1971). *Attitudes of young people to games and pastimes*. Dublin: Economic and Social Research Institute.

O'Donnell, I. (2005). Lethal violence in Ireland, 1841 to 2003. *British Journal of Criminology, 45*(5), 671–695.

O'Donoghue, N. (1987). *Proud and upright men*. Indreabhán, Galway: Clódóirí Lurgan Teo.

O'Malley, E. (1992). Problems of industrialisation in Ireland. In J. H. Goldthorpe & C. T. Whelan (Eds.), *The development of industrial society in Ireland* (pp. 31–52). Oxford: Oxford University Press.

O'Sullivan, J. (2002). *Men in black*. Dublin: Sliabh Bán Publications.

O'Sullivan, T. F. (1916). *The story of the G.A.A.* Printed at 49 Middle Abbey Street, Dublin.

Robinson, R. J. (1987). The civilizing process: Some remarks on Elias's social history. *Sociology, 21*(1), 1–17.

Rothstein, B. (2009). Creating political legitimacy: Electoral democracy versus quality of government. *American Behavioral Scientist, 53*(3), 311–330.

Rouse, P. (1993). The politics of culture and sport in Ireland: A history of the GAA ban on foreign games 1884–1971. *International Journal of the History of Sport, 10*(3), 333–360.

Rouse, P. (2015). *Sport & Ireland.* Oxford: Oxford University Press.

Sheard, K. (1999). A twitch in time saves nine: Birdwatching, sport, and civilizing processes. *Sociology of Sport Journal, 16*, 181–205.

Syson, I. (2013). The 'chimera' of origins: Association football in Australia before 1880. *International Journal of the History of Sport, 30*(5), 453–468.

Toms, D. (2015). *Soccer in Munster: A social history 1877–1937.* Cork: Cork University Press.

Tynan, M. P. (2013). *Association football and Irish society during the inter-war period, 1918–1939.* PhD thesis, University of Ireland, Maynooth, Maynooth.

Weber, M. (1991). *From Max Weber: Essays in sociology.* London: Routledge.

Wouters, C. (1987). Developments in the behavioural codes between the sexes: The formalization of informalization in the Netherlands, 1930–1985. *Theory, Culture & Society, 4*(2/3), 405–207.

Wouters, C. (2007). *Informalization: Manners and emotions since 1890.* London: Sage.

Index[1]

A

Achievement striving, 101, 110, 182, 183
Affiliation, 72–76, 78, 79, 97, 101, 103, 118, 119, 139, 140, 142
Agrarian, 34, 70
Agricultural, 33, 34, 63
Allegiance, 29, 35, 44, 58, 70, 72, 75, 83, 117, 119, 148, 168
Amateur, 3, 13, 93–113, 117–136, 170, 175
  amateurism, 3, 4, 13, 14, 93–113, 117–136, 188
Ambivalence, 25, 26, 35, 49, 97, 112, 158
Anger, 10, 11, 30, 40, 41, 43, 54–57, 62, 64, 144
Anglo-Irish, 69–71, 93–95
Annual convention, 54, 79, 146
Anxieties, 98, 99, 106, 110, 123, 124, 145, 146
Aristocracy, 93

Armagh, xi, 126
Assault, 11, 25, 28, 29, 33, 41, 46, 49, 56, 59, 60
Australia, 15, 65, 161–167, 172, 173, 176
Australian Rules football, 15, 65, 161, 163–165, 167, 169, 177n1
Authoritarian, 150, 151, 158

B

Bairner, Alan, 39, 156
Ball, 1, 2, 21, 26, 27, 29, 40, 121, 140, 165, 170, 171, 174–176
Ban, 29, 103, 104, 118, 126, 139, 140, 142, 145, 149, 150, 154
Behind the scenes, 15
Belfast, 69, 119
Belonging, 43, 50, 52, 57, 58, 61, 63, 168
Biological, 42
Blame gossip, 98, 119, 120, 144–146

[1] Note: Page numbers followed by 'n' refer to notes.

© The Author(s) 2020
J. Connolly, P. Dolan, *Gaelic Games in Society*, Palgrave Studies on Norbert Elias, https://doi.org/10.1007/978-3-030-31699-0

Bonding
  functional, 58, 59, 63
  segmental, 58, 63
Bourgeoisie, 43, 45
Boyle, Raymond, 145
Britain, 5, 9, 10, 16n1, 19, 20, 25, 51,
  61, 69, 70, 81, 82, 93–95, 119,
  163, 164
Broken-time payments, 100, 103, 122
Bureaucratisation, 99–103, 106, 107

C
Caid, 20, 164
Carey, Tim, 28
Celtic Times, 21, 22, 24, 26, 49, 71,
  74–76, 97
Centralisation, 3, 13, 15, 28, 76,
  88, 119
Children, 132, 147, 173, 176
Choice, 121, 148, 149, 151, 155
Civilisation, 43, 55, 60
Civilising processes, 7, 12, 42–48, 52,
  57, 61
ClannaGael Fontenoy, 156
Clare, 83, 100, 135
Clark, Samuel, 34, 51
Class
  middle, 25, 61, 69–72, 93–96,
    98–100, 113n1, 119
  working, 43, 46, 58, 71, 93, 96, 100
Clergy, 74–76
  clerical, 76
Club Players Association (CPA), 187
Clubs, 8, 13, 20, 21, 27, 29, 42, 49,
  54, 60, 69, 71–84, 86–88, 89n1,
  97, 98, 101, 102, 109, 111,
  113n3, 113n4, 117–119, 121,
  126, 129, 130, 134, 140, 142,
  146, 148, 154, 156, 164, 171,
  173, 176, 184, 187
Coaches, 33, 104, 105, 128, 129,
  132–136, 168, 171, 188

Codes, 11, 13, 15, 21, 73, 95, 110,
  111, 117, 118, 120, 140, 155,
  157, 158, 161–177
Codification, 19, 23, 97
Cognitive, 29
Collins, Randall, 43, 45, 47, 62
Collins, Tony, 164
Commercialisation, 33, 34, 51, 70,
  107, 130
Communications, 106, 129, 133, 151,
  152, 158n2, 173
Competition, 15, 54, 74–76, 78,
  80–84, 94, 96, 100, 101,
  103–106, 117, 120–122,
  124–129, 132, 135, 142–144,
  151, 156, 158, 166, 167, 173,
  175, 177, 182, 184–188, 189n4
Conboy, Tony, 102, 103, 128
Condemnation, 21, 31, 50, 60, 144,
  157, 169, 185
Conduct, 8, 9, 11, 12, 21, 23, 26, 28,
  29, 33, 35, 36, 39–43, 45,
  47–49, 52–54, 56, 57, 59, 61,
  62, 167, 169, 171–174, 176
Connaught, 79
Connolly, John, 2, 6, 10, 12, 54,
  110, 146
Cooney, M., 47, 60
Cooperation, 14, 15, 63, 166
Cork, 77, 106, 121, 131, 184
Corry, Eoghan, 2, 107
Courtney, Pat, 29
Cricket, 24, 34, 69, 72, 119, 140, 141
Croke Park, xi, 27, 40, 60, 106,
  156, 175
Cronin, Mike, 2, 142, 165, 166
Crowds, 29, 47, 49, 50, 52, 53, 59,
  101, 169, 184
Culture, x, 14, 23, 45, 70, 71, 111,
  112, 120, 184
Curran, Conor, 96, 118, 120,
  140, 142
Curtis Jr, L P, 25

Cusack, Dónal Óg, 134
Cusack, Michael, 5, 20, 22, 24, 25, 49, 95, 97, 113n2

D
Daly, Mary, 73
Dangerous, 24–26, 29, 47
Darby, Paul, 171
Data, 6, 8–10, 96, 189
Davin, Maurice, 95, 97
De Búrca, Marcus, 2, 19, 49, 71, 74, 75, 78, 80, 82, 86
Decentralisation, 3, 13
De-civilising, 43
Democratisation, functional, 7, 43
Derry, 57
Detachment, 10–12, 50
Development, x, 2–4, 8–12, 14–16, 16n1, 19, 23, 25, 28, 32–35, 43–45, 50, 60, 69–89, 101, 103, 104, 106–108, 119, 122, 124, 126, 128–130, 134, 151–153, 156, 161–177, 181–189
  developmental, 15, 181–184
Devine, Liam, 28, 123
Devlin, P. J., 123
Discipline, 4, 6, 22, 24, 26, 28, 104, 131, 172
Discourse, 3, 14, 118, 123–126, 129, 130, 139
Disgrace, 33, 52, 54
Disintegration, 44, 77
Distinction, 5, 20, 21, 35, 42, 45, 46, 62, 70, 158, 161, 162, 167, 175, 176
Dolan, Paddy, x, 2, 6, 10, 12, 23, 35, 51, 54, 70, 94, 110, 131, 145–147, 149, 152, 158, 163
Double bind, 53, 101, 102, 139, 162, 167
Down, 25, 32, 77, 98, 105, 129, 132, 148, 169, 175

Drag effect, 162
Dublin, xi, 20, 27, 61, 77, 82, 106, 110, 123, 141, 145, 156, 187
Duncan, Mark, 2
Dunning, Eric, 4, 6, 8, 9, 11, 20, 23, 26, 27, 32, 39, 42, 44–47, 54, 57–59, 62–65, 72, 93, 97, 99, 102, 104–106, 108, 109, 122, 166, 173, 182, 189
Durkheim, Émile, 20, 46, 55, 58, 64, 144, 171

E
Economic, 4, 61, 63, 69, 97, 107, 122, 166
Elias, Norbert, ix–xi, 2–4, 6–8, 10, 11, 20, 23, 25–28, 34, 35, 42–48, 52, 53, 55, 57–64, 72, 73, 82, 87, 102, 108, 119, 120, 139, 144, 149, 158, 162–164, 166, 168, 173, 175, 181, 184–186, 188, 189
Elite, 14, 15, 24, 61, 69, 70, 93, 95, 99, 104, 105, 111–113, 113n1, 134, 136, 173, 176, 183
Embarrassment, 54, 144, 149, 158
Emigration, 171
Emotion
  controlled decontrolling of emotions, 44
  entrainment, 43 (*see also* Collins, Randall)
Employment, 35, 70, 100, 122, 146
English, 24, 61, 62, 71, 73, 95, 110, 118, 139, 141, 164
Eriksen, Thomas Hyland, 166
Essentialising, 161–177
Established and outsiders, 182
Ethnic, 5, 7, 21, 25, 34, 35, 43, 51, 57, 72, 94, 162

Excitement, 27, 35, 40, 45, 50,
    52, 53, 72, 108, 109, 127,
    143, 161, 172, 177
Exciting, 27, 30, 62, 168
Expenses, 95, 97, 99–101, 103, 105,
    112, 127, 129, 131

F
Face-to-face, 5, 47, 59, 62
Faction fights, 25
Farmers, 34, 69, 70
    tenant farmers, 25, 51, 62, 63, 70
Fear, 47, 55, 78, 87, 102, 125, 176
Feelings, 3, 7, 10, 15, 24, 33, 41, 43,
    44, 52, 54, 72, 83, 109, 120,
    144, 149, 150, 152, 153, 156,
    158, 166–168, 185, 186, 189
Felson, R B, 47
Feminisation, 182, 183
Fighting, 27, 53, 128
Figurational sociology, 6–8, 184
Figurations, 4–7, 9, 11, 12, 21,
    33–35, 43, 44, 55, 59, 60, 62,
    64, 78, 85, 88, 96, 102, 110,
    111, 126–130, 132, 139, 166,
    167, 187, 188
Financial, 74, 76, 97, 102, 103,
    105–107, 111, 113n4, 118, 123,
    124, 132, 134, 136, 166, 188
Finnane, M, 61
Fitzgerald, Dick, 122
Folk games, 19, 20, 26, 163, 176
Football hooliganism, 12
Foreign games, 142–146, 184
Forward panics, 42–48
    See also Collins, Randall
France, 163
Free fights, 42, 50–52
Free State, 120, 146
Fullam, Brendan, 2, 24
Fulton, Gareth, 156

Function, x, 6, 14, 15, 23, 27, 32, 34,
    40, 45, 46, 48, 50, 54, 55, 59–61,
    63, 70, 71, 73–76, 78–81, 83–88,
    94, 99, 101, 102, 106, 111, 122,
    124, 126–131, 133, 135, 143–145,
    149, 151, 152, 157, 163, 168,
    171, 175, 177, 182, 187
Functional differentiation, 7, 13, 87,
    88, 109
Functional specialisation, 13, 33, 48,
    50, 55, 56, 64, 80, 86, 105, 110,
    128, 158
Functionaries, 3, 13, 27, 54, 63, 85,
    86, 89, 102, 103, 106, 122, 124,
    132, 143, 144, 151, 152, 188

G
Gaelic Athletic Association (GAA)
    administrators, 3, 10, 14, 33, 53,
        54, 60, 96, 100, 101, 103,
        106, 110, 112, 118, 120–125,
        128, 130, 132–136, 141, 143,
        145–154, 156, 158, 161–162,
        171, 184–187
    Central Council, 86, 87, 89, 28, 32,
        56, 85
    central executive, 73, 74, 82, 85, 87
    congress, 86–89, 98, 103, 112, 123,
        124, 127, 134, 140, 143, 144,
        151, 152
    county board, 54, 128
    county committees, 73, 77, 82, 84,
        87, 88, 102, 124, 131
    delegate, 85–87, 124, 125, 127,
        146, 153
    executive committee, 85, 131
    general secretary, 77, 127, 143,
        144, 188
    management committee, 85, 86, 89
    motions, 27, 85, 88, 103, 123
    vigilance committees, 141, 150

Gaelic football, 1, 2, 15, 19–21, 25, 28, 31, 32, 34, 40, 57, 65, 83, 117, 153, 155, 161–167, 169, 171, 174, 175, 189n1

Gaelic games, ix, x, 1–16, 19–36, 39–42, 45, 48, 49, 51, 55, 57, 58, 61, 62, 65, 72, 99, 103, 104, 108–110, 112, 120, 121, 123, 126, 127, 133, 139–145, 147–149, 151–155, 157, 161, 171, 176, 181–184, 186–189, 189n1, 189n4
   all-Ireland, 58

Gaelic Players Association (GPA), 133–136, 183, 187, 188

Galway, 105

Garnham, Neil, 25, 69, 72, 89n1, 96–99, 118, 119, 121, 140, 142

Garrison games, 141

Garvin, Tom, 71

Gate-taking, 97, 101, 103, 107–108, 124, 127

Gender, 6, 15, 62, 181–184

Generations, 5, 8, 9, 42, 45, 46, 48, 111, 112, 131, 146–148, 150, 158, 171, 173–174, 183, 187, 188

Gentlemanly, 93, 94

Gilroy, Paul, 163

Goffman, Erving, 47

Goudsblom, Joop, 59, 64, 173

Grimes, P, 54

Guilt, 52

Guiney, David, 21

H

Habitus, x, 5–7, 11, 16, 29, 33–36, 43–45, 48–51, 54, 59, 62–64, 70, 110, 112, 147, 149, 150, 152, 154, 158, 173–176, 181–183, 185–187

Hassan, David, 51, 171

Hay, Roy, 164

Hayes, Maurice, 128

Hegarty, Roddy, 2

Hess, R., 164

Hibbins, G. M., 164

Historians, xi, 2–5, 96, 164

Historical, 4–6, 8–11, 33, 35, 47, 162, 164, 189

Holton, Robert, 162

Homo clausus, 60, 158

Honour, 13, 161, 169

Hooliganism, 39, 45, 56
   football, 12

Hostility, 21, 25, 49, 51, 70, 76, 84, 86, 141, 143, 144, 156

Hunt, Tom, 21, 22, 72–74, 96, 118, 140

Hurley, 1, 24, 27, 30, 32, 53

Hurling, ix, 1, 2, 19–21, 23–25, 27, 31, 32, 34, 48, 53, 69, 75, 83, 112, 117, 135, 140, 153, 157, 176, 188, 189n1

Hybrid, 15, 65, 161–164, 166–169, 171–177

Hybridisation, 161–177

Hyde, Douglas, 143

I

Identification, ix, 13, 14, 29, 34, 43, 44, 61, 63, 64, 70, 73, 76–78, 80–83, 88, 94, 108, 109, 117, 122, 127, 133, 134, 136, 139–158, 161, 165, 175, 176, 186
   scope of, 43, 64

I-identity, 149, 150, 157, 186

Impulse, 23, 41, 48–55, 64, 145, 157

Impulsiveness, 44, 62

Incorporation, 46

Indigenous, 161, 166, 167

Individualisation, 13, 16, 39–65, 106, 152, 157, 158, 185, 186

Industrialisation, 33, 43, 93, 94, 130

Injury, 40, 47, 53, 60, 172, 183
Insecurity, 93, 144, 145
Integrating, 132, 139–158
Intellectualisation, 13, 104
Interaction, 20, 31, 33, 40, 46–48,
    59, 62, 162, 172
  face-to-face, 47, 62
Interactional, 47
Inter-county, 32, 53, 56, 80–83, 99,
    101, 104, 105, 124–128,
    130–136, 156, 187
Internalisation, 62, 183
International, 5, 15, 51, 65, 110, 130,
    142–145, 153, 155, 156,
    161–177, 189n4
International Rules football,
    15, 161–177
Involvement–detachment (Elias), 10
Ireland
  Act of Union with Great Britain, 69
  Irish society, x, 69, 94, 146
  partition, 16n1, 51, 137n1
Irish Amateur Athletic Association
    (IAAA), 71, 95, 96, 139
Irish Football Association (IFA), 69,
    117–119, 140
Irish Republican Brotherhood (IRB),
    72, 74–78, 80, 140
Irish Rugby Football Union (IRFU),
    89n1, 117, 156

J
John J. Higgins collection, ix, xi
Journalists, 2, 9, 14, 24, 27–32, 42,
    48, 50–54, 56, 57, 60, 121, 123,
    124, 133, 151, 157, 167, 169,
    170, 172–175, 177, 183, 185

K
Kee, Robert, 25, 27
Kelly, Seán, 88, 156

Kerry, 57, 77, 118, 122, 140, 156
Kilkenny, 122, 123
Kilminster, Richard, 10, 11

L
Labour, 34, 47, 55, 63, 72
Labourers, 34, 63, 70, 94
Ladies Gaelic football, 182
Land, 25, 26, 61, 63, 69
Landlords, 25, 34, 35, 62, 63, 70
Laois, 100, 123
Laws of Hurley, 23
League of Ireland, 156
Lee, Joe, 25
Legislation, 88
Legitimacy, x, 9, 15, 44, 46, 49, 51,
    52, 54, 57–59, 62–64, 72, 119,
    134, 187
Leinster, xi, 40, 60, 79, 84, 100,
    123, 185
Leisure, 45, 48, 96, 108, 140, 146,
    149, 161
Lennon, Joe, 20–24, 26, 30–32, 49,
    53, 78, 88
Limerick, xi, 100, 102
Linesmen, 29, 30
Liston, Katie, 182–184
Longford, 56
Looney, Tom, 82, 121
Louth, 40–42

M
Mac Lua, Brendan, 141, 144
Maguire, Caroline, 70, 75, 182, 184
Mahon, Jack, 20
Manager, 2, 33, 40, 50, 104, 105,
    129, 133, 135, 136, 158n2,
    169, 170
Mandle, William F., 2, 20, 22, 27,
    49, 72–78, 80, 82, 83, 95, 96,
    140, 142

Manuals, 8, 128
Martin, Henry, 40, 129
Masculinity, 46
Match, 12, 20–22, 24, 27, 30, 32, 41,
    42, 49, 50, 52–57, 60, 64, 65,
    76, 77, 101, 104, 119, 121,
    143–145, 156, 157, 172, 184
McAnallen, Dónal, xi, 2, 95, 97–99,
    103, 104
McCabe, Conor, 142, 143
McConville, C, 161, 164
McDevitt, Patrick F., 70, 139, 142
McElligott, Richard, 74, 77, 96, 99,
    100, 118, 140
McGee, Owen, 71, 74, 75, 77, 78, 169
McKeever, Jim, 128
Meath, 40, 84, 165
Media
    amplification, 54, 136
    mediatisation, 133
Meetings, 8, 9, 77, 78, 85, 139, 153
Mennell, Stephen, ix, xi, 43, 48, 58,
    63, 188
Micro-sociology, 42–43
Migration, 70
Militant, 72, 82, 120, 135, 142
Miller, Liam, 184
Mimetic, x, 27, 46, 62, 72
Monopolisation, 7, 43, 52, 57, 62,
    63, 173
Moore, Cormac, 143
Moortown, 28, 29
Morals, 8, 10, 23, 27, 29, 31, 33,
    39–42, 47, 50, 51, 54, 59, 60,
    64, 161, 169
Motivations, x, xi, 14, 93, 110, 142,
    150, 151, 154, 158, 189
Mulvey, Johnny, 73, 82
Munster, ix, 27, 31, 53, 79
Murphy, Patrick, 2, 9, 32, 45, 54, 65
Murphy, William, 39, 45
Mutual accommodation, 154, 156

Mutual dependencies, 43, 163
Mutual identification, 13, 44,
    80–83, 175

N
Narrative, 5, 58, 65, 71, 102,
    119, 120, 136, 139, 147,
    158, 164, 177
Nation
    national, x, 5, 8, 14, 15, 21, 24,
        25, 28, 33–35, 43, 45, 51, 52,
        56–58, 61–65, 69, 70, 72, 73,
        75, 76, 78, 80–89, 95, 97, 98,
        101, 106, 110, 125, 127, 133,
        134, 139–158, 161–163,
        165–171, 175–177, 186
    nationalism, 2, 25, 50, 51, 72, 83,
        94, 120, 166, 168
    nationalist, 25–27, 51, 61, 71, 72,
        75, 80, 83, 139, 140, 142
    nationality, 24, 145, 149
Native, 34, 69–71, 77, 94, 95, 124,
    145, 163
Natural, 26, 42, 43, 45, 47, 77, 100,
    173, 175
Nederveen Pieterse, Jan, 162, 163
Needs, 5, 10, 14, 45, 64, 73–76,
    78, 79, 84, 86, 97, 108–110,
    112, 124, 134, 148–151, 158,
    172, 177
Network, 4, 5, 29, 33, 34, 42, 43, 70,
    88, 149, 163, 166
Newspapers, 40, 101, 143, 164, 167,
    169
New York, 56
Nobility, 25, 43, 45
Nolan, William, 72, 74, 80, 82
Norms, 6, 8, 19, 29, 46, 47, 50,
    56, 59, 62–64, 70, 132, 167,
    169, 183
Northern Ireland, 16n1, 51, 54, 57

O

O'Callaghan, Liam, 99, 140, 142
O'Connor, Christy, 129
O'Connor, Muiris, 35
O'Connor, Robert, 152
O'Donnell, I., 62
O'Donoghue, Noel, 72, 118, 121
Ó'Gráda, Cormac, 34
Ó hAnnrachain, Tadhg, 142
O'Kane, P., 51
O'Malley, Eoin, 35
Ó Maonaigh, Aaron, 120, 142
Ó Riain, Seamus, 71, 94, 95
O'Sullivan, Jim, 32
O'Sullivan, Thomas F., 73, 74, 76, 78,
    79, 83
Offaly, 131
Organic solidarity, 46, 58
Organisations
  inter-organisational, 13, 15, 98,
    106, 118, 128, 135, 151,
    184–187
  intra-organisational, 15, 76–78, 84,
    86, 106, 125
Origin, ix, 5, 42, 60, 163, 164
  origin myths, 164–165

P

Pacification, 24, 44–46, 57, 61, 62, 64
Parliamenterisation, 35
Parnell, Charles Stewart, 77, 78
Parsons, Talcott, 8
Payments, 97, 100, 103, 122, 124,
    129, 133, 134, 136
Personality structure, 145
Physical, 12, 23–32, 35, 41, 44, 52,
    62, 104, 120, 123, 135, 172, 174
Physiological, 62
Pitch invasions, 49, 52–55
Play, 12, 19–24, 26, 28, 30, 31, 33,
    48–50, 55, 63–65, 97, 101, 102,

109, 111, 113n3, 117, 122, 125,
    133, 140, 141, 148, 149, 161,
    163–165, 168, 170, 172–176,
    183, 184, 188
  rough, 20, 26, 30, 48
Player power, 3, 14, 117–136
Polarities, 58
Police, 40, 42, 46, 47, 50, 51, 53, 56,
    57, 59, 63, 94, 140
Politicians, 35, 142, 185
Power balance, 3, 4, 7, 8, 15, 16,
    45, 75, 76, 79, 89, 94, 111,
    126, 129–131, 136, 146, 182,
    183, 187
Power ratio, 6, 12, 81, 87, 132, 136
Power sources, 70, 83–85, 135–136
Praise gossip, 14, 120, 139, 142, 144,
    145
President, 26, 28, 42, 95, 106, 112,
    134, 143, 144, 146–148, 151,
    153, 165
Pressures, 7, 13, 24, 26, 32, 43,
    77–79, 82, 84–86, 102, 104,
    106, 108–112, 118, 126, 133,
    140, 183, 184, 188
Pride, 13, 15, 24, 31, 35, 56, 63, 148,
    166–168, 170, 176
Private, 63, 101
Professionalism, 3, 13, 14, 95, 98, 99,
    101–103, 107–110, 112, 113,
    117–136, 176, 188
Promotion, 19, 70, 110, 127, 130,
    131, 151, 171, 173
Protection, 26, 42, 46, 49, 55–58
Provincial council, 78–81, 84, 87,
    89, 99
Psychic, 64, 158
Psychological, 4, 15, 104
Public, 3, 23, 30, 31, 52, 54, 63, 94,
    100, 120, 123, 124, 130, 141,
    143, 155, 184, 185
Punishment, 50

Q

Quest for excitement, 144

R

Radio Éireann, 145, 152, 153
Radió Teilifís Éireann (RTÉ), 40, 107, 159n3
Rational, 58, 59, 188
  calculation, 11
Referee, 8, 9, 12, 22, 26, 28–33, 40–42, 46, 48–53, 55–57, 59, 60, 64, 172
Representation, 84, 85, 161–163, 165, 167, 168, 171, 175, 176
Republic of Ireland, 16n1, 40, 51, 137n2, 145, 149, 158n1, 159n4, 184
Repugnance, 27, 29, 33, 39, 40, 51, 59
  thresholds of, 2, 7, 12, 16, 23, 26, 29, 30, 33
Rituals, 47, 165, 171, 177
Robinson, R. J., 44
Rothstein, B., 46
Rouse, Paul, 2, 4, 69, 96–98, 100, 139–142
Routinisation, 45, 61
Rugby, 1–3, 9, 10, 19, 21, 34, 35, 45, 69, 72, 98, 99, 106, 111, 113n4, 117–120, 140–145, 153–156, 164–166, 184, 187, 189n4
Rulebook, 45
Rules
  Rule 27, 154
  Rule 42, 156

S

Scotson, John, 44, 119, 120, 139
Scottish, 69, 110, 118
Scrummages, 21
Self-presentation, 42

Self-restraint, 2, 7, 8, 12–14, 23, 26, 29, 30, 45, 59, 64, 148–151, 158, 173
Self-steering, 43, 44
Sensitivities, 24, 30, 33, 35, 40, 125, 151
Seriousness of involvement, 3, 13, 14, 99–105, 109, 113, 121–126, 128, 129, 131, 136, 182, 183
Shame, 23, 36, 54, 57, 145, 149, 158, 166, 176
  thresholds of, 9, 23, 39, 48, 52, 168
Sheard, Ken, 7–9, 11, 45, 93, 97, 104–106, 166
Skill, 30, 121, 122, 145, 155, 170, 174
Sliotar, 1, 128
Soccer, 2, 3, 9, 10, 12, 21, 34, 39, 45, 56, 69, 72, 98, 99, 101, 110, 111, 113n3, 113n4, 117–121, 123, 140–145, 154–156, 164, 166, 169, 184–187, 189n4
Social change, 2, 4, 5, 8, 9, 24, 42, 152
Social class, 5, 13, 43, 61, 70, 94, 97, 98, 110, 119, 120, 140
Social control, 29, 63, 139–152, 167
Social integration, 13, 44, 60, 61, 63, 88, 108, 128, 162, 168
Socialisation, 15
Social meaning, 65, 109, 122, 125, 127
Social structures, x, 6, 42, 58, 63, 96, 158, 189
Sociogenesis, 69–89, 187
Socio-temporal structure, 42
Soldiers, 24
Solidarity, 13, 46, 50, 57, 58, 177
Spectators, 2, 3, 8–13, 20, 22, 27, 30, 33, 39–65, 72, 96, 97, 101, 107–109, 119, 135, 145, 150, 172, 173, 177, 182, 186, 189n4
Sportisation, 15, 26, 45, 50, 57, 143, 163, 165–167

Standardisation, 12, 19–22, 48, 76, 166
Static, 3, 58
Status, 6, 63, 70, 79, 81, 83–85, 93,
    94, 96, 124, 125, 127, 128, 131,
    134, 135, 144, 149, 166, 169,
    175, 187, 189n4
Stigmatisation, 14, 93, 96, 118, 121,
    140, 142, 143
Strength, 24, 82, 118, 121, 131,
    133–136, 149, 155, 157, 176, 186
Superiority, 3, 15, 16, 144, 152–158,
    168, 184
  diminishing displays of superiority,
    14, 139–158
Supporters, 28, 29, 51–53, 55–58, 64,
    65, 150, 154, 155, 173
Symbols, 13, 15, 34, 35, 57, 61, 64,
    161, 176
Syson, I., 164

T
Taboo, 152, 157
Taxation, 7, 44
Teams, 1, 2, 19–22, 25–28, 31, 32,
    40–42, 50, 52–59, 63, 65, 75,
    77, 78, 83, 100–105, 112, 118,
    121–129, 131, 132, 134, 135,
    143–145, 165, 168, 170, 174,
    177n1, 184, 189n4
Tension, 3, 8, 13, 15, 25–27, 34, 35,
    40, 43, 45, 47, 48, 62, 64,
    69–89, 93, 94, 98, 99, 101, 103,
    104, 111, 112, 117–122, 125,
    127, 129, 131, 139, 152, 163,
    167, 171–173, 177, 182, 188
  balance, 3, 93–113, 188
They-groups, 109, 175
They-image, 83
Tipperary, 53
Toms, David, 118, 120, 140
Trade, 34, 70, 130

Traditions, 5, 11, 19, 31, 39, 44, 51,
    60, 148, 164
Training, 27, 100, 102–105, 111,
    112, 121–126, 128, 129, 133,
    135, 174
  camps, 100, 102, 104, 124
Transgressions, 12, 19, 28, 40, 50, 54,
    55, 60, 64, 81, 163, 168, 173
Traynor, Oscar, 144
Trust, 47, 136, 149
Tyrone, 28

U
Ulster, 87, 118
Umpires, 23, 29–31, 49, 55, 56, 64, 165
Unintended consequences, 8, 30, 162
United Kingdom (UK), 34, 51, 61
United States of America (USA), 133
Urbanisation, 93, 152, 185

V
Values, x, 6, 7, 19, 29, 62, 63, 70, 78,
    94–97, 107, 111, 112, 131, 149,
    150, 158, 185, 186
Victorian, 164
Violence
  collective violence, 48, 49, 51, 52,
    54, 58
  demonopolisation of violence, 57
  individual violence, 13, 39–65
  instrumental, 23, 32, 33
  stabbing, 25
Voluntary, 99, 106, 107, 111, 112,
    124, 130
  volunteerism, 3, 98, 111, 112

W
War, 29
Waterford, 53

Weber, Max, 43, 44
We-feelings, 14, 63, 83, 85, 86, 122,
    132, 133, 143, 144, 154, 159n4,
    167–171, 173–176, 186, 187
We-group, 52, 63, 64, 109, 149,
    171, 176
We–I balances, 60, 186
We-identifications, 73, 81–83, 88,
    109, 111, 133, 154, 157, 166,
    177, 186
Wexford, 120
Wicklow, 76

Women, 150, 152, 182, 189n1
Work, ix, x, 2, 4, 5, 10–12, 42, 44,
    46, 47, 86, 96, 97, 99, 101,
    102, 105–107, 112, 123, 130,
    132, 165
Wouters, Cas, 59, 64, 150, 151,
    156, 173
Wrestling, 21

Y
Youth, 57, 132, 139–158

Printed by Printforce, the Netherlands